McDougal Littell
LITERATURE

InterActive
READER & WRITER
for Critical Analysis

Grade 7

McDougal Littell
EVANSTON, ILLINOIS • BOSTON • DALLAS

COVER
Untitled (1986), Jerry N. Uelsmann. © Jerry N. Uelsmann.

Copyright © 2008 McDougal Littell, a division of Houghton Mifflin Company. All rights reserved.

Warning: No part of this work may be reproduced or transmitted in any form or by any means, electronic or mechanical, including photocopying and recording, or by any information storage or retrieval system without the prior written permission of McDougal Littell unless such copying is expressly permitted by federal copyright law. With the exception of not-for-profit transcription in Braille, McDougal Littell is not authorized to grant permission for further uses of copyrighted selections reprinted in this text without the permission of their owners. Permission must be obtained from the individual copyright owners as identified herein. Address inquiries to Supervisor, Rights and Permissions, McDougal Littell, P.O. Box 1667, Evanston, IL 60204.

ISBN 13: 978-0-618-92132-4   ISBN 10: 0-618-92132-X

Printed in the United States of America.

6 7 8 9–0928–12 11 10
4500244530

SENIOR PROGRAM CONSULTANTS

Janet Allen
Internationally-known Reading and Literacy Specialist

Arthur N. Applebee
Leading Professor, School of Education, University of Albany, State University of New York; Director of the Center on English Learning and Achievement

Jim Burke
Lecturer, Author, English Teacher, Burlingame, California

Douglas Carnine
Professor of Education, University of Oregon

Yvette Jackson
Executive Director, National Urban Alliance for Effective Education

Robert Jiménez
Professor of Language, Literacy, and Culture, Vanderbilt University

Judith A. Langer
Distinguished Professor, University of Albany, State University of New York; Director of the Center on English Learning and Achievement; Director of the Albany Institute for Research in Education

Robert J. Marzano
Senior Scholar, Mid-Continent Research for Education and Learning (McREL), Denver, Colorado

Donna M. Ogle
Professor of Reading and Language, National-Louis University, Chicago, Illinois; Past President, International Reading Association

Carol Booth Olson
Senior Lecturer, Department of Education, University of California, Irvine

Carol Ann Tomlinson
Professor of Educational Research, Foundations, and Policy, University of Virginia; Co-Director of the University's Institutes on Academic Diversity

ENGLISH LEARNER SPECIALISTS

Mary Lou McCloskey
Past President, TESOL; Director of Teacher Development and Curriculum Design for Educo, Atlanta, Georgia

Lydia Stack
Past President, TESOL; International ESL Consultant

CURRICULUM SPECIALIST

William L. McBride
Nationally-known Speaker, Educator, and Author

TABLE OF CONTENTS

Introducing *The InterActive Reader & Writer* viii
User's Guide x
Skills and Strategies xxiv

UNIT 1 — PLOT, CONFLICT, AND SETTING 2

Skills & Standards
Plot, Conflict, Setting
Identify Text Features

ANCHOR SELECTION: SHORT STORY
Rikki-tikki-tavi — Rudyard Kipling 5

RELATED NONFICTION:
- **King Cobras: Feared, Revered** MAGAZINE ARTICLE 25
- **Fight or Flight?** ONLINE ARTICLE 29

Learn the Terms: Academic Vocabulary	4
Assessment Practice I	22
Responding in Writing: Short Response	23
Learn the Skill: **Identify Text Features**	24
Assessment Practice II	32
Timed Writing Practice: **Definition Essay**	33

UNIT 2 — ANALYZING CHARACTER AND POINT OF VIEW 34

Character, Point of View
Identify Author's Purpose

ANCHOR SELECTION: SHORT STORY
A Retrieved Reformation — O. Henry 37

RELATED NONFICTION:
- **When the Curtain Comes Up on a Second Act** MAGAZINE ARTICLE 50
- **Juvenile Justice on Trial** EDITORIAL 53

Learn the Terms: Academic Vocabulary	36
Assessment Practice I	47
Responding in Writing: Short Response	48
Learn the Skill: **Identify Author's Purpose**	49
Assessment Practice II	56
Timed Writing Practice: **Opinion Essay**	57

iv THE INTERACTIVE READER & WRITER

UNIT 3 — UNDERSTANDING THEME — 58

Skills & Standards

Theme

ANCHOR SELECTION: SHORT STORY
The War of the Wall — Toni Cade Bambara — 61

Identify Characteristics of Forms

RELATED NONFICTION:
- *Veterans' Mural Honors Those Who Served* NEWSPAPER ARTICLE — 73
- *Mural-Making Manual* HOW-TO MANUAL — 76

Learn the Terms: Academic Vocabulary	60
Assessment Practice I	70
Responding in Writing: Short Response	71
Learn the Skill: **Identify Characteristics of Forms**	72
Assessment Practice II	78
Timed Writing Practice: **Personal Response to Literature**	79

UNIT 4 — MOOD, TONE, AND STYLE — 80

Mood, Tone, Style

ANCHOR SELECTION: SHORT STORY
Dark They Were, and Golden-Eyed — Ray Bradbury — 83

Identify Text Clues

RELATED NONFICTION:
How Terraforming Mars Will Work SCIENCE ARTICLE — 104

Learn the Terms: Academic Vocabulary	82
Assessment Practice I	101
Responding in Writing: Short Response	102
Learn the Skill: **Identify Text Clues**	103
Assessment Practice II	108
Timed Writing Practice: **Fictional Narrative**	109

UNIT 5A — APPRECIATING POETRY: IMAGERY AND FIGURATIVE LANGUAGE — 110

Imagery, Figurative Language

ANCHOR SELECTIONS: POETRY
the earth is a living thing — Lucille Clifton — 113
Sleeping in the Forest — Mary Oliver — 114
Gold — Pat Mora — 115

Evaluate Information

RELATED NONFICTION:
- *What's Your Ecological Footprint?* TEXTBOOK — 119
- *Cool School* MAGAZINE ARTICLE — 120

Learn the Terms: Academic Vocabulary	112
Assessment Practice I	116
Responding in Writing: Short Response	117
Learn the Skill: **Evaluate Information**	118
Assessment Practice II	124
Timed Writing Practice: **Expository Essay**	125

UNIT 5B — APPRECIATING POETRY: SOUND DEVICES — 126

Skills & Standards

Sound Devices

ANCHOR SELECTIONS: POETRY

Scaffolding	Seamus Heaney	129
The World Is Not a Pleasant Place to Be	Nikki Giovanni	130
Annabel Lee	Edgar Allan Poe	131

Evaluate Sources for Usefulness

RELATED NONFICTION:
Guidelines for Keeping Your Friendships Strong **BROCHURE** — 136

Learn the Terms: Academic Vocabulary	128
Assessment Practice I	133
Responding in Writing: Short Response	134
Learn the Skill: **Evaluate Sources for Usefulness**	135
Assessment Practice II	140
Timed Writing Practice: **Personal Narrative**	141

UNIT 6 — MYTHS, LEGENDS, AND TALES — 142

ANCHOR SELECTIONS: GREEK MYTHS

Characteristics of Myths

Prometheus	Bernard Evslin	145
Orpheus and Eurydice	Olivia Coolidge	149

Recognize Cause-and-Effect Relationships

RELATED NONFICTION:
- An American Prometheus **HISTORY ARTICLE** — 157
- Discoveries That Changed the World **TIMELINE** — 160

Learn the Terms: Academic Vocabulary	144
Assessment Practice I	154
Responding in Writing: Short Response	155
Learn the Skill: **Recognize Cause-and-Effect Relationships**	156
Assessment Practice II	162
Timed Writing Practice: **Cause-and-Effect Essay**	163

UNIT 7 — BIOGRAPHY AND AUTOBIOGRAPHY — 164

Characteristics of Autobiographical Writing

ANCHOR SELECTION: PERSONAL ESSAY

Names/Nombres	Julia Alvarez	167

Synthesize Sources

RELATED NONFICTION:
Name That Child: How Culture and Tradition Influence Choices **ONLINE ARTICLE** — 176

Learn the Terms: Academic Vocabulary	166
Assessment Practice I	173
Responding in Writing: Short Response	174
Learn the Skill: **Synthesize Sources**	175
Assessment Practice II	182
Timed Writing Practice: **Autobiographical Narrative**	183

THE INTERACTIVE READER & WRITER

Skills & Standards	**UNIT 8A INFORMATION, ARGUMENT, AND PERSUASION**		**184**
Text Features	**ANCHOR SELECTION: MAGAZINE ARTICLE** **What Do You Know About Sharks?**	Sharon Guynup	**187**
Examine Treatment	**RELATED NONFICTION:** **A Real Can of Worms: Animal Figures of Speech** **MAGAZINE ARTICLE**		**197**

Learn the Terms: Academic Vocabulary — 186
Assessment Practice I — 194
Responding in Writing: Short Response — 195
Learn the Skill: **Examine Treatment** — 196
Assessment Practice II — 202
Timed Writing Practice: **Expository Essay** — 203

	UNIT 8B INFORMATION, ARGUMENT, AND PERSUASION		**204**
Argument and Persuasion	**ANCHOR SELECTION: SPEECH** **Remarks at the Dedication of the Aerospace Medical Health Center**	John F. Kennedy	**207**
Analyze Patterns of Organization	**RELATED NONFICTION:** **Inventions Inspired by Apollo** **ONLINE ARTICLE**		**215**

Learn the Terms: Academic Vocabulary — 206
Assessment Practice I — 212
Responding in Writing: Short Response — 213
Learn the Skill: **Analyze Patterns of Organization** — 214
Assessment Practice II — 220
Timed Writing Practice: **Persuasive Essay** — 221

Nonfiction Skills Handbook — **R2**
Test-Taking Handbook — **R26**
   Successful Test Taking — R26
   Functional Reading Test — R30
   Revising-and-Editing Test — R34

Introducing The InterActive Reader & Writer

The InterActive Reader & Writer is a literature book to mark on, write in, and make your own. As you will see, this book helps you become an active reader. It also helps you become a better writer.

An Easy-to-Carry Literature Text

This book won't weigh you down. It fits as comfortably in your hand as it can in your backpack. Yet it is packed with great things to read and do:

- Important works of literature by leading authors
- A rich selection of nonfiction texts—Web pages, magazine articles, and more
- A variety of genres—such as short stories, biographies, speeches, poems, and myths
- Activities that will help you think more deeply about yourself and the world beyond

Becoming a Critical Reader

Most people get more out of a work of literature the second time they read it. To help you get the most out of the literature in *The InterActive Reader & Writer,* you'll read each core literary work two times.

- You'll read it once on your own, marking the text as you choose.
- You'll read it a second time, using the notes in the margins to help you think critically about the text.

BEFORE READING ACTIVITIES

Big Question The first activity in each unit gets you thinking about a real-life question that the literature addresses.

Learn the Terms A brief skill lesson helps you understand the most important features of the literature and teaches terms you will need in order to talk and write about the selection. Additional skills terms increase your ability to think critically about literature.

DURING READING ACTIVITIES

A wide variety of side column notes challenges you to dig deeply into each selection.

VOCABULARY SUPPORT

Words to Know Important words are underlined and boldfaced in blue. Their definitions appear nearby in the side column.

Specialized Vocabulary Vocabulary notes in nonfiction selections explain special words used in certain careers or fields of study.

Special Features

TEST PREPARATION

No one likes tests, but everyone likes doing well on them. *The Interactive Reader & Writer* will help you become a better test-taker.

TestSmart TestSmart questions appear right next to the text you are reading. These give you an opportunity to practice answering multiple-choice questions about literature—without worrying about being scored!

Test Tips You'll be given helpful strategies to use when answering test questions.

Assessment Practice Multiple-choice test items help you focus on how well you've read the texts provided. They also help you prepare for real tests.

Written Responses Many tests ask you to write one or more paragraphs about a reading passage. This book gives you the opportunity to write about each selection you read. A **Test-Taker's Toolkit** shows you how to develop each written response, step-by-step.

NONFICTION READING

Each main literature selection in *The InterActive Reader & Writer* is paired with one or two nonfiction selections that are related in some way to the literature. You will learn many different strategies for getting the most out of the nonfiction you read. These strategies will help you on tests, in other classes, and in the world outside of school. For example, you will learn how to:

- Use text features to preview a text
- Identify main ideas and details
- Understand how ideas are organized
- Synthesize information

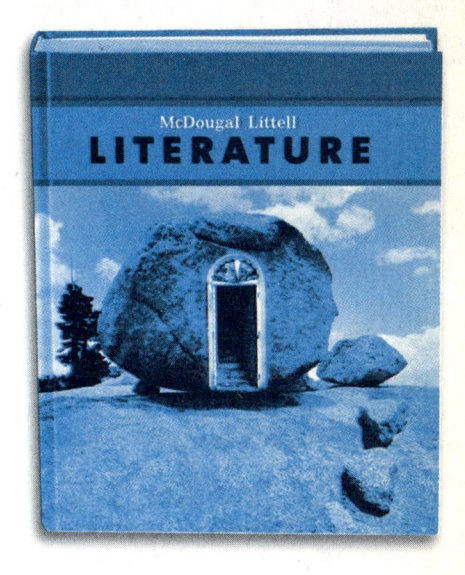

LINKS TO
McDougal Littell Literature

If you are using **McDougal Littell Literature**, you will find the **InterActive Reader & Writer** to be the perfect companion. *The InterActive Reader & Writer* helps you read certain core selections from *McDougal Littell Literature* more carefully and more carefully and in greater depth.

Read on to learn more!

INTRODUCTION ix

User's Guide

The InterActive Reader & Writer with for Critical Analysis has an easy-to-follow organization, as shown by these sample pages from the science fiction story "Dark They Were, and Golden-Eyed" by Ray Bradbury.

UNIT 4
MOOD, TONE, AND STYLE

Dark They Were, and Golden-Eyed ①
BY RAY BRADBURY

RELATED NONFICTION
How Terraforming Mars Will Work ②

① Anchor Selection
Each unit is made up of a cluster of readings. The main literature selection is called the **anchor selection.** You will read this first.

② Related Nonfiction
The titles in smaller type are the **Related Nonfiction** pieces. As you preview each unit, read the titles and think about how all the readings might be related.

x   INTERACTIVE READER & WRITER

Can where you are ③
CHANGE *who you are?*

Your hobbies, interests, and habits often depend on the climate you are used to and the people and places you encounter every day. If you were to move away from everything you know, how much of who you are would change? How much would stay the same?

DISCUSS IT With a group, discuss the question at the top of the page. Take turns answering the question and explaining your reasons. Record your group's responses in the notebook.

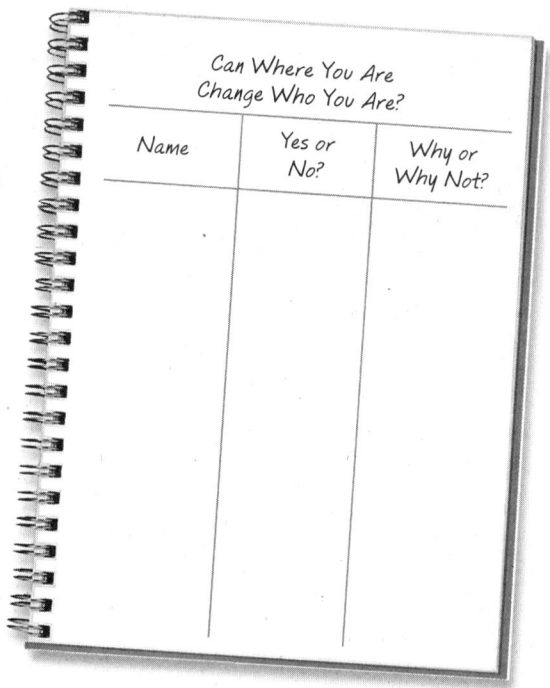

Can Where You Are Change Who You Are?

Name	Yes or No?	Why or Why Not?

④
ASSESSMENT GOALS

By the end of this lesson, you will be able to...
- analyze mood, tone, and style
- apply critical thinking skills to analyze text
- identify text clues in nonfiction texts
- analyze a writing prompt and plan a fictional narrative

DARK THEY WERE, AND GOLDEN-EYED 81

③ **Big Question**
Each unit begins with an activity that gets you thinking about a real-life question that the literature addresses. Sometimes you'll work in a group to complete this activity. After reading, you'll return to this question. Don't be surprised if you have a different perspective.

④ **Assessment Goals**
This box sums up the unit's main learning goals. The first goal names the unit's **literature skill.** The second goal is your overall **critical thinking objective.** The third goal names the skill you'll be learning with the **nonfiction** selections. The last goal names the **writing activity** you'll complete at the end of the unit.

USER'S GUIDE   **xi**

1) Learn the Terms: Academic Vocabulary

This page presents a brief, easy-to-understand lesson that introduces important terms and explains what to look for in the literature you read.

2) You will come back to these academic terms several times during the unit. For example, in Unit 4 you will come across the terms *mood, tone,* and *style* in the side notes of the main selection.

3) Additional Terms for Critical Analysis

Additional terms for critical analysis will challenge you to think and write about the literature even more deeply.

---

1) LEARN THE TERMS: ACADEMIC VOCABULARY

Mood, Tone, and Style

Think of a story as a homemade meal. You've learned about the basic ingredients: plot, characters, setting, and theme. What gives a writer's work a unique flavor? What makes you tear hungrily through one story, while another is hard to digest? The answer is the blend of spices known as mood, tone, and style.

2)

MOOD

MOOD is the feeling that a writer creates for a reader.

Words to describe mood
- eerie
- romantic
- peaceful
- wondrous
- frightning
- anxious

A writer creates mood through
- descriptions of setting
- characters' speech or feelings
- imagery, or words and phrases that appeal to the readers' five senses

TONE

TONE is a writer's attitude toward his or her subject.

Words to describe tone
- humorous
- angry
- sarcastic
- serious
- sympathetic
- admiring

A writer creates tone through
- words that let the reader "hear" the author's attitude
- details that make a subject appear a certain way

STYLE

STYLE is the unique way a writer puts words together. Style is not *what* is said but *how* it's said.

Words to describe style
- conversational
- lively
- economical
- flowery

Writer's create their unique style through the use of
- word choice
- sentence structure
- imagery

3) ADDITIONAL TERMS FOR CRITICAL ANALYSIS

Ray Bradbury is one of the world's most famous science fiction writers, but he writes other kinds of stories as well. The following terms can help you discuss both the selection you're about to read and Bradbury's general style:

- **SCIENCE FICTION** is fiction in which a writer imagines unexpected possibilities of the past or the future, using known scientific data and theories as well as his or her own creative ideas.

- **SYNTAX** is the way in which words are put together to form phrases and sentences. Syntax includes the order of words in a sentence.

82   UNIT 4: MOOD, TONE, AND STYLE

DARK THEY WERE, AND Golden-Eyed

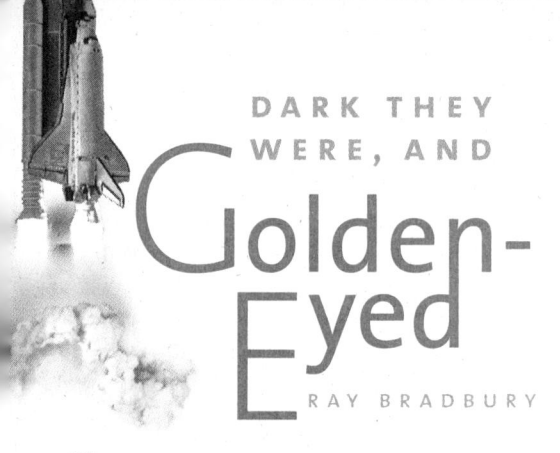

RAY BRADBURY

④ SECOND READ: CRITICAL ANALYSIS

MARK & ANALYZE
Read this selection once on your own, marking the text in any way that's helpful to you.

Then read the story a second time, using the questions in the margins to help you analyze the literature. When you see this pencil ⑤, you'll be asked to mark up the text.

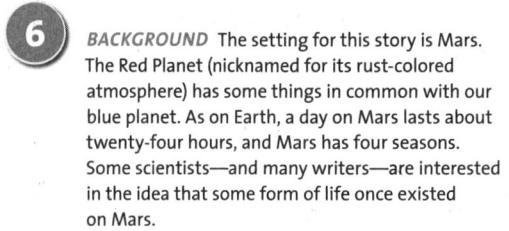

⑥ BACKGROUND The setting for this story is Mars. The Red Planet (nicknamed for its rust-colored atmosphere) has some things in common with our blue planet. As on Earth, a day on Mars lasts about twenty-four hours, and Mars has four seasons. Some scientists—and many writers—are interested in the idea that some form of life once existed on Mars.

The rocket metal cooled in the meadow winds. Its lid gave a bulging *pop*. From its clock interior stepped a man, a woman, and three children. The other passengers whispered away across the Martian meadow, leaving the man alone among his family.

The man felt his hair flutter and the tissues of his body draw tight as if he were standing at the center of a vacuum. His wife, before him, seemed almost to whirl away in smoke. The children, small seeds, might at any instant be sown to all
10 the Martian climes.

The children looked up at him, as people look to the sun to tell what time of their life it is. His face was cold.

"What's wrong?" asked his wife.

"Let's get back on the rocket."

DARK THEY WERE, AND GOLDEN-EYED   **83**

---

④ SECOND READ: CRITICAL ANALYSIS
You'll read each selection once on your own, marking the text as you wish. Then you'll read it a second time, using the questions in the margins to provide a deeper understanding of the selection.

⑤ The pencil symbol appears whenever you are being asked to circle, underline, or mark the text in other ways.

⑥ BACKGROUND
This paragraph gives important information about the selection you are about to read. Always read this section before starting the main text.

USER'S GUIDE **xiii**

1 ▶

When you come to this symbol, follow the arrow to the side column. Answer the question. Then read on.

2 💡 **TestSmart**

TestSmart questions will give you practice answering multiple-choice questions typically found on tests.

Each **TestSmart** question has a **TIP** that gives you useful strategies for figuring out answers to multiple-choice questions.

A tip may ask you to underline or circle things in the text. The blue lines show how one student used this tip to mark up the text. Notice how the underlined phrases all suggest one answer—C.

ANALYZE

Reread the boxed text. What later events are foreshadowed, or hinted at, in this passage?

_____
_____
_____
_____

💡 **TestSmart** **2**

Which word *best* describes the overall mood created by the characters' speech and feelings in lines 34–45?

Ⓐ peaceful
Ⓑ lively
Ⓒ anxious
Ⓓ weary

TIP When a question asks you to define a story's **mood**, think about your own emotional response. What feeling do you have at this point in the story? Decide which answer choice is closest to your feeling. Then make sure you can support your answer with evidence from the text. For this question, underline the words that help create a distinct mood in lines 34–45.

"Go back to Earth?"

"Yes! Listen!"

The wind blew as if to flake away their identities. At any moment the Martian air might draw his soul from him, as marrow comes from a white bone. He felt submerged in a chemical that could dissolve his intellect and burn away his past. ◀ **1**

They looked at Martian hills that time had worn with a crushing pressure of years. They saw the old cities, lost in their meadows, lying like children's delicate bones among the blowing lakes of grass.

"Chin up, Harry," said his wife. "It's too late. We've come over sixty million miles."

The children with their yellow hair hollered at the deep dome of Martian sky. There was no answer but the racing hiss of wind through the stiff grass.

He picked up the luggage in his cold hands. "Here we go," he said—a man standing on the edge of a sea, ready to wade in and be drowned.

They walked into town.

Their name was Bittering. Harry and his wife Cora; Dan, Laura, and David. They built a small white cottage and ate good breakfasts there, but the fear was never gone. It lay with Mr. Bittering and Mrs. Bittering, a third unbidden partner at every midnight talk, at every dawn awakening.

"I feel like a salt crystal," he said, "in a mountain stream, being washed away. We don't belong here. We're Earth people. This is Mars. It was meant for Martians. For heaven's sake, Cora, let's buy tickets for home!"

But she only shook her head. "One day the atom bomb will fix Earth. Then we'll be safe here."

"Safe and insane!" ◀

Tick-tock, seven o'clock sang the voice-clock; *time to get up.* And they did.

Something made him check everything each morning— warm hearth, potted blood-geraniums—precisely as if he expected something to be amiss. The morning paper was

84 UNIT 4: MOOD, TONE, AND STYLE

xiv INTERACTIVE READER & WRITER

toast-warm from the 6 A.M. Earth rocket. He broke its seal and tilted it at his breakfast place. He forced himself to be <u>convivial</u>.

"Colonial days all over again," he declared. "Why, in ten years there'll be a million Earthmen on Mars. Big cities, everything! They said we'd fail. Said the Martians would resent our invasion. But did we find any Martians? Not a living soul! Oh, we found their empty cities, but no one in them. Right?"

A river of wind submerged the house. When the windows
60 ceased rattling Mr. Bittering swallowed and looked at the children. ▶

"I don't know," said David. "Maybe there're Martians around we don't see. Sometimes nights I think I hear 'em. I hear the wind. The sand hits my window. I get scared. And I see those towns way up in the mountains where the Martians lived a long time ago. And I think I see things moving around those towns, Papa. And I wonder if those Martians *mind* us living here. I wonder if they won't do something to us for coming here." ▶

70 "Nonsense!" Mr. Bittering looked out the windows. "We're clean, decent people." He looked at his children. "All dead cities have some kind of ghosts in them. Memories, I mean." He stared at the hills. "You see a staircase and you wonder what Martians looked like climbing it. You see Martian paintings and you wonder what the painter was like. You make a little ghost in your mind, a memory. It's quite natural. Imagination." He stopped. "You haven't been prowling up in those ruins, have you?"

"No, Papa." David looked at his shoes.

80 "See that you stay away from them. Pass the jam."

"Just the same," said little David, "I bet something happens."

---

3 convivial (kən-vĭv′ē-əl) *adj.* enjoying the company of others; sociable

4 💡 TestSmart
VOCABULARY
The word *submerged* means "covered in water." What is the most likely meaning of the prefix *sub-*, which is used to form *submerged* in line 59?
Ⓐ over
Ⓑ under
Ⓒ beside
Ⓓ between

TIP When a test question asks you about the meaning of a **prefix**, the definition of a word that includes the prefix can help you find the answer. In this case, think about the definition of *submerged*. If you know that to submerge something is to place it under water, what does that tell you about the meaning of *sub-*?

5 **INTERPRET**
Bradbury uses wind **imagery** throughout this story. Underline two examples of this kind of imagery in lines 59–69.

Look for other examples as you continue your second read. What do you think the wind might represent?

_____
_____
_____
_____

DARK THEY WERE, AND GOLDEN-EYED   **85**

---

3 **Vocabulary**
Important vocabulary words are underlined and boldfaced in the text. A definition and a respelling appear in the side column.

4 **TestSmart Vocabulary**
Some TestSmart questions will ask about words found in the selection. The **TIP** that follows will help strengthen your word-attack skills in testing situations.

5 **Challenging Questions**
Questions such as this one ask you to use high-level critical thinking skills in order to achieve a deeper understanding of the selection.

The selection continues...

USER'S GUIDE   **XV**

① Big Question
At the end of each main literature selection, you'll be asked to think again about the **Big Question** you discussed before reading.

② Footnotes
Some selections in this book include definitions of special words and phrases. When you see a number in the text, look down at the bottom of the page for an explanation of the meaning.

ANALYZE
Reread the boxed text. What are the rocket men doing that has been done before?

_____
_____
_____

The authors of **science fiction** stories sometimes include a message or comment about human civilization. What comment do you think Bradbury is making about civilization in this story?

_____
_____
_____
_____
_____

Big Question ①
Look back at the question on page 81. Which answer does this story support? Why?

_____
_____
_____
_____
_____

"Lots to be done, Lieutenant." His voice droned on and
560 quietly on as the sun sank behind the blue hills. "New settlements. Mining sites, minerals to be looked for. Bacteriological specimens[5] taken. The work, all the work. And the old records were lost. We'll have a job of remapping to do, renaming the mountains and rivers and such. Calls for a little imagination.

"What do you think of naming those mountains the Lincoln Mountains, this canal the Washington Canal, those hills—we can name those hills for you, Lieutenant. Diplomacy. And you, for a favor, might name a town for me.
570 Polishing the apple.[6] And why not make this the Einstein Valley, and farther over . . . are you _listening_, Lieutenant?"

The lieutenant snapped his gaze from the blue color and the quiet mist of the hills far beyond the town.

"What? Oh, _yes_, sir!"

---

② 5. **bacteriological specimens:** samples of different kinds of single-celled living things.
6. **polishing the apple:** acting in a way to get on the good side of another person.

100   UNIT 4: MOOD, TONE, AND STYLE

Assessment Practice I

Reading Comprehension

DIRECTIONS *Answer these questions by filling in the correct ovals.*

1. Which element of Bradbury's style is most obvious in lines 6–7?
   - Ⓐ his use of vivid imagery
   - Ⓑ his choice of unusual words
   - Ⓒ his description of the story's setting
   - Ⓓ his short sentences and sentence fragments

2. Which pair of words *best* describes the mood created in lines 59–69?
   - Ⓐ pleasant, happy
   - Ⓒ bitter, angry
   - Ⓑ eerie, fearful
   - Ⓓ sad, lonely

3. Which element most contributes to the mood in lines 532–534?
   - Ⓐ the description of the setting
   - Ⓑ the conversation between the rocket men
   - Ⓒ the attitude of the Martians
   - Ⓓ the imagery used to describe the spacecraft

4. Which sentence from the story uses unusual syntax?
   - Ⓐ "He looked at his children."
   - Ⓑ "Nevertheless, man lives by symbol and label."
   - Ⓒ "The paths were covered with a thin film of cool water all summer long."
   - Ⓓ "They moved along in the canal, the father, the mother, the racing children in their swimsuits."

5. Which event below could only happen in a science fiction story?
   - Ⓐ Humans build space rockets.
   - Ⓑ Atom bombs cause destruction on Earth.
   - Ⓒ Food can be stored in a deep freeze.
   - Ⓓ Humans learn the Martian language.

6. At the end of the story, why do the Martians learn English so quickly?
   - Ⓐ Martian and English are very similar.
   - Ⓑ The rocket men are good teachers.
   - Ⓒ The Martians used to be humans.
   - Ⓓ They had met Earthlings before.

7. The word *bidden* means "invited or asked to come." What is the most likely meaning of the prefix *un-*, which is used to form *unbidden* in line 37?
   - Ⓐ the opposite of
   - Ⓒ always
   - Ⓑ not finished
   - Ⓓ again

8. Read this sentence from the story:

   > Rubber tires upon which children had swung in back yards hung suspended like stopped clock pendulums in the blazing air.

   In this sentence, *suspended* means
   - Ⓐ sent away
   - Ⓑ full of suspense
   - Ⓒ delayed
   - Ⓓ hung from above

DARK THEY WERE, AND GOLDEN-EYED 101

---

③ Assessment Practice I: Reading Comprehension
After reading each main literature selection, you'll have an opportunity to practice your test-taking skills and strategies by answering questions about the selection. The direction line will tell you how to mark the answers.

④ Literary Skills
Certain test items, such as 1 through 5, will ask questions that are related to the literary skills. You can review these skills by rereading **Learn the Terms,** page 82.

⑤ Test Strategies
Some test items will give you a chance to use the **TestSmart TIPs** you learned earlier in the lesson. Here, notice how the **TIP** on page 84 can help answer test items 2 and 3. The **TIP** on page 85 can help answer test item 7.

⑥ Critical Analysis
Test items 4 and 5 address the **Additional Terms for Critical Analysis,** which you learned about on page 82. If you want to review these terms, turn back to this page.

⑦ Vocabulary
The last two test items focus on vocabulary. Remember to use the line numbers to help locate and reread the sentences in which the words appear.

USER'S GUIDE xvii

① Responding in Writing

After each main literature selection, you'll write a short response. This activity might ask you to use some of the literary terms you have studied.

② Test-Taker's Toolkit

The **Test-Taker's Toolkit** helps you plan your response. Completing the graphic organizer will give you the ideas you'll use in your writing.

Assessment Practice I

Responding in Writing ①

9. Short Response In a paragraph, analyze how the imagery in "Dark They Were, and Golden-Eyed" adds to the story's mood.

For help, use the **Test-Taker's Toolkit** below.

② Test-Taker's Toolkit

ACADEMIC VOCABULARY When you're asked to **analyze** how an element in a story works, you first need to look at specific examples of that element. Then you need to explain how those examples affect the whole selection. To complete this response, start by identifying the story's **mood**. Then find three specific images that help to create that mood.

GRAPHIC ORGANIZER Use the chart below to help you plan your response.

WORDS THAT DESCRIBE THE MOOD OF THIS STORY:

↑ ↑ ↑

IMAGES THAT HELP CREATE THIS MOOD:

What's the Connection? ④

"Dark They Were, and Golden-Eyed" is a purely fictional account of a human settlement on Mars. The science article "How Terraforming Mars Will Work" describes what it would actually take to make the Red Planet suitable for human habitation.

PLAN IT? To support human life, Mars would need to be much warmer and much wetter. Which two of the following ideas seem like the most reasonable ways to make this happen? Check them. Then draw a simple sketch of how one of the plans might work.

- ☐ Use giant mirrors to reflect sunlight toward Mars to melt its polar ice caps.
- ☐ Send rockets full of water to Mars and fill the empty seas.
- ☐ Hurl asteroids at Mars to raise its temperature and melt the ice caps.
- ☐ Use hydrogen bombs to interrupt Mars's orbit and move it closer to the sun.

LEARN THE SKILL: IDENTIFY TEXT CLUES ⑤

Authors of nonfiction try to organize their writing so that readers can easily keep track of the flow of ideas. Here are three **text clues** you can look for to help you follow along as new ideas are introduced.

- **Transitions** are words or phrases that signal a change in idea. A new idea may be introduced using transition phrase such as *Another option for*. Headings also signal a change in idea.
- **Signal words** help you understand how ideas relate to each other. For example, the word *but* can signal that a contrasting idea is coming up. Words such as *if* signal a cause-effect relationship.
- **Demonstrative pronouns** such as *this*, *these*, and *those* are often used to make relationships between topics and ideas clear. Notice the people, places, or ideas to which these words refer.

For more on transitions and other text clues, see *Nonfiction Handbook* page R24.

---

③ **Related Nonfiction**

- How Terraforming Mars Will Work
  SCIENCE ARTICLE

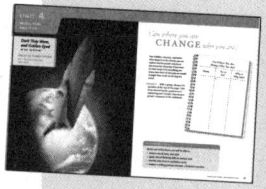

Use with "Dark They Were, and Golden-Eyed," p. 80

RELATED NONFICTION **103**

---

③ **Related Nonfiction**
Once you've completed the literature section, you'll get ready to read the **Related Nonfiction.**

④ **What's the Connection?**
This activity gets you thinking and talking about the nonfiction selections you are about to read. It also explains how they connect to the literature selection.

⑤ **Learn the Skill**
Before you read the **Related Nonfiction,** you will learn a useful skill or strategy. You will encounter the boldfaced terms later as you are reading and as you complete the practice test.

USER'S GUIDE **xix**

1. Set a Purpose
You will begin each nonfiction selection by setting a purpose for reading. One student's purpose for reading appears on the lines provided. Yours may be different.

2. Text Clues
These notes ask you to apply the skill or strategy you learned before reading.

CLOSE READ

1 SET A PURPOSE

My purpose for reading is to find out what terraforming is and why it might be necessary to terraform Mars.

2 TEXT CLUES

The underlined text presents a problem and its possible solution. Identify these below:

Problem: _____
_____
_____

Possible solution: _____
_____
_____

Circle the **demonstrative pronoun** that helps make clear the relationship between the problem and the action we might need to take to address it.

104 UNIT 4: MOOD, TONE, AND STYLE

---

http://www.howstuffworks.com

howstuffworks
It's good to know   HOME SCIENCE HEALTH COMPUTER

1 | 2 | 3 | 4 ▶

How Terraforming Mars Will Work
by Kevin Bonsor

Why would we ever want to go to Mars? It has a very thin atmosphere and no signs of existing life—but Mars does hold some promise for the continuation of the human race. <u>There are more than six billion people on Earth, and that number continues to grow unabated. This overcrowding, or the possibility of planetary disaster, will force us to eventually consider new homes in our solar system, and Mars may have more to offer us than the photos of its barren landscape now show.</u>

Recently, NASA probes[1] have discovered hints to a warmer past on Mars, one in which water may have flowed and life might have existed.
10 . . . [A]n effort to colonize Mars would begin with altering the current climate and atmosphere to more closely resemble that of Earth. The process of transforming the Martian atmosphere to create a more habitable living environment is called terraforming. . . . ◀

WHY MARS?

Mars is the next closest planet to us. And although it is a cold, dry planet today, it holds all of the elements that are needed for life to exist, including

- Water, which may be frozen at the polar ice caps
- Carbon and oxygen in the form of carbon dioxide (CO_2)
20 - Nitrogen

There are amazing similarities between the Martian atmosphere that exists today and the atmosphere that existed on Earth billions of years ago. . . . [T]he similarity [between] the early Earth and modern

---
1. **probes:** small, unmanned spacecraft that gather and send back information.

---

xx INTERACTIVE READER & WRITER

http://www.howstuffworks.com

◁ 1 | **2** | 3 | 4 ▷

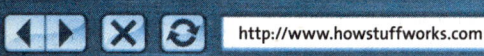

Mars atmospheres has led some scientists to speculate [that] the same process that turned the Earth's atmosphere from mostly carbon dioxide into breathable air could be repeated on Mars. [This process] would thicken the atmosphere and create a greenhouse effect[2] that would heat the planet and provide a suitable living environment for plants and animals. . . .

30   Other worlds have been considered as possible candidates for terraforming, including Venus, Europa (a Jupiter moon), and Titan (a Saturn moon). However, Europa and Titan are too far from the sun, and Venus is too close (the average temperature on Venus is about 900 degrees Fahrenheit [482.22 Celsius]). Mars stands alone as the one planet in our solar system, not including Earth, that might be able to support
40 life. In the next section, learn how scientists plan to transform the dry, cold landscape of Mars into warm, livable habitat. ▶

This photograph of Mars was taken by the rover *Spirit* in 2007.

CREATING A MARTIAN GREENHOUSE

Terraforming Mars will be a huge undertaking, if it is ever done at all. Initial stages of terraforming Mars could take several decades
50 or centuries. Terraforming the entire planet into an Earth-like habitat would have to be done over several millennia.[3] Some have even

---
2. **greenhouse effect:** the warming of the lower atmosphere of a planet due to gases in the upper atmosphere that trap heat from the sun.
3. **millennia** (mə-lĕn′ē-ə): plural form of millennium, meaning "one thousand years."

RELATED NONFICTION   **105**

3 TEXT CLUES

In the boxed text, underline the **signal word** that alerts you to a change in topic.

What topic is the writer addressing in and before the sentence containing the signal word?

_____
_____

What topic is the writer addressing after the sentence containing the signal word?

_____
_____

3 As you move through the **Related Nonfiction,** you'll have additional opportunities to use the nonfiction skills you've learned.

The selection continues...

USER'S GUIDE   **xxi**

① Assessment Practice II: Reading Comprehension

In this second practice test, you'll answer test items about all the selections you have read in the unit.

② Nonfiction Skill

Some test items ask about the nonfiction skill or strategy you learned. If there are page or line references in the question, use them to locate and reread the text you are being asked about before you choose an answer.

③ Connecting Texts

Test items such as 5 and 6 ask you to connect information from more than one source. You can look back at the selections if you need to.

---

① Assessment Practice II

Reading Comprehension

DIRECTIONS Answer these questions by filling in the correct ovals.

1. What must be done to colonize Mars?
   - Ⓐ discover life on that planet
   - Ⓑ send a probe to learn about Mars
   - Ⓒ alter the climate and atmosphere
   - Ⓓ learn to grown crops in terra firma

2. What is the purpose of the bulleted list on page 104?
   - Ⓐ It notes why Mars is cold and dry.
   - Ⓑ It tells what we must add to Mars.
   - Ⓒ It cites the elements needed for life.
   - Ⓓ It states the similarities between Mars's atmosphere and Earth's.

3. According to the article, what positive result would greenhouse gases have on Mars?
   - Ⓐ They would trap the sun's radiation and make Mars cooler.
   - Ⓑ They would make the atmosphere thinner.
   - Ⓒ They would trap the sun's radiation and make Mars warmer.
   - Ⓓ They would take the place of poisonous gases.

4. What text clue in lines 76–79 signals the introduction of a new idea?
   - Ⓐ the signal words "in turn"
   - Ⓑ the demonstrative pronoun "this"
   - Ⓒ the synonyms "Mars" and "the planet"
   - Ⓓ the transitional phrase "another option"

5. The main purpose of the section "Creating a Martian Greenhouse" is to explain
   - Ⓐ how to build factories on Mars
   - Ⓑ why we should hurl asteroids at Mars
   - Ⓒ how mirrors can warm Mars
   - Ⓓ various ideas for making Mars livable

6. According to the facts presented in "Terraforming Mars," what problems have the humans solved in "Dark They Were"?
   - Ⓐ They sent a rocket to Mars and back.
   - Ⓑ They heated Mars, located water, and thickened the atmosphere.
   - Ⓒ They added ammonia, carbon dioxide, and nitrogen to Mars.
   - Ⓓ They got rid of the old Martian civilization and renamed the hills.

7. Read the following sentence from the text:

   > It will take many centuries of human ingenuity and labor to develop a habitable environment and bring life to the cold, dry world of Mars.

   In this sentence, the word *ingenuity* means
   - Ⓐ geniuses   Ⓒ needs
   - Ⓑ rockets   Ⓓ creativity

8. What does *unabated* mean in line 4?
   - Ⓐ illegally   Ⓒ without control
   - Ⓑ naturally   Ⓓ without worry

108 UNIT 4: MOOD, TONE, AND STYLE

Timed Writing Practice ④

PROMPT
Write a (fictional narrative) about an imaginary event that happens on Mars. Create characters, a plot, and details with your imagination. Also include facts about Mars and space exploration that you learned from the Related Nonfiction.

⑤ **BUDGET YOUR TIME**
You have 45 minutes to complete this assignment. Decide how much time to spend on each step.

Analyze ___5___
Plan ___10___
Write ___20___
Review ___10___

⑥ Test-Taker's Toolkit

1. ANALYZE THE PROMPT
- **A.** **Read the prompt** carefully. Draw lines between the sentences to help you focus on each one.
- **B.** **Note key words** that tell you exactly what you must do. The writing form has been circled for you. Circle the topic, and underline the sources you need to consult to find relevant details.

2. PLAN YOUR RESPONSE
- **A.** **Plan your story** Use a story map like the one shown to help you plan your story.
- **B.** **Gather facts** Look back through the nonfiction selections you read. Find some facts you might include to make your story details seem realistic. List these facts below. They might provide inspiration.

SETTING:
CHARACTERS:
PROBLEM:
PLOT/EVENTS:
RESOLUTION:

3. WRITE AND REVIEW
- **A.** **Write an interest-grabbing opening** Try to reveal your story's setting in the first paragraph.
- **B.** **Write out your story** Leave enough time to read through it. Make sure you have met all the requirements. Also check your spelling and grammar.

RELATED NONFICTION **109**

---

④ **Timed Writing Practice**
This writing activity is an opportunity to practice responding to a prompt on a writing test—without the stress of test-taking!

⑤ **Budget Your Time**
This feature helps you plan how much time to spend on each step. The blue text shows how one student budgeted her time.

⑥ **Test-Taker's Toolkit**
The Test-Taker's Toolkit shows you how to break the writing process into three easy steps. Fill in the graphic organizer provided. This will help you gather the information you'll need to write your full response. (You may want to copy the graphic organizer onto a larger sheet of paper.)

USER'S GUIDE **xxiii**

Skills and Strategies

Thinking Critically

The skills and strategies found in this book will help you tackle critical thinking questions you encounter in school—and on tests in particular. Critical thinking questions are often challenging because the answers are usually not directly stated in the text. But you will find that tackling these types of questions is worth the extra brain power it takes to answer them. That's because they help you get more out of the selections you read. Here is a list of the critical thinking skills and strategies you will encounter most often in this book:

Make Inferences
Make logical guesses based on details in the text and your own experiences.
- Keep track of important details in your reading.
- Ask: How can what I already know help me "read between the lines"?

Draw Conclusions
Decide what's happening based on evidence, experience, and reasoning.
- Start by making inferences as you read.
- Then combine your inferences to reach a logical conclusion.

Analyze
Break things down to gain a better understanding.
- Consider the experiences and feelings that make a character act a certain way.
- In nonfiction, look for details to help you learn how something works or is defined.

Interpret
Find deeper meaning in what you read.
- Consider the outcome of events and what they might mean.
- Think about what the author is trying to tell the reader.

Evaluate
Examine something to decide its value or worth.
- You can decide to evaluate the actions of a particular character, for example.
- You can also decide on the value of what you are reading.

Make Judgments
Form an opinion based on information given.
- Gather evidence from the text.
- Be ready to support your opinion.

continued on next page

Compare/Contrast
Identify similarities and differences in two or more subjects.

- Make a list of the qualities of each subject. In what ways are the lists the same? Different?
- Decide if the subjects are more alike or more different.

Synthesize
Combine information together to gain a better understanding.

- Think of what you already know about the subject.
- Add this to the facts, details, and ideas presented in your reading.

Make Generalizations
Form a broad statement about a subject.

- Gather evidence.
- Then decide what ideas are suggested by this evidence.

Classify
Decide how pieces of information might fit into categories.

- Look for common characteristics in the information provided.
- Cite evidence from your reading to show why you classified as you did.

Examine Perspectives
Think about the values and beliefs presented.

- Look for a writer's statements of opinion.
- Decide how perspective affects the information you get.

UNIT 1
PLOT, CONFLICT, AND SETTING

Rikki-tikki-tavi
BY RUDYARD KIPLING

RELATED NONFICTION
King Cobras: Feared, Revered
Fight or Flight?

What makes you BRAVE?

You see a small child stepping in front of a speeding car. You get the chance to sing in front of a thousand people. Your best friend needs help standing up to a bully. All of these are occasions that require you to be brave—to overcome your fears and take action. But what is bravery, exactly?

DISCUSS IT The writer Mark Twain once said that courage is not the *absence* of fear, but the *mastery* of fear. Answer the questions in the notebook. Based on your answers, do you agree with Mark Twain? Discuss your opinions with a partner.

                                      Yes No

1. Is a boy who gets nervous in small spaces brave every time he gets in an elevator? ☐ ☐

2. Is a professional snowboarder brave when she tackles the steepest trail on the mountain? ☐ ☐

3. Is a cat brave when she goes into a burning house to get her kittens? ☐ ☐

4. Is a student brave who says no to his friends when they try to get him to do something risky? ☐ ☐

Do you agree with Mark Twain? _____
_____

ASSESSMENT GOALS

By the end of this lesson, you will be able to...

- analyze plot, conflict, and setting in a work of fiction
- apply critical thinking skills to analyze text
- use text features to navigate nonfiction text
- analyze a writing prompt and plan a definition essay

LEARN THE TERMS: ACADEMIC VOCABULARY

Plot, Conflict, and Setting

"Rikki-tikki-tavi" is a classic adventure tale that pits a small mammal called a mongoose against a dangerous enemy. Review the following terms before beginning your analysis of the story:

- **CONFLICT** is a struggle between different forces. Almost every story has a main conflict—a problem that is the story's focus. For example, a fight between enemies is a conflict.

- **SETTING** is the time and place of the action. The time includes the historical era, the season, and the time of day. The place might be a country, a neighborhood, or a room. In many stories, setting affects the plot.

- **PLOT** is what happens in a story. A plot can usually be broken down into five stages.

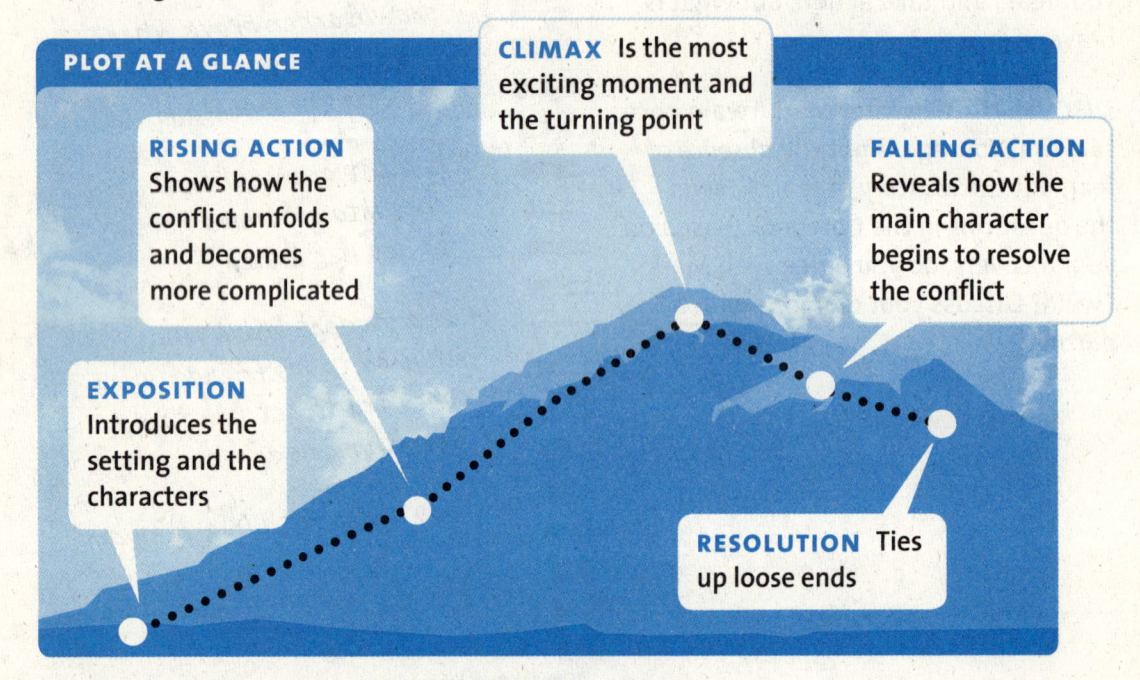

PLOT AT A GLANCE

CLIMAX Is the most exciting moment and the turning point

RISING ACTION Shows how the conflict unfolds and becomes more complicated

FALLING ACTION Reveals how the main character begins to resolve the conflict

EXPOSITION Introduces the setting and the characters

RESOLUTION Ties up loose ends

ADDITIONAL TERMS FOR CRITICAL ANALYSIS

Rudyard Kipling uses these elements to create an exciting plot.

- **FORESHADOWING** is a writer's use of hints or clues to suggest events that will occur later in a story. Foreshadowing creates suspense and makes readers eager to find out what will happen next.

- **SUSPENSE** is the excitement or tension that readers feel as they wait to find out how a story ends or a conflict is resolved. Writers create suspense by raising questions in readers' minds about what might happen next.

Rikki-*tikki*-tavi
Rudyard Kipling

BACKGROUND The setting of this story is India during the late 1800s. At that time the British ruled India. British families lived in airy one-story homes called bungalows. It was not uncommon to find snakes, insects, or wild animals near or even inside a bungalow. Two wild creatures that are found in India are the mongoose, a small mammal that grows to about 16 inches, and the cobra, a poisonous snake that can grow to 18 feet in length. The cobra and the mongoose are natural enemies.

This is the story of the great war that Rikki-tikki-tavi fought single-handed, through the bathrooms of the big bungalow in Segowlee cantonment.[1] Darzee, the tailorbird, helped him, and Chuchundra,[2] the muskrat, who never comes out into the middle of the floor but always creeps round by the wall, gave him advice; but Rikki-tikki did the real fighting. ▶

He was a mongoose, rather like a little cat in his fur and his tail but quite like a weasel in his head and his habits. His eyes and the end of his restless nose were pink; he could scratch himself anywhere he pleased with any leg, front or back, that he chose to use; he could fluff up his tail till it looked like a bottle-brush, and his war cry as he scuttled through the long grass was: *Rikk-tikk-tikki-tikki-tchk!*

---

1. **Segowlee** (sə-gou′lē) **cantonment:** area in India that was home to a British military base.
2. **Chuchundra** (chə-chōōn′drə).

SECOND READ: CRITICAL ANALYSIS

MARK & ANALYZE
Read this selection once on your own, marking the text in any way that is helpful to you.

Then read the story a second time, using the questions in the margins to help you analyze the literature. When you see this pencil, you'll be asked to mark up the text.

ANALYZE
Usually in the **exposition** of a story, the author introduces the characters and **setting** and might hint at the **conflict** to come. What's unique about the way this story begins? Tell why you think Kipling might have chosen to open the story in this way.

_____
_____
_____
_____
_____

revive (rĭ-vīv′) *v.* to return to life or consciousness

One day, a high summer flood washed him out of the burrow where he lived with his father and mother and carried him, kicking and clucking, down a roadside ditch. He found a little wisp of grass floating there and clung to it till he lost his senses. When he **revived**, he was lying in the hot sun on the middle of a garden path, very draggled indeed, and a small boy was saying, "Here's a dead mongoose. Let's have a funeral."

"No," said his mother, "let's take him in and dry him. Perhaps he isn't really dead."

They took him into the house, and a big man picked him up between his finger and thumb and said he was not dead but half choked; so they wrapped him in cotton wool and warmed him over a little fire, and he opened his eyes and sneezed. "Now," said the big man (he was an Englishman who had just moved into the bungalow), "don't frighten him, and we'll see what he'll do."

It is the hardest thing in the world to frighten a mongoose, because he is eaten up from nose to tail with curiosity. The motto of all the mongoose family is "Run and Find Out"; and Rikki-tikki was a true mongoose. He looked at the cotton wool, decided that it was not good to eat, ran all round the table, sat up and put his fur in order, scratched himself, and jumped on the small boy's shoulder.

"Don't be frightened, Teddy," said his father. "That's his way of making friends."

"Ouch! He's tickling under my chin," said Teddy.

Rikki-tikki looked down between the boy's collar and neck, snuffed at his ear, and climbed down to the floor, where he sat rubbing his nose.

"Good gracious," said Teddy's mother, "and that's a wild creature! I suppose he's so tame because we've been kind to him." ◀

"All mongooses are like that," said her husband. "If Teddy doesn't pick him up by the tail or try to put him in a cage,

---

EVALUATE

In the **exposition**, Kipling reveals Rikki-tikki's core character traits. Which of these traits is most critical in his later battles? Underline the sentence that describes it.

Why is this trait so important?

_____

_____

he'll run in and out of the house all day long. Let's give him something to eat."

They gave him a little piece of raw meat. Rikki-tikki liked it immensely; and when it was finished, he went out into the veranda and sat in the sunshine and fluffed up his fur to make it dry to the roots. Then he felt better.

"There are more things to find out about in this house," he said to himself, "than all my family could find out in all their lives. I shall certainly stay and find out."

He spent all that day roaming over the house. He nearly drowned himself in the bathtubs, put his nose into the ink on a writing table, and burnt it on the end of the big man's cigar, for he climbed up in the big man's lap to see how writing was done. At nightfall he ran into Teddy's nursery to watch how kerosene lamps were lighted, and when Teddy went to bed, Rikki-tikki climbed up too; but he was a restless companion, because he had to get up and attend to every noise all through the night and find out what made it. Teddy's mother and father came in, the last thing, to look at their boy, and Rikki-tikki was awake on the pillow.

"I don't like that," said Teddy's mother; "he may bite the child."

"He'll do no such thing," said the father. "Teddy is safer with that little beast than if he had a bloodhound to watch him. If a snake came into the nursery now—"

But Teddy's mother wouldn't think of anything so awful. ▶

Early in the morning Rikki-tikki came to early breakfast in the veranda, riding on Teddy's shoulder, and they gave him banana and some boiled egg; and he sat on all their laps one after the other, because every well-brought-up mongoose always hopes to be a house mongoose some day and have rooms to run about in; and Rikki-tikki's mother (she used

---

TestSmart

In lines 59–76, which phrase or sentence foreshadows an important event that occurs later in the story?

- A "He may bite the child."
- B "If a snake came into the nursery now—"
- C "At nightfall he ran into Teddy's nursery . . ."
- D "He nearly drowned himself in the bathtubs . . ."

TIP A question about **foreshadowing** requires you to think about more than one event in the story. Remember that these events may be far apart from each other.

to live in the general's house at Segowlee) had carefully told Rikki what to do if ever he came across white men.

Then Rikki-tikki went out into the garden to see what was to be seen. It was a large garden, only half-cultivated, with bushes, as big as summerhouses, of Marshal Niel roses, lime and orange trees, clumps of bamboos, and thickets of high grass. Rikki-tikki licked his lips. "This is a splendid hunting ground," he said, and his tail grew bottlebrushy at the thought of it; and he scuttled up and down the garden, snuffing here and there till he heard very sorrowful voices in a thorn bush. It was Darzee, the tailorbird, and his wife. They had made a beautiful nest by pulling two big leaves together and stitching them up the edges with fibers and had filled the hollow with cotton and downy fluff. The nest swayed to and fro, as they sat on the rim and cried.

"What is the matter?" asked Rikki-tikki.

"We are very miserable," said Darzee. "One of our babies fell out of the nest yesterday, and Nag ate him."

"H'm!" said Rikki-tikki, "that is very sad—but I am a stranger here. Who is Nag?"

Darzee and his wife only **cowered** down in the nest without answering, for from the thick grass at the foot of the bush there came a low hiss—a horrid, cold sound that made Rikki-tikki jump back two clear feet. Then inch by inch out of the grass rose up the head and spread hood[3] of Nag, the big black cobra, and he was five feet long from tongue to tail. When he had lifted one-third of himself clear of the ground, he stayed, balancing to and fro exactly as a dandelion tuft balances in the wind; and he looked at Rikki-tikki with the wicked snake's eyes that never change their expression, whatever the snake may be thinking of. ◀

"Who is Nag?" said he. "*I* am Nag. The great god Brahm[4] put his mark upon all our people when the first cobra spread

---

cower (kou′ər) *v.* to crouch or shrink down in fear

CLASSIFY

Reread lines 98–113. In your opinion, is this section part of the **exposition,** or is it the beginning of the **rising action?**

☐ exposition
☐ rising action

Consider what you know about the rest of the story as you explain your answer.

_____
_____
_____
_____

---

3. **hood:** an expanded part on or near the head of an animal.
4. **Brahm** (bräm): another name for Brahma, creator of the universe in the Hindu religion.

his hood to keep the sun off Brahm as he slept. Look, and be afraid!"

He spread out his hood more than ever, and Rikki-tikki saw the spectacle mark on the back of it that looks exactly like the eye part of a hook-and-eye fastening. He was afraid for the minute, but it is impossible for a mongoose to stay frightened for any length of time; and though Rikki-tikki had never met a live cobra before, his mother had fed him on dead ones, and he knew that all a grown mongoose's business in life was to fight and eat snakes. Nag knew that too, and at the bottom of his cold heart, he was afraid.

"Well," said Rikki-tikki, and his tail began to fluff up again, "marks or no marks, do you think it is right for you to eat **fledglings** out of a nest?"

Nag was thinking to himself and watching the least little movement in the grass behind Rikki-tikki. He knew that mongooses in the garden meant death sooner or later for him and his family; but he wanted to get Rikki-tikki off his guard. So he dropped his head a little, and put it on one side.

"Let us talk," he said. "You eat eggs. Why should not I eat birds?" ▶

"Behind you! Look behind you!" sang Darzee.

Rikki-tikki knew better than to waste time in staring. He jumped up in the air as high as he could go, and just under him whizzed by the head of Nagaina,[5] Nag's wicked wife. She had crept up behind him as he was talking, to make an end of him; and he heard her savage hiss as the stroke missed. He came down almost across her back, and if he had been an old mongoose, he would have known that then was the time to break her back with one bite; but he was afraid of the terrible lashing return stroke of the cobra. He bit, indeed, but did not bite long enough; and he jumped clear of the whisking tail, leaving Nagaina torn and angry.

"Wicked, wicked Darzee!" said Nag, lashing up as high as he could reach toward the nest in the thorn bush; but

---

5. **Nagaina** (nä-gə-ē′nə).

fledgling (flĕj′lĭng) *n.* a young bird that has recently grown its flight feathers

EVALUATE

Review lines 103–136. Put a box around words and phrases that create a positive impression of Rikki-tikki. Circle words and phrases that describe Nag in negative ways.

Both animals feel they are protecting something. Why do you think Kipling presents one animal as cute, lively, and brave and the other as evil and ominous?

_____
_____
_____
_____

Darzee had built it out of reach of snakes, and it only swayed to and fro.

Rikki-tikki felt his eyes growing red and hot (when a mongoose's eyes grow red, he is angry), and he sat back on his tail and hind legs like a little kangaroo and looked all around him and chattered with rage. But Nag and Nagaina had disappeared into the grass. When a snake misses its stroke, it never says anything or gives any sign of what it means to do next. Rikki-tikki did not care to follow them, for he did not feel sure that he could manage two snakes at once. So he trotted off to the gravel path near the house and sat down to think. It was a serious matter for him. ◀

If you read the old books of natural history, you will find they say that when the mongoose fights the snake and happens to get bitten, he runs off and eats some herb that cures him. That is not true. The victory is only a matter of quickness of eye and quickness of foot—snake's blow against mongoose's jump—and as no eye can follow the motion of a snake's head when it strikes, this makes things much more wonderful than any magic herb. Rikki-tikki knew he was a young mongoose, and it made him all the more pleased to think that he had managed to escape a blow from behind.

It gave him confidence in himself, and when Teddy came running down the path, Rikki-tikki was ready to be petted. But just as Teddy was stooping, something wriggled a little in the dust, and a tiny voice said, "Be careful. I am Death!" It was Karait,[6] the dusty brown snakeling that lies for choice on the dusty earth; and his bite is as dangerous as the cobra's. But he is so small that nobody thinks of him, and so he does the more harm to people.

Rikki-tikki's eyes grew red again, and he danced up to Karait with the peculiar rocking, swaying motion that he had inherited from his family. It looks very funny, but it is

---

DRAW CONCLUSIONS
Reread lines 153–162. What character trait does Rikki-tikki display when he decides not to follow the snakes? Tell how this trait affects the outcome of his next encounter with Nag and Nagaina.

---

6. **Karait** (kə-rīt′).

so perfectly balanced a **gait** that you can fly off from it at any angle you please; and in dealing with snakes this is an advantage.

If Rikki-tikki had only known, he was doing a much more dangerous thing than fighting Nag; for Karait is so small and can turn so quickly, that unless Rikki bit him close to the back of the head, he would get the return stroke in his eye or his lip. But Rikki did not know: his eyes were all red, and he rocked back and forth, looking for a good place to hold. Karait struck out. Rikki jumped sideways and tried to run in, but the wicked little dusty gray head lashed within a fraction of his shoulder, and he had to jump over the body, and the head followed his heels close. ▶

Teddy shouted to the house, "Oh, look here! Our mongoose is killing a snake"; and Rikki-tikki heard a scream from Teddy's mother. His father ran out with a stick, but by the time he came up, Karait had lunged out once too far, and Rikki-tikki had sprung, jumped on the snake's back, dropped his head far between his forelegs, bitten as high up the back as he could get hold, and rolled away.

That bite paralyzed Karait, and Rikki-tikki was just going to eat him up from the tail, after the custom of his family at dinner, when he remembered that a full meal makes a slow mongoose; and if he wanted all his strength and quickness ready, he must keep himself thin. He went away for a dust bath under the castor-oil bushes, while Teddy's father beat the dead Karait. "What is the use of that?" thought Rikki-tikki; "I have settled it all."

And then Teddy's mother picked him up from the dust and hugged him, crying that he had saved Teddy from death; and Teddy's father said that he was a providence, and Teddy looked on with big scared eyes. Rikki-tikki was rather amused at all the fuss, which, of course, he did not understand. Teddy's mother might just as well have petted Teddy for playing in the dust. Rikki was thoroughly enjoying himself. ▶

---

gait (gāt) *n.* a manner of walking or moving on foot

ANALYZE
Reread the boxed text. How does Kipling build **suspense** by giving readers this information?

_____

_____

_____

_____

TestSmart

VOCABULARY
What does the word *providence* mean in line 214?

Ⓐ hunter
Ⓑ blessing
Ⓒ vindication
Ⓓ professional

TIP When asked to find the meaning of an unfamiliar word, look for **context clues** in the surrounding text, such as the words underlined here. In this case, the positive connotation of the word *hugged* and the importance of saving Teddy from death suggest the correct answer.

That night at dinner, walking to and fro among the wineglasses on the table, he might have stuffed himself three times over with nice things; but he remembered Nag and Nagaina, and though it was very pleasant to be patted and petted by Teddy's mother and to sit on Teddy's shoulder, his eyes would get red from time to time, and he would go off into his long war cry of "*Rikk-tikk-tikki-tikki-tchk!*"

Teddy carried him off to bed and insisted on Rikki-tikki sleeping under his chin. Rikki-tikki was too well-bred to bite or scratch, but as soon as Teddy was asleep, he went off for his nightly walk around the house; and in the dark he ran up against Chuchundra, the muskrat, creeping around by the wall. Chuchundra is a brokenhearted little beast. He whimpers and cheeps all the night, trying to make up his mind to run into the middle of the room; but he never gets there.

"Don't kill me," said Chuchundra, almost weeping. "Rikki-tikki, don't kill me!"

"Do you think a snake killer kills muskrats?" said Rikki-tikki scornfully.

"Those who kill snakes get killed by snakes," said Chuchundra, more sorrowfully than ever. "And how am I to be sure that Nag won't mistake me for you some dark night?"

"There's not the least danger," said Rikki-tikki; "but Nag is in the garden, and I know you don't go there."

"My cousin Chua,[7] the rat, told me—" said Chuchundra, and then he stopped.

"Told you what?"

"H'sh! Nag is everywhere, Rikki-tikki. You should have talked to Chua in the garden."

"I didn't—so you must tell me. Quick, Chuchundra, or I'll bite you!"

Chuchundra sat down and cried till the tears rolled off his whiskers. "I am a very poor man," he sobbed. "I never had spirit enough to run out into the middle of the room. H'sh! I mustn't tell you anything. Can't you *hear*, Rikki-tikki?"

---

7. **Chua** (chōō′ə).

ANALYZE
Underline the details that help create **suspense** in lines 239–250.

In what way does Chuchundra's hesitancy add to the tension?
_____
_____
_____
_____

Rikki-tikki listened. The house was as still as still, but he thought he could just catch the faintest *scratch-scratch* in the world—a noise as faint as that of a wasp walking on a windowpane—the dry scratch of a snake's scales on brickwork.

"That's Nag or Nagaina," he said to himself, "and he is crawling into the bathroom sluice. You're right, Chuchundra; I should have talked to Chua."

He stole off to Teddy's bathroom, but there was nothing there, and then to Teddy's mother's bathroom. At the bottom of the smooth plaster wall, there was a brick pulled out to make a sluice for the bath water, and as Rikki-tikki stole in by the masonry curb where the bath is put, he heard Nag and Nagaina whispering together outside in the moonlight.

"When the house is emptied of people," said Nagaina to her husband, "*he* will have to go away, and then the garden will be our own again. Go in quietly, and remember that the big man who killed Karait is the first one to bite. Then come out and tell me, and we will hunt for Rikki-tikki together."

"But are you sure that there is anything to be gained by killing the people?" said Nag.

"Everything. When there were no people in the bungalow, did we have any mongoose in the garden? So long as the bungalow is empty, we are king and queen of the garden; and remember that as soon as our eggs in the melon bed hatch (as they may tomorrow), our children will need room and quiet."

"I had not thought of that," said Nag. "I will go, but there is no need that we should hunt for Rikki-tikki afterward. I will kill the big man and his wife, and the child if I can, and come away quietly. Then the bungalow will be empty, and Rikki-tikki will go."

DRAW CONCLUSIONS

In lines 263–268, underline details that describe the bathroom in this 19th-century Indian bungalow.

How would the plot be affected if the **setting** changed to a more modern home?

_____
_____
_____
_____
_____

ANALYZE

At key plot points, Kipling uses dialogue to intensify the **conflict**. What does the reader learn through the dialogue on this page?

_____
_____
_____

COMPARE & EVALUATE

What do both Rikki-tikki and Nag consider when planning their attacks? In your opinion, is one character smarter than the other? Explain.

_____
_____
_____
_____

Rikki-tikki tingled all over with rage and hatred at this, and then Nag's head came through the sluice, and his five feet of cold body followed it. Angry as he was, Rikki-tikki was very frightened as he saw the size of the big cobra. Nag coiled himself up, raised his head, and looked into the bathroom in the dark, and Rikki could see his eyes glitter.

"Now, if I kill him here, Nagaina will know; and if I fight him on the open floor, the odds are in his favor. What am I to do?" said Rikki-tikki-tavi.

Nag waved to and fro, and then Rikki-tikki heard him drinking from the biggest water jar that was used to fill the bath. "That is good," said the snake. "Now, when Karait was killed, the big man had a stick. He may have that stick still, but when he comes in to bathe in the morning, he will not have a stick. I shall wait here till he comes. Nagaina—do you hear me?—I shall wait here in the cool till daytime." ◀

There was no answer from outside, so Rikki-tikki knew Nagaina had gone away. Nag coiled himself down, coil by coil, around the bulge at the bottom of the water jar, and Rikki-tikki stayed still as death. After an hour he began to move, muscle by muscle, toward the jar. Nag was asleep, and Rikki-tikki looked at his big back, wondering which would be the best place for a good hold. "If I don't break his back at the first jump," said Rikki, "he can still fight; and if he fights— O Rikki!" He looked at the thickness of the neck below the hood, but that was too much for him; and a bite near the tail would only make Nag savage.

"It must be the head," he said at last; "the head above the hood. And, when I am once there, I must not let go." ◀

Then he jumped. The head was lying a little clear of the water jar, under the curve of it; and, as his teeth met, Rikki braced his back against the bulge of the red earthenware to hold down the head. This gave him just one second's purchase, and he made the most of it. Then he was battered to and fro as a rat is shaken by a dog—to and fro on the floor,

UNIT 1: PLOT, CONFLICT, AND SETTING

up and down, and round in great circles; but his eyes were red, and he held on as the body cart-whipped over the floor, upsetting the tin dipper and the soap dish and the flesh brush, and banged against the tin side of the bath.

As he held, he closed his jaws tighter and tighter, for he made sure he would be banged to death; and, for the honor of his family, he preferred to be found with his teeth locked. He was dizzy, aching, and felt shaken to pieces when something went off like a thunderclap just behind him; a hot wind knocked him senseless, and red fire **singed** his fur. The big man had been awakened by the noise and had fired both barrels of a shotgun into Nag just behind the hood. ▶

Rikki-tikki held on with his eyes shut, for now he was quite sure he was dead; but the head did not move, and the big man picked him up and said, "It's the mongoose again, Alice; the little chap has saved *our* lives now."

Then Teddy's mother came in with a very white face and saw what was left of Nag, and Rikki-tikki dragged himself to Teddy's bedroom and spent half the rest of the night shaking himself tenderly to find out whether he really was broken into forty pieces, as he fancied.

When morning came, he was very stiff but well pleased with his doings. "Now I have Nagaina to settle with, and she will be worse than five Nags, and there's no knowing when the eggs she spoke of will hatch. Goodness! I must go and see Darzee," he said. ▶

Without waiting for breakfast, Rikki-tikki ran to the thorn bush where Darzee was singing a song of triumph at the top of his voice. The news of Nag's death was all over the garden, for the sweeper had thrown the body on the rubbish heap.

"Oh, you stupid tuft of feathers!" said Rikki-tikki angrily. "Is this the time to sing?"

---

singe (sĭnj) *v.* to burn lightly

MAKE JUDGMENTS
Rising action leads to a story's **climax,** or point of maximum tension. Recall the rest of the story. In your opinion, should Rikki-tikki's battle with Nag be considered the climax? Explain.

☐ yes   ☐ no

_____
_____
_____
_____
_____

ANALYZE
Rikki-tikki has now fought two snakes. What has he learned from these fights that prepares him for his final battle?

_____
_____
_____
_____

RIKKI-TIKKI-TAVI

valiant (văl′yənt) *adj.* brave; courageous

"Nag is dead—is dead—is dead!" sang Darzee. "The **valiant** Rikki-tikki caught him by the head and held fast. The big man brought the bang stick, and Nag fell in two pieces! He will never eat my babies again."

"All that's true enough; but where's Nagaina?" said Rikki-tikki, looking carefully round him.

"Nagaina came to the bathroom sluice and called for Nag," Darzee went on; "and Nag came out on the end of a stick—the sweeper picked him up on the end of a stick and threw him upon the rubbish heap. Let us sing about the great, the red-eyed Rikki-tikki!" And Darzee filled his throat and sang.

"If I could get up to your nest, I'd roll your babies out!" said Rikki-tikki. "You don't know when to do the right thing at the right time. You're safe enough in your nest there, but it's war for me down here. Stop singing a minute, Darzee."

"For the great, the beautiful Rikki-tikki's sake I will stop," said Darzee. "What is it, O Killer of the terrible Nag?"

"Where is Nagaina, for the third time?"

"On the rubbish heap by the stables, mourning for Nag. Great is Rikki-tikki with the white teeth."

"Bother my white teeth! Have you ever heard where she keeps her eggs?"

"In the melon bed, on the end nearest the wall, where the sun strikes nearly all day. She hid them there weeks ago."

"And you never thought it worthwhile to tell me? The end nearest the wall, you said?" ◀

"Rikki-tikki, you are not going to eat her eggs?"

"Not 'eat' exactly, no. Darzee, if you have a grain of sense, you will fly off to the stables and pretend that your wing is broken and let Nagaina chase you away to this bush. I must get to the melon bed, and if I went there now, she'd see me."

Darzee was a featherbrained little fellow who could never hold more than one idea at a time in his head; and just because he knew that Nagaina's children were born in eggs like his own, he didn't think at first that it was fair to kill

EVALUATE

This page of dialogue contains both humor and **suspense.** Circle the words and phrases that add to the humor; box the words and phrases that add to the suspense.

In your opinion, does the humor enhance or detract from the suspense?

_____

_____

_____

_____

them. But his wife was a sensible bird, and she knew that cobra's eggs meant young cobras later on; so she flew off from the nest and left Darzee to keep the babies warm and continue his song about the death of Nag. Darzee was very like a man in some ways.

She fluttered in front of Nagaina by the rubbish heap and cried out, "Oh, my wing is broken! The boy in the house threw a stone at me and broke it." Then she fluttered more desperately than ever.

Nagaina lifted up her head and hissed, "You warned Rikki-tikki when I would have killed him. Indeed and truly, you've chosen a bad place to be lame in." And she moved toward Darzee's wife, slipping along over the dust.

"The boy broke it with a stone!" shrieked Darzee's wife.

"Well! It may be some **consolation** to you when you're dead to know that I shall settle accounts[8] with the boy. My husband lies on the rubbish heap this morning, but before night the boy in the house will lie very still. What is the use of running away? I am sure to catch you. Little fool, look at me!" ▶

Darzee's wife knew better than to do *that,* for a bird who looks at a snake's eyes gets so frightened that she cannot move. Darzee's wife fluttered on, piping sorrowfully, and never leaving the ground, and Nagaina quickened her pace.

Rikki-tikki heard them going up the path from the stables, and he raced for the end of the melon patch near the wall. There, in the warm litter above the melons, very **cunningly** hidden, he found twenty-five eggs, about the size of a bantam's eggs[9] but with whitish skins instead of shells.

"I was not a day too soon," he said, for he could see the baby cobras curled up inside the skin, and he knew that the minute they were hatched they could each kill a man or a mongoose. He bit off the tops of the eggs as fast as he could, taking care to crush the young cobras, and turned over the litter from time to time to see whether he had missed any. At last there

---

8. **settle accounts:** even things out by getting revenge.
9. **bantam's eggs:** the eggs of a small hen.

---

consolation (kŏn′sə-lā′shən) *n.* a comfort

TestSmart

In lines 389–407, why does Darzee's wife pretend to have a broken wing?

Ⓐ She hopes Nagaina will feel sorry for her.

Ⓑ She wants Nagaina to settle her account with the boy.

Ⓒ She is trying to trick Nagaina into entering the bungalow.

Ⓓ She is acting as a decoy to get Nagaina away from her eggs.

TIP When line numbers appear in a test question, always reread those lines. If the answer is not directly stated in the text, you have to **infer** the answer, or combine clues from the text with your own knowledge to make an educated guess. Circle a phrase or sentence on this page that helps you guess the right answer.

cunningly (kŭn′ĭng-lē) *adv.* in a clever way that is meant to trick or deceive

were only three eggs left, and Rikki-tikki began to chuckle to himself when he heard Darzee's wife screaming.

"Rikki-tikki, I led Nagaina toward the house, and she has gone into the veranda and—oh, come quickly—she means killing!"

Rikki-tikki smashed two eggs and tumbled backward down the melon bed with the third egg in his mouth and scuttled to the veranda as hard as he could put foot to the ground. Teddy and his mother and father were there at early breakfast; but Rikki-tikki saw that they were not eating anything. They sat stone still, and their faces were white. Nagaina was coiled up on the matting by Teddy's chair, within easy striking distance of Teddy's bare leg; and she was swaying to and fro, singing a song of triumph.

"Son of the big man that killed Nag," she hissed, "stay still. I am not ready yet. Wait a little. Keep very still, all you three! If you move, I strike, and if you do not move, I strike. Oh, foolish people who killed my Nag!"

Teddy's eyes were fixed on his father, and all his father could do was to whisper, "Sit still, Teddy. You mustn't move. Teddy, keep still."

Then Rikki-tikki came up and cried, "Turn round, Nagaina; turn and fight!"

"All in good time," said she, without moving her eyes. "I will settle my account with you presently. Look at your friends, Rikki-tikki. They are still and white. They are afraid. They dare not move, and if you come a step nearer, I strike."

"Look at your eggs," said Rikki-tikki, "in the melon bed near the wall. Go and look, Nagaina!"

The big snake turned half round and saw the egg on the veranda. "Ah-h! Give it to me," she said.

Rikki-tikki put his paws one on each side of the egg, and his eyes were blood-red. "What price for a snake's egg? For a young cobra? For a young king cobra? For the last—the very

---

INTERPRET

Do you think Rikki-tikki intentionally saved the last cobra egg, or did he just run off with it in a rush?

☐ intentionally
☐ unintentionally

Underline details on this page and the next that support your opinion.

last of the brood? The ants are eating all the others down by the melon bed."

Nagaina spun clear round, forgetting everything for the sake of the one egg; and Rikki-tikki saw Teddy's father shoot out a big hand, catch Teddy by the shoulder, and drag him across the little table with the teacups, safe and out of reach of Nagaina. ▶

"Tricked! Tricked! Tricked! *Rikk-tck-tck!*" chuckled Rikki-tikki. "The boy is safe, and it was I—I—I that caught Nag by the hood last night in the bathroom." Then he began to jump up and down, all four feet together, his head close to the floor. "He threw me to and fro, but he could not shake me off. He was dead before the big man blew him in two. I did it! *Rikki-tikki-tck-tck!* Come then, Nagaina. Come and fight with me. You shall not be a widow long."

Nagaina saw that she had lost her chance of killing Teddy, and the egg lay between Rikki-tikki's paws. "Give me the egg, Rikki-tikki. Give me the last of my eggs, and I will go away and never come back," she said, lowering her hood.

"Yes, you will go away, and you will never come back, for you will go to the rubbish heap with Nag. Fight, widow! The big man has gone for his gun! Fight!"

Rikki-tikki was bounding all round Nagaina, keeping just out of reach of her stroke, his little eyes like hot coals. Nagaina gathered herself together and flung out at him. Rikki-tikki jumped up and backwards. Again and again and again she struck, and each time her head came with a whack on the matting of the veranda, and she gathered herself together like a watch spring. Then Rikki-tikki danced in a circle to get behind her, and Nagaina spun round to keep her head to his head, so that the rustle of her tail on the matting sounded like dry leaves blown along by the wind. ▶

He had forgotten the egg. It still lay on the veranda, and Nagaina came nearer and nearer to it, till at last, while Rikki-tikki was drawing breath, she caught it in her mouth, turned to the veranda steps, and flew like an arrow down the path,

COMPARE
What similarities do you see between Nagaina's reaction to news of her eggs and the family's reaction to their predicament?

VISUALIZE
Kipling uses imagery to vividly describe the battle between Nagaina and Rikki-tikki. Underline words and phrases in lines 464–488 that help you to see and hear the events as if you were there.

TestSmart

Rikki-tikki momentarily forgets about the egg on the porch. How does his forgetfulness advance the plot?

- Ⓐ The outcome remains uncertain.
- Ⓑ The resolution becomes clear.
- Ⓒ Foreshadowed events occur.
- Ⓓ Loose ends are tied up.

TIP When asked how an event relates to a stage in the **plot**, you're often being asked to identify a **cause and effect relationship**. Locate the event in the text. What does it cause to happen?

EVALUATE

Earlier in the story, Kipling created **suspense** by describing Rikki-tikki's battles in great detail. Note what's different about the way this final fight is presented. Which of the battle scenes do you find most suspenseful? Tell why.

_____
_____
_____
_____

---

with Rikki-tikki behind her. When the cobra runs for her life, she goes like a whiplash flicked across a horse's neck. Rikki-tikki knew that he must catch her, or all the trouble would begin again. ◀

She headed straight for the long grass by the thorn bush, and as he was running, Rikki-tikki heard Darzee still singing his foolish little song of triumph. But Darzee's wife was wiser. She flew off her nest as Nagaina came along and flapped her wings about Nagaina's head. If Darzee had helped, they might have turned her; but Nagaina only lowered her hood and went on. Still, the instant's delay brought Rikki-tikki up to her, and as she plunged into the rat hole where she and Nag used to live, his little white teeth were clenched on her tail, and he went down with her—and very few mongooses, however wise and old they may be, care to follow a cobra into its hole.

It was dark in the hole; and Rikki-tikki never knew when it might open out and give Nagaina room to turn and strike at him. He held on savagely and stuck out his feet to act as brakes on the dark slope of the hot, moist earth.

Then the grass by the mouth of the hole stopped waving, and Darzee said, "It is all over with Rikki-tikki! We must sing his death song. Valiant Rikki-tikki is dead! For Nagaina will surely kill him underground." ◀

So he sang a very mournful song that he made up on the spur of the minute;[10] and just as he got to the most touching part, the grass quivered again, and Rikki-tikki, covered with dirt, dragged himself out of the hole leg by leg, licking his whiskers. Darzee stopped with a little shout. Rikki-tikki shook some of the dust out of his fur and sneezed. "It is all over," he said. "The widow will never come out again." And the red ants that live between the grass stems heard him

---

10. **on the spur of the minute:** on a sudden impulse, without previous thought or planning.

and began to troop down one after another to see if he had spoken the truth.

Rikki-tikki curled himself up in the grass and slept where he was—slept and slept till it was late in the afternoon, for he had done a hard day's work.

"Now," he said, when he awoke, "I will go back to the house. Tell the coppersmith, Darzee, and he will tell the garden that Nagaina is dead."

The coppersmith is a bird who makes a noise exactly like the beating of a little hammer on a copper pot; and the reason he is always making it is because he is the town crier to every Indian garden and tells all the news to everybody who cares to listen. As Rikki-tikki went up the path, he heard his "attention" notes like a tiny dinner gong, and then the steady "*Ding-dong-tock!* Nag is dead—*dong!* Nagaina is dead! *Ding-dong-tock!*" That set all the birds in the garden singing and the frogs croaking, for Nag and Nagaina used to eat frogs as well as little birds.

When Rikki got to the house, Teddy and Teddy's mother (she looked very white still, for she had been fainting) and Teddy's father came out and almost cried over him; and that night he ate all that was given him till he could eat no more and went to bed on Teddy's shoulder, where Teddy's mother saw him when she came to look late at night.

"He saved our lives and Teddy's life," she said to her husband. "Just think, he saved all our lives."

Rikki-tikki woke up with a jump, for the mongooses are light sleepers.

"Oh, it's you," said he. "What are you bothering for? All the cobras are dead; and if they weren't, I'm here."

Rikki-tikki had a right to be proud of himself; but he did not grow too proud, and he kept that garden as a mongoose should keep it, with tooth and jump and spring and bite, till never a cobra dared show its head inside the walls. ▸

ANALYZE

What's the most important thing you learn in the **falling action**? Underline it.

What loose ends are tied up in the **resolution**?

Big Question

In this story, the animals are given human characteristics, yet they also behave on instinct. Do you think Rikki-tikki was **brave** for fighting the snakes? Explain why or why not.
MAKE JUDGMENTS

Assessment Practice I

Reading Comprehension

DIRECTIONS *Answer these questions about "Rikki-tikki-tavi" by filling in the correct ovals.*

1. What do the details in lines 85–97 reveal about the setting?
   - A India is very hot.
   - B Snakes live in India.
   - C The garden is partly wild.
   - D It is early in the evening.

2. How are Darzee and his wife different?
   - A Darzee is evil, but his wife is kind-hearted.
   - B Darzee is foolish, but his wife is wise.
   - C Darzee is brave, but his wife is timid.
   - D Darzee is large, but his wife is small.

3. The most likely cause of Rikki-tikki's conflict with the cobras is that
   - A the cobras killed Rikki-tikki's parents
   - B Rikki-tikki was born to fight and eat snakes
   - C Rikki-tikki wants to be the most feared animal in the garden
   - D the birds need Rikki-tikki's help to defend their nest from the cobras

4. Lines 425–443 are suspenseful because
   - A Darzee's wife is screaming.
   - B Teddy's father doesn't have the gun.
   - C Rikki-tikki might break the third egg.
   - D Nagaina is within striking distance of Teddy.

5. Which event leads directly to the climax of the story?
   - A Rikki-tikki hears Nag and Nagaina plotting to kill the people.
   - B Nagaina grabs her last egg and heads for the garden.
   - C Darzee sings a victory song for Rikki-tikki.
   - D Rikki-tikki killed a snakeling in the garden.

6. From the story's resolution, you can tell that
   - A Darzee the tailorbird bird has learned his lesson.
   - B Rikki-tikki will eventually be killed by a snake.
   - C Teddy's mother will learn to love Rikki-tikki.
   - D Teddy and his family will be safe.

7. What does the word *purchase* mean in line 319?
   - A to buy
   - B to rest
   - C a firm hold
   - D a storebought item

8. From its description in lines 255–261, you can tell that a *sluice* is
   - A hollow
   - B flexible
   - C curved
   - D tasty

22 UNIT 1: PLOT, CONFLICT, AND SETTING

Responding in Writing

9. Short Response Write a paragraph that summarizes "Rikki-tikki-tavi."

Test-Taker's Toolkit

ACADEMIC VOCABULARY When you're asked to **summarize** a story, you need to identify its **setting** and key characters and briefly explain the **conflict,** main events, and **resolution** in your own words.

GRAPHIC ORGANIZER Use the story map below to help you plan your response. Look back at the story to help you remember the details.

TITLE:	AUTHOR:
SETTING:	
KEY CHARACTERS:	
CONFLICT:	

MAIN PLOT EVENTS:

RESOLUTION:

For help, use the Test-Taker's Toolkit below.

RIKKI-TIKKI-TAVI

Related Nonfiction

- **King Cobras: Feared, Revered**
  MAGAZINE ARTICLE
- **Fight or Flight?**
  ONLINE ARTICLE

Use with "Rikki-tikki-tavi," p. 2

What's the Connection?

Like many people, the family in "Rikki-tikki-tavi" would do anything to avoid a close encounter with a venomous cobra. However, some people have a different perspective about snakes. In the magazine article "King Cobras: Feared, Revered" a writer tells about her visit to a village in Thailand where people perform perilous tricks with wild king cobras. When a cobra approaches the writer herself, she nearly panics. The science article "Fight or Flight?" explores the physiological factors that govern our response to frightening encounters such as these.

THINK ABOUT FEAR On the lines below, list the different effects fear can have on a person or an animal. Then answer the question.

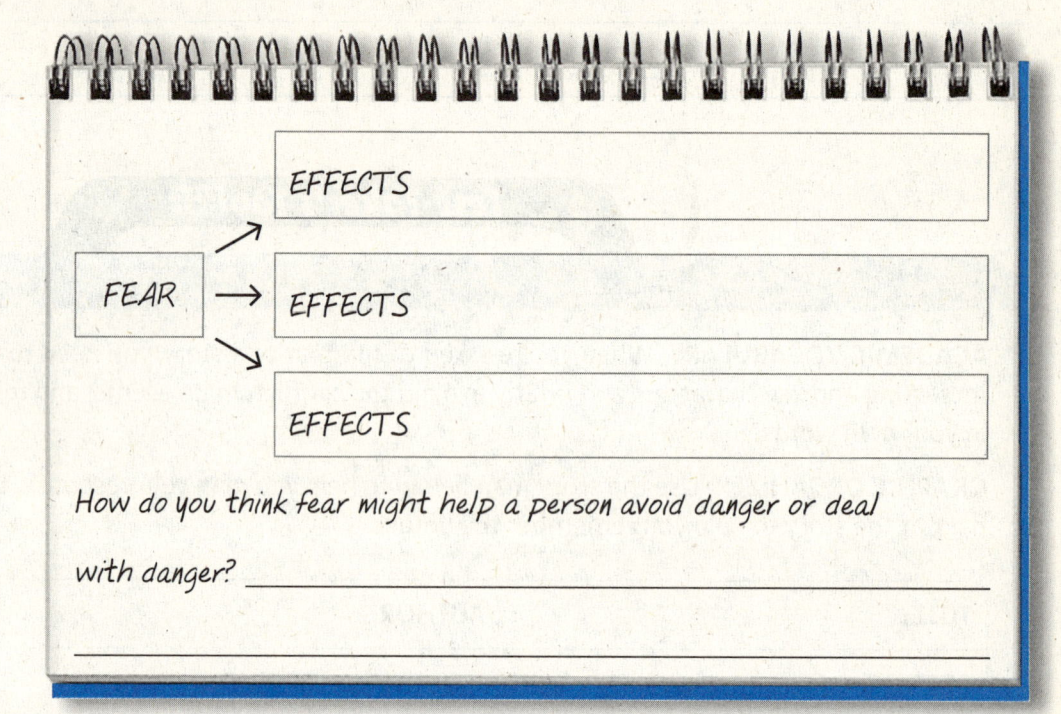

FEAR → EFFECTS
FEAR → EFFECTS
FEAR → EFFECTS

How do you think fear might help a person avoid danger or deal with danger? _____

LEARN THE SKILL: IDENTIFY TEXT FEATURES

Many nonfiction writers use design elements called **text features** to organize text and to point out key ideas and important information. Here are some of the most common text features:

- A **title** suggests an article's topic.
- **Subheadings** usually name the main ideas, or the most important points the writer makes.
- **Graphic aids** such as diagrams, charts, and maps provide information in visual form.
- **Captions** give information about photos or other graphics.

For more on text features, see *Nonfiction Handbook* page R22.

UNIT 1: PLOT, CONFLICT, AND SETTING

KING COBRAS
Feared, Revered
by Mattias Klum
from *National Geographic*

CLOSE READ

SET A PURPOSE
My purpose for reading is

TEXT FEATURES
Preview the article. What information do you learn from the **title** and **subheadings**? In which section would you expect to find information about the author's meeting with a cobra?

Lightning fast and just as deadly, an agitated king cobra strikes in self-defense during a "boxing match" between man and serpent. Villagers of Ban Khok Sa-nga in northeastern Thailand perform this perilous dance for coins from visitors and respect from peers. The act began as a way to lure potential buyers of herbal medicines and snakebite cures.

As if lit from within, the mist-drenched rain forest of Borneo's Danum Valley awakens with me before sunrise. Somewhere below stirs the king cobra—the inspiration

"Though snakes strike fear in many Westerners, in the East the cobra is often an object of worship and reverence . . ."

RELATED NONFICTION 25

SPECIALIZED Vocabulary

If the word **neurotoxin** in line 18 is new to you, look to see whether you recognize any of the word's parts. If you do, put a box around the familiar word that appears within the larger word.

Write the word's likely meaning. **WORD ANALYSIS**

_____

_____

_____

DRAW CONCLUSIONS

What changes might the over-cutting of Southeast Asian forests result in for the humans and wildlife who live in the area?

---

for my journey to the villages and forests of Southeast Asia. The longest venomous snake, it produces startling amounts of **neurotoxin**—enough to kill an elephant with a single bite. But this serpent that can stand up like a man in a terrifying pose
20 is shy and retreating, aggressive only if provoked. We know little about its populations, but fragmented forests and illegal wildlife trade may be putting it at risk. Though snakes strike fear in many Westerners, in the East the cobra is often an object of worship and reverence—and, in some places, a part of peoples' livelihoods. So I have come here to pay my respects to Ophiophagus hannah, with hopes that I might observe this king of snakes in its natural realm. ◀

At home in tropical Asia, the king cobra requires dense undergrowth, such as mangrove swamps or forests near streams.
30 "King cobras don't adapt well to heavily cultivated areas like rice fields," says biologist Wolfgang Wuster of the University of Wales, Bangor. "So if the forests go, so do the kings."

Close Encounters

Once fearful of all that slithered in their wild, brimming forests, the villagers of Ban Khok Sa-nga for decades made use of venomous snakes by killing and eating them. Today locals, who rely on rice cultivation and a diminishing supply of wood, bring in much needed income by entertaining with, rather than stir-frying, the deadly king
40 cobra. Waving and yelling "King cobra!" in Thai and English, roving shills[1] enticed me and other passersby into a small building where, for 10 baht (about 25 cents), we watched the ladies of the King Cobra Club dance holding snakes' heads in their mouths. No one could tell me the origins of the performance, but it makes economic sense—and sends chills through an uninitiated crowd. ◀

> "Snakes aren't evil or mean... They just want to be left alone."

---

1. **shills:** slang for people who lure customers.

UNIT 1: PLOT, CONFLICT, AND SETTING

CLOSE READ

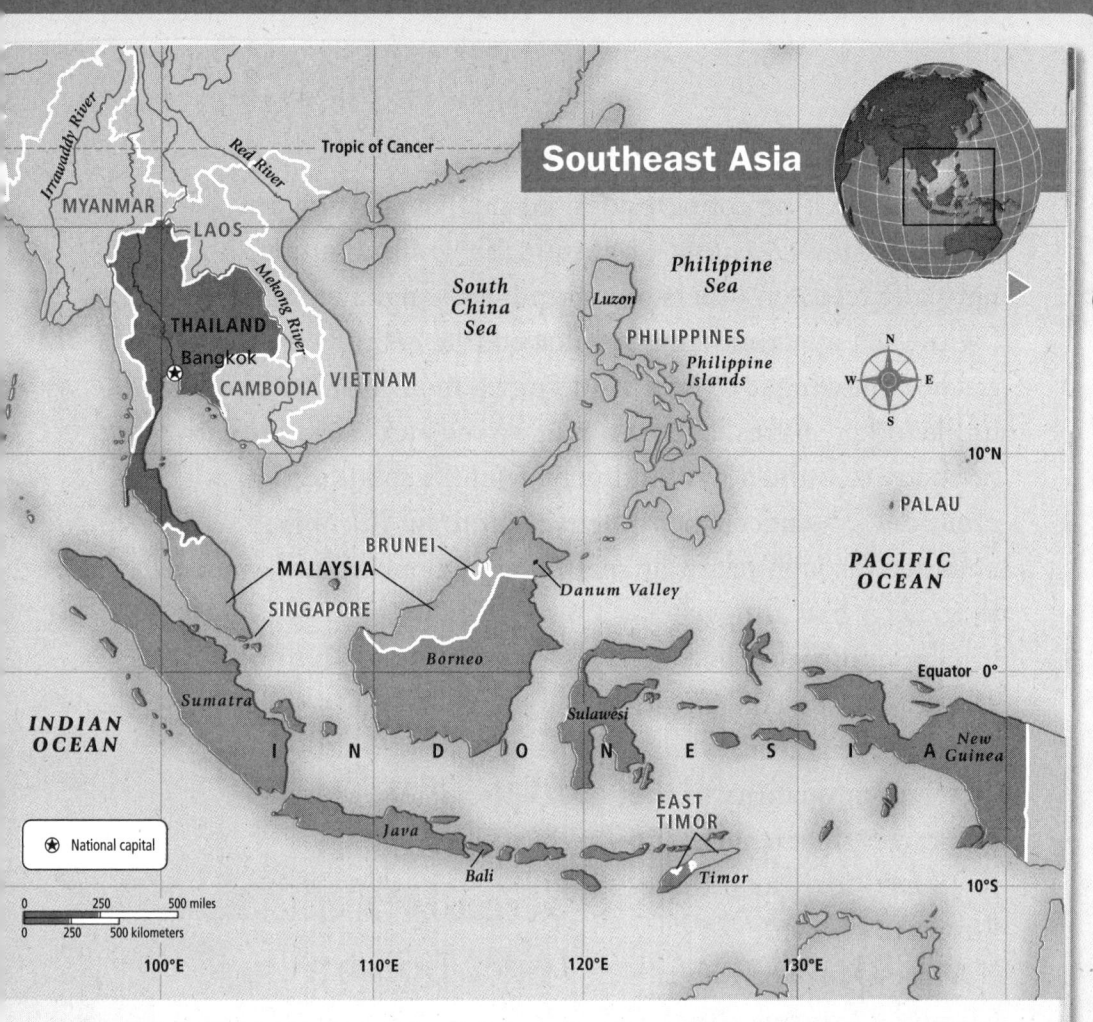

TEXT FEATURES

According to this map, what countries are found in Southeast Asia? Circle their names.

In what country is the Danum Valley?

---

50   A man for whom cobras are family, village elder Komchai Pimsaimoon has spent years learning the rhythms of the serpent—what calms it and what makes it fighting mad. Mad was in force back at the boxing ring, where a now rested king whipped toward me on release from its wooden enclosure. Though I managed to skirt its strike, I took some comfort knowing I had cobra antivenom in my pack. Locals assured me that their herbal remedy was also on hand—just in case mine failed to work.

With no room for error, snake handler Othman Ayib intensely
60 eyes his student, who attempts to calm—and kiss—a wild king cobra. Ayib caught the agitated snake on a Malaysian golf course, where it had strayed from the forest, and later freed it on wilder lands. "Snakes aren't evil or mean," he says. "They just want to be left alone."

RELATED NONFICTION   27

The Forest's Deadly King

Where the king cobra resides, no smaller snake of any species is safe. *O. hannah,* a formidable ground hunter, normally feeds on others of its kind. In Langkawi, Malaysia, I witnessed a victim being swallowed, the cobra's visible trachea allowing it to breathe despite a mouthful. In a behavior unlike other snakes, a female king rounds up leaf litter with her body to build a nest and may defend a small territory around it. She injects her potent neurotoxin in copious amounts through relatively small fangs (about ten millimeters long). Her hatchlings—usually numbering between 20 and 40—emerge already loaded with poison, which increases in quantity as they attain the great lengths (up to 18 feet) for which the kings are known.

At the Queen Saovabha Memorial Institute's Snake Farm in Bangkok, antivenom, the modern snakebite remedy, is made. Adult cobras are milked every few weeks, and small doses of venom are injected into horses, which develop antibodies to it. Horse plasma is collected and treated to make the final product—which, if given to a victim in time, stops the venom's toxic effects. ◀

After a frantic chase for the ultimate photograph, I at last faced a wild king in a Danum Valley stream. With a growling hiss and flared hood the defensive cobra stood its ground, landed a forceful strike on my camera lens, then dropped flat and fled downstream—14 feet of muscle and scales sweeping my leg as it made its escape.

> "Her hatchlings—usually numbering between 20 and 40—emerge already loaded with poison . . ."

TestSmart

Which step is *not* part of the process of making antivenom?

- **A** Adult cobras are milked.
- **B** Venom is injected into horses.
- **C** Antibodies are withdrawn from cobras.
- **D** Horse plasma is collected and treated.

TIP When a test question includes the word *not*, use the **process of elimination** to find the answer. Even if you think you already know it, double check by locating each lettered choice in the text. One choice has been found for you. Underline the others. The one you cannot find is the correct answer.

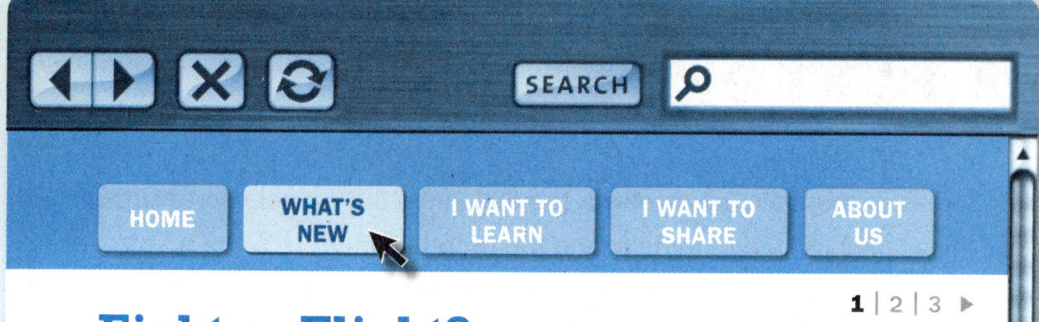

Fight or Flight?

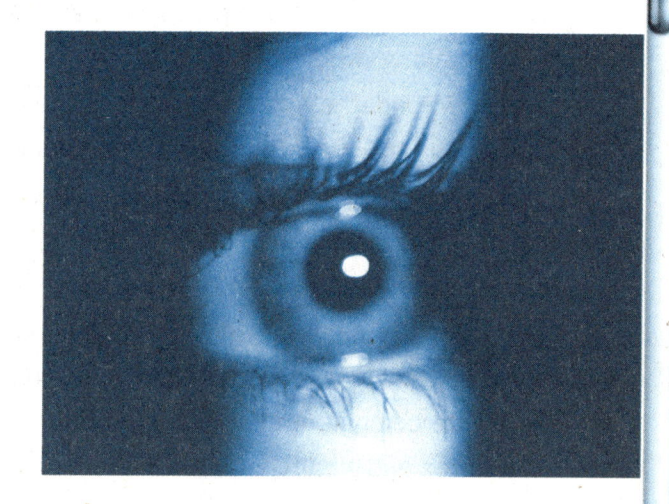

Picture this: You go out to the garage to get your bicycle, and as you open the door, you find yourself staring into the eyes of a king cobra. Its hood is flared, its fangs are showing, and it's hissing, ready to strike. There's no time to wonder where this deadly snake came from, or what it's doing there. You have to act—now. ▶

BRAIN WORK

Before you even begin to think about what to do, though, your brain goes into high gear. It begins triggering a series of chemical and physiological reactions in your body that will help you deal with this terrifying threat. Your heart begins to pound, your breathing becomes rapid, your muscles get tense, the pupils of your eyes dilate, and you may sweat or get goose bumps. Internal changes are also taking place: the level of glucose in your blood increases to provide energy, the smooth muscles that line your organs relax so oxygen can flood your lungs, and your digestive and immune systems stop functioning to free up nutrients your body needs to take action fast.

These external and internal physical reactions are part of the fight-or-flight response, a survival mechanism you share with all other animals. When you experience a frightening stimulus, such as a cobra in your path, your brain immediately begins processing the information. Five primary

PREDICT

From what you've read so far, what do you think this article will be about? Give evidence to support your answer.

areas of the brain are involved: the thalamus, the sensory cortex, the hippocampus, the amygdala, and the hypothalamus.

YOU TAKE THE HIGH ROAD, AND I'LL TAKE THE LOW ROAD

First, the message "Possible danger!" is received in the thalamus. It is then sent along two separate pathways: the low road and the high road. The low road, the shortest pathway, goes first to the amygdala and then to the hypothalamus. It kicks in without complete details about the stimulus, to save you in case the danger does turn out to be life threatening. This instant-messaging system quickly gets the body geared up either to take on the threat or to take off.

At the same time, sensory details—the shape, color, size, hissing sound, smell, and feel of the cobra (if you were unfortunate enough to touch it)—are being sent along the high road from the thalamus to the sensory cortex and hippocampus. On the high road, the information is interpreted and evaluated before being forwarded to the amygdala. The sensory cortex tries to determine what all the details mean and then sends this information to the hippocampus for further evaluation. The hippocampus compares the data with what's stored in your memory and checks to see if your senses have registered additional clues, like a slithery trail in the dust on the garage floor. If the hippocampus decides there is no danger—that the snake is just a model your older brother built for the science fair, for example—it signals the amygdala, which tells the hypothalamus to shut down the fight-or-flight response. On the other hand, if everything indicates that you're face-to-face with a real cobra, the message is "Full speed ahead."

HOW THE HUMAN BRAIN REACTS TO A THREAT

The hypothalamus gets this message to the body through both the nervous system and the bloodstream. The nervous system causes the body to speed up, become tense, and get ready to act. At the same time, it sends messages to your smooth muscles and glands that release the stress hormones epinephrine and norepinephrine into your blood. It's these hormones that cause your heart rate and blood pressure to

---

MONITOR

Reread the boxed paragraph. Why is it important for our brains to have a short pathway? Underline the answer in the text.

SPECIALIZED Vocabulary

If the specialized vocabulary in a science article such as this one is interfering with your comprehension, use context clues and information found in **graphic aids** to help you get what you need to know. Circle clues that help you understand the role of the hippocampus in the fight-or-flight response.
WORD ANALYSIS

PATHWAYS IN THE BRAIN

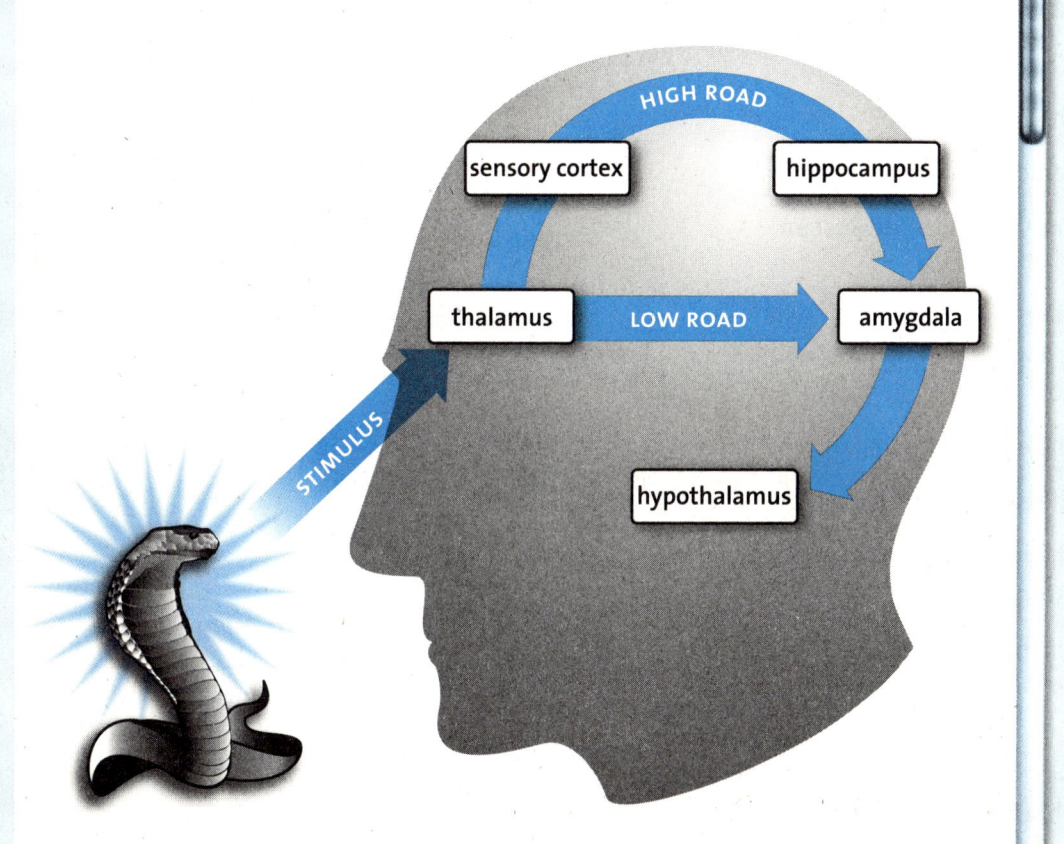

TEXT FEATURES

Use the diagram plus clues in the text to write each detail below where it belongs in the chart.
- shortest pathway
- full details
- few details
- longer pathway

Low Road	
High Road	

increase. The hypothalamus also stimulates the pituitary gland, which causes the release of other hormones that prepare you to deal with the venomous snake.

So now your body is totally mobilized and ready for action. All that remains is to decide what to do. In a split second, you have to consider what action will be the bravest, the most sensible, or just the most likely to get you out of the situation alive. You're perfectly prepared for fight or flight. Now, which will it be?

Assessment Practice II

Reading Comprehension

DIRECTIONS *Answer these questions about the three selections in this lesson by filling in the correct ovals.*

1. Which subheading *best* sums up the last paragraph of "King Cobras"?
   - A A King Attacks
   - B The Broken Lens
   - C Perilous Snake Dance
   - D Antivenom to the Rescue

2. According to "King Cobras," what is unique about a female king cobra's behavior?
   - A She eats other snakes.
   - B She attacks humans aggressively.
   - C She has one or two hatchlings per litter.
   - D She builds a nest and defends the area around it.

3. According to "Fight or Flight?" what part of the brain first perceives danger?
   - A thalamus
   - B amygdala
   - C hippocampus
   - D sensory cortex

4. Which of the following reactions is *not* a response to fear?
   - A pupils dilate
   - B glucose levels drop
   - C oxygen floods lungs
   - D digestive system stops functioning

5. In "Fight or Flight?", which text feature helps the reader to visualize the pathways in the brain?
   - A map
   - B diagram
   - C captions
   - D subheadings

6. Which of Nag's characteristics in "Rikki-tikki-tavi" is *not* supported by information in "King Cobras"?
   - A his lightning-quick speed
   - B his venomous bite
   - C his flared head
   - D his evil heart

7. Read this sentence from "King Cobras":

   > She injects her potent neurotoxin in copious amounts through relatively small fangs (lines 73–74).

   From the sentence, you can tell that *copious* means
   - A deadly
   - B large
   - C tiny
   - D valuable

8. In line 64 of "Fight or Flight?" the word *mobilized* means
   - A made ready for movement
   - B made perfectly still
   - C already in motion
   - D motorized

Timed Writing Practice

PROMPT

What does being brave mean to you? Write an essay in which you define the concept of (bravery). Provide at least three examples of brave people or deeds to support your ideas. Draw the examples from your own life as well as from two of the selections you have read.

BUDGET YOUR TIME

You have 45 minutes to complete this assignment. Decide how much time to spend on each step.

Analyze _____
Plan _____
Write _____
Review _____

45

Test-Taker's Toolkit

1. ANALYZE THE PROMPT

A. **Find key words** Read the prompt carefully. Circle key words in each sentence. One example has been circled for you.

B. **Find key elements** Based on the circled words, jot down a list of the key elements you need to include in your essay to get a good score.

2. PLAN YOUR RESPONSE

A. **Make notes** Find details and examples that meet the requirements of the prompt. Use a planning chart like the one shown.

B. **Organize your information** Your chart can help you structure your essay. Start with your introduction and definition. Then write a paragraph for each example. End with a conclusion that wraps everything up.

Definition:
Example 1: (personal)
Example 2: (selection 1)
Example 3: (selection 2)

3. WRITE AND REVIEW

A. **Craft an opening** that introduces the topic and shows you understand the prompt. For this prompt, you would want to mention the idea of bravery and say that you will be explaining what it means to you. Write a draft of your opening below.

_____
_____
_____

B. **Write out your full response.** Leave enough time to read through it and make sure you have met all the requirements of the prompt.

RELATED NONFICTION   33

UNIT 2
ANALYZING CHARACTER AND POINT OF VIEW

A Retrieved Reformation
BY O. HENRY

RELATED NONFICTION
When the Curtain Comes Up on a Second Act

Juvenile Justice on Trial

Who deserves a second CHANCE?

Everybody makes mistakes—sometimes big ones. But even people who have made serious mistakes in their lives can change their ways. Why might such a person deserve a second chance?

LIST IT With a partner, think of two or three people who have made some serious errors. Perhaps it's a coach who had great players but led the team to a losing season. Maybe it's someone who betrayed the trust of all her friends. Should these people get a chance to try again and make it right? Discuss why or why not. Then write a list of criteria, or factors, determining who should get a second chance.

Someone deserves a second chance if...

1. _____
2. _____
3. _____

ASSESSMENT GOALS

By the end of this lesson, you will be able to . . .

- analyze character and point of view in a work of fiction
- apply critical thinking skills to analyze a text
- determine the author's purpose in nonfiction texts
- analyze a writing prompt and plan an opinion essay

LEARN THE TERMS: ACADEMIC VOCABULARY

Character and Point of View

To fully understand a story, you have to think about the characters you meet within it. What kind of personality does each one have? How is he or she affected by events? Knowing the following terms can help you explore these types of questions:

- The **NARRATOR** is the voice that tells the story. A writer's choice of narrator is referred to as **POINT OF VIEW**.

- In **FIRST-PERSON POINT OF VIEW**, the narrator is a character in the story and uses the pronouns *I* and *me* to refer to himself or herself. The narrator can describe only his or her own thoughts and feelings.

- In **THIRD-PERSON POINT OF VIEW**, the narrator is not a character in the story and tells the story the way an outside observer would.

- The **MAIN CHARACTER** is the most important character in the story. A story may have more than one main character. A **MINOR CHARACTER** is less important in a story.

- A **CHARACTER TRAIT** is a quality of a character, such as sloppiness, bravery, or honesty.

- **CHARACTERIZATION** is the way writers communicate characters' traits and help readers understand what the characters are like. There are four methods of characterization.

METHODS OF CHARACTERIZATION

PHYSICAL APPEARANCE
A character's appearances, including clothing, hairstyle, gestures, and expressions, can tell you a great deal about him or her.

THOUGHTS, SPEECH, AND ACTIONS
What a character says, does, and believes can reveal his or her personality. Think about how the character treats others and what he or she values.

OTHER CHARACTERS
Other characters' reactions can be clues to what a character is like. Pay attention to what other characters say or think about the person.

NARRATOR'S COMMENTS
Sometimes the narrator tells you directly what a character is like. Notice whether the narrator likes or respects the character, or whether the narrator is critical of him or her.

ADDITIONAL TERMS FOR CRITICAL ANALYSIS

Knowing these additional terms will help you discuss O. Henry's work more precisely:

- The word *omniscient* means "all-knowing." In a story told from the **THIRD-PERSON OMNISCIENT POINT OF VIEW**, the narrator knows what all the characters in the story are thinking and feeling.

- A **DYNAMIC CHARACTER** is one that undergoes important changes as the plot unfolds. These changes happen because of the character's actions and experiences in the story. A **STATIC CHARACTER** is one that remains the same. The character may experience events and interact with other characters, but he or she does not change as a result.

A Retrieved REFORMATION

O. Henry

BACKGROUND The main character in this story, Jimmy Valentine, is a safecracker. He opens safes illegally and steals the money stored inside. The story takes place in the early years of the 20th century, a time in which banks were more vulnerable to robbery than they are now.

A guard came to the prison shoe shop, where Jimmy Valentine was assiduously stitching uppers,[1] and escorted him to the front office. There the warden handed Jimmy his pardon, which had been signed that morning by the governor. Jimmy took it in a tired kind of way. He had served nearly ten months of a four-year sentence. He had expected to stay only about three months, at the longest. When a man with as many friends on the outside as Jimmy Valentine had is received in the "stir" it is hardly worthwhile to cut his hair.

"Now, Valentine," said the warden, "you'll go out in the morning. Brace up, and make a man of yourself. You're not a bad fellow at heart. Stop cracking safes, and live straight." ▶

"Me?" said Jimmy, in surprise. "Why, I never cracked a safe in my life."

---

1. **assiduously** (ə-sĭj′ōō-əs-lē) **stitching uppers:** carefully and industriously sewing together the top portions of shoes.

SECOND READ: CRITICAL ANALYSIS

MARK & ANALYZE
Read this selection once on your own, marking the text in any way that is helpful to you.

Then read the story a second time, using the questions in the margins to help you analyze the literature. When you see this pencil, you'll be asked to mark up the text.

ANALYZE
Underline the sentence that states the warden's opinion of Jimmy's character.

How does this early **characterization** of Jimmy make the outcome of the story more believable?

virtuous (vûr′chōō-əs) *adj.* morally good; honorable

DRAW CONCLUSIONS
The warden's statements make it clear that Jimmy is guilty. Why would Jimmy still deny that he committed the crime?

_____
_____
_____
_____

Who do you think would be most surprised at Jimmy's later actions, the warden or Jimmy? Explain.

_____
_____
_____
_____
_____

compulsory (kəm-pŭl′sə-rē) *adj.* forced; required

rehabilitate (rē′hə-bĭl′ĭ-tāt′) *v.* to restore to useful life, as through therapy and education

DRAW CONCLUSIONS
Jimmy only has five dollars. Underline the details in the text that show he isn't concerned about having so little money.

What do you learn later in the story that explains his attitude?

_____
_____
_____

"Oh, no," laughed the warden. "Of course not. Let's see, now. How was it you happened to get sent up on that Springfield job? Was it because you wouldn't prove an alibi for fear of compromising somebody in extremely high-toned society? Or was it simply a case of a mean old jury that had it in for you? It's always one or the other with you innocent victims."

"Me?" said Jimmy, still blankly **virtuous**. "Why, warden, I never was in Springfield in my life!" ◀

"Take him back, Cronin," smiled the warden, "and fix him up with outgoing clothes. Unlock him at seven in the morning, and let him come to the bull-pen. Better think over my advice, Valentine."

At a quarter past seven on the next morning Jimmy stood in the warden's outer office. He had on a suit of the villainously fitting, ready-made clothes and a pair of the stiff, squeaky shoes that the state furnishes to its discharged **compulsory** guests.

The clerk handed him a railroad ticket and the five-dollar bill with which the law expected him to **rehabilitate** himself into good citizenship and prosperity. The warden gave him a cigar, and shook hands. Valentine, 9762, was chronicled[2] on the books "Pardoned by Governor," and Mr. James Valentine walked out into the sunshine.

Disregarding the song of the birds, the waving green trees, and the smell of the flowers, Jimmy headed straight for a restaurant. There he tasted the first sweet joys of liberty in the shape of a broiled chicken and a bottle of white wine—followed by a cigar a grade better than the one the warden had given him. From there he proceeded leisurely to the depot. He tossed a quarter into the hat of a blind man sitting by the door, and boarded his train. Three hours set him down in a little town near the state line. He went to the café of one Mike Dolan and shook hands with Mike, who was alone behind the bar. ◀

---

2. **chronicled** (krŏn′ĭ-kəld): written down in a record book or ledger book.

"Sorry we couldn't make it sooner, Jimmy, me boy," said Mike. "But we had that protest from Springfield to buck against, and the governor nearly balked. Feeling all right?"

"Fine," said Jimmy. "Got my key?"

He got his key and went upstairs, unlocking the door of a room at the rear. Everything was just as he had left it. There on the floor was still Ben Price's collar-button that had been torn from that eminent detective's shirt-band when they had overpowered Jimmy to arrest him. ▶

Pulling out from the wall a folding-bed, Jimmy slid back a panel in the wall and dragged out a dust-covered suitcase. He opened this and gazed fondly at the finest set of burglar's tools in the East. It was a complete set, made of specially tempered steel, the latest designs in drills, punches, braces and bits, jimmies, clamps, and augers, with two or three novelties invented by Jimmy himself, in which he took pride. Over nine hundred dollars they had cost him to have made at _____, a place where they make such things for the profession.

In half an hour Jimmy went downstairs and through the café. He was now dressed in tasteful and well-fitting clothes, and carried his dusted and cleaned suitcase in his hand.

"Got anything on?"[3] asked Mike Dolan, genially.

"Me?" said Jimmy, in a puzzled tone. "I don't understand. I'm representing the New York Amalgamated Short Snap Biscuit Cracker and Frazzled Wheat Company."

This statement delighted Mike to such an extent that Jimmy had to take a seltzer-and-milk on the spot. He never touched "hard" drinks. ▶

A week after the release of Valentine, 9762, there was a neat job of safe-burglary done in Richmond, Indiana, with no clue to the author. A scant eight hundred dollars was all

---

3. **Got anything on?** *slang expression*: Mike Dolan is asking whether Jimmy has any robberies planned.

---

balk (bôk) *v.* to refuse to move or act

eminent (ĕm′ə-nənt) *adj.* famous; well-respected

ANALYZE

Reread the boxed text. Circle the name of the **character** who will be important later on in the story.

Why do you think O. Henry mentions the character at this point in the story?

_____

_____

_____

genially (jēn′yəl-lē) *adv.* in a pleasant, friendly manner

MAKE INFERENCES

One way that O. Henry **characterizes** Jimmy is through the description of Jimmy's possessions. Circle and reread the paragraph that describes Jimmy's tools and his reaction to them.

List three things you can infer about Jimmy's personality from the description.

1. _____

_____

2. _____

_____

3. _____

A RETRIEVED REFORMATION 39

that was secured. Two weeks after that a patented, improved, burglar-proof safe in Logansport was opened like a cheese to the tune of fifteen hundred dollars, currency; securities and silver untouched. That began to interest the rogue catchers.[4] Then an old-fashioned bank safe in Jefferson City became active and threw out of its crater an eruption of banknotes amounting to five thousand dollars. The losses were now high enough to bring the matter up into Ben Price's class of work. By comparing notes, a remarkable similarity in the methods of the burglaries was noticed. Ben Price investigated the scenes of the robberies, and was heard to remark: "That's Dandy Jim Valentine's autograph. He's resumed business. Look at that combination knob—jerked out as easy as pulling up a radish in wet weather. He's got the only clamps that can do it. And look how clean those tumblers were punched out! Jimmy never has to drill but one hole. Yes, I guess I want Mr. Valentine. He'll do his bit next time without any short-time or clemency foolishness."[5]

Ben Price knew Jimmy's habits. He had learned them while working up the Springfield case. Long jumps, quick get-aways, no confederates,[6] and a taste for good society—these ways had helped Mr. Valentine to become noted as a successful dodger of **retribution**. It was given out that Ben Price had taken up the trail of the **elusive** cracksman, and other people with burglar-proof safes felt more at ease. ◀

One afternoon Jimmy Valentine and his suitcase climbed out of the mailhack in Elmore, a little town five miles off the railroad down in the blackjack country of Arkansas. Jimmy, looking like an athletic young senior just home from college, went down the board sidewalk toward the hotel.

A young lady crossed the street, passed him at the corner, and entered a door over which was the sign "The Elmore

---

retribution (rĕt′rə-byōō′shən) *n.* punishment for bad behavior

elusive (ĭ-lōō′sĭv) *adj.* tending to elude capture

ANALYZE
From **what point of view is this story told?**

☐ third-person limited point of view

☐ third-person omniscient point of view

☐ first-person point of view

How does this point of view add suspense to the story?

---

4. **rogue** (rōg) **catchers:** people who chase after criminals.
5. **He'll do his bit . . . foolishness:** He'll serve his full term in prison without anyone shortening the length of it or pardoning him.
6. **confederates** (kən-fĕd′ər-ĭts): accomplices or associates in crime.

Bank." Jimmy Valentine looked into her eyes, forgot what he was, and became another man. She lowered her eyes and colored slightly. Young men of Jimmy's style and looks were scarce in Elmore.

Jimmy collared a boy that was loafing on the steps of the bank as if he were one of the stockholders, and began to ask him questions about the town, feeding him dimes at intervals. By and by the young lady came out, looking royally unconscious of the young man with the suitcase, and went her way.

"Isn't that young lady Miss Polly Simpson?" asked Jimmy, with specious guile.[7]

"Naw," said the boy. "She's Annabel Adams. Her pa owns this bank. What'd you come to Elmore for? Is that a gold watch-chain? I'm going to get a bulldog. Got any more dimes?"

Jimmy went to the Planters' Hotel, registered as Ralph D. Spencer, and engaged a room. He leaned on the desk and declared his platform to the clerk. He said he had come to Elmore to look for a location to go into business. How was the shoe business, now, in the town? He had thought of the shoe business. Was there an opening? ▶

The clerk was impressed by the clothes and manner of Jimmy. He, himself, was something of a pattern of fashion to the thinly gilded youth of Elmore, but he now perceived his shortcomings. While trying to figure out Jimmy's manner of tying his four-in-hand[8] he cordially gave information.

Yes, there ought to be a good opening in the shoe line. There wasn't an exclusive shoe store in the place. The dry-goods and general stores handled them. Business in all lines was fairly good. Hoped Mr. Spencer would decide to locate in Elmore. He would find it a pleasant town to live in, and the people very sociable. ▶

---

7. **specious guile** (spē′shəs gīl): innocent charm masking real slyness.
8. **four-in-hand:** a necktie tied in the usual way, that is, in a slipknot with the ends left hanging.

TestSmart

VOCABULARY
In line 129, the word *engaged* means

A agreed to get married
B rented
C fought over
D put into gear

TIP A test question may ask about a word that has more than one meaning, such as *engaged*. Even if you are familiar with the word, reread the sentence in which it is used before answering the question. The meaning you are familiar with might not be the correct answer. Use **context clues** to figure out which meaning makes the most sense.

ANALYZE

Underline passages on pages 40–41 in which O. Henry **characterizes** Jimmy through what other characters think or say about him. Circle passages in which O. Henry characterizes Jimmy through the narrator's comments.

A RETRIEVED REFORMATION 41

Mr. Spencer thought he would stop over in the town a few days and look over the situation. No, the clerk needn't call the boy. He would carry up his suitcase, himself; it was rather heavy.

Mr. Ralph Spencer, the phoenix[9] that arose from Jimmy Valentine's ashes—ashes left by the flame of a sudden and alterative attack of love—remained in Elmore, and prospered. He opened a shoe store and secured a good run of trade.

Socially he was also a success and made many friends. And he accomplished the wish of his heart. He met Miss Annabel Adams, and became more and more captivated by her charms.

At the end of a year the situation of Mr. Ralph Spencer was this: he had won the respect of the community, his shoe store was flourishing, and he and Annabel were engaged to be married in two weeks. Mr. Adams, the typical, plodding, country banker, approved of Spencer. Annabel's pride in him almost equaled her affection. He was as much at home in the family of Mr. Adams and that of Annabel's married sister as if he were already a member. ◀

One day Jimmy sat down in his room and wrote this letter, which he mailed to the safe address of one of his old friends in St. Louis:

Dear Old Pal:

I want you to be at Sullivan's place, in Little Rock, next Wednesday night, at nine o'clock. I want you to wind up some little matters for me. And, also, I want to make you a present of my kit of tools. I know you'll be glad to get them—you couldn't duplicate the lot for a thousand dollars. Say, Billy, I've quit the old business—a year ago. I've got a nice store. I'm making an honest living, and I'm going to marry the finest girl on earth two weeks from now. It's

CLASSIFY

Reread lines 148–163 and underline the details that show Jimmy is a **dynamic character.**

---

9. **phoenix** (fē´nĭks): a mythological bird that lived for 500 years and then burned itself to death, only to rise from its own ashes to live another long life.

the only life, Billy—the straight one. I wouldn't touch a dollar of another man's money now for a million. After I get married I'm going to sell out and go West, where there won't be so much danger of having old scores brought up against me. I tell you, Billy, she's an angel. She believes in me; and I wouldn't do another crooked thing for the whole world. Be sure to be at Sully's, for I must see you. I'll bring along the tools with me.

*Your old friend,
Jimmy* ▶

On the Monday night after Jimmy wrote this letter, Ben Price jogged unobtrusively into Elmore in a livery buggy.¹⁰ He lounged about town in his quiet way until he found out what he wanted to know. From the drugstore across the street from Spencer's shoe store he got a good look at Ralph D. Spencer.

"Going to marry the banker's daughter are you, Jimmy?" said Ben to himself, softly. "Well, I don't know!"

The next morning Jimmy took breakfast at the Adamses. He was going to Little Rock that day to order his wedding suit and buy something nice for Annabel. That would be the first time he had left town since he came to Elmore. It had been more than a year now since those last professional "jobs," and he thought he could safely venture out. ▶

After breakfast quite a family party went down together—Mr. Adams, Annabel, Jimmy, and Annabel's married sister with her two little girls, aged five and nine. They came by the hotel where Jimmy still boarded, and he ran up to his room and brought along his suitcase. Then they went on to the bank. There stood Jimmy's horse and buggy and Dolph Gibson, who was going to drive him over to the railroad station.

All went inside the high, carved oak railings into the banking room—Jimmy included, for Mr. Adams's future son-in-law was welcome anywhere. The clerks were pleased to be

---

10. **livery** (lĭv′ə-rē) **buggy:** a hired horse and carriage.

CONTRAST
Reread Jimmy's letter to his friend. In what way has Jimmy's attitude toward "living straight" changed?

ANALYZE
Why is it important to know the thoughts and actions of both Jimmy and Ben Price?

greeted by the good-looking, agreeable young man who was going to marry Miss Annabel. Jimmy set his suitcase down. Annabel, whose heart was bubbling with happiness and lively youth, put on Jimmy's hat and picked up the suitcase. "Wouldn't I make a nice drummer?"[11] said Annabel. "My! Ralph, how heavy it is. Feels like it was full of gold bricks."

"Lot of nickel-plated shoehorns in there," said Jimmy, coolly, "that I'm going to return. Thought I'd save express charges by taking them up. I'm getting awfully economical."

The Elmore Bank had just put in a new safe and vault. Mr. Adams was very proud of it, and insisted on an inspection by everyone. The vault was a small one, but it had a new patented door. It fastened with three solid steel bolts thrown simultaneously with a single handle, and had a time lock. Mr. Adams beamingly explained its workings to Mr. Spencer, who showed a courteous but not too intelligent interest. The two children, May and Agatha, were delighted by the shining metal and funny clock and knobs. ◀

While they were thus engaged Ben Price **sauntered** in and leaned on his elbow, looking casually inside between the railings. He told the teller that he didn't want anything; he was just waiting for a man he knew.

Suddenly there was a scream or two from the women, and a commotion. **Unperceived** by the elders, May, the nine-year-old girl, in a spirit of play, had shut Agatha in the vault. She had then shot the bolts and turned the knob of the combination as she had seen Mr. Adams do.

The old banker sprang to the handle and tugged at it for a moment. "The door can't be opened," he groaned. "The clock hasn't been wound nor the combination set."

Agatha's mother screamed again, hysterically.

"Hush!" said Mr. Adams, raising his trembling hand. "All be quiet for a moment. Agatha!" he called as loudly as he could. "Listen to me." During the following silence they

---

ANALYZE

Irony is the contrast between appearance and reality. What is ironic about the scene in the boxed paragraph?

_____

_____

_____

_____

saunter (sôn′tər) v. to stroll in a casual manner

unperceived (ŭn-pər-sēvd′) adj. not seen or noticed

---

11. **drummer:** an old-fashioned word for traveling salesman.

could just hear the faint sound of the child wildly shrieking in the dark vault in a panic of terror.

"My precious darling!" wailed the mother. "She will die of fright! Open the door! Oh, break it open! Can't you men do something?"

"There isn't a man nearer than Little Rock who can open that door," said Mr. Adams, in a shaky voice. "My God! Spencer, what shall we do? That child—she can't stand it long in there. There isn't enough air, and, besides, she'll go into convulsions from fright." ▶

Agatha's mother, frantic now, beat the door of the vault with her hands. Somebody wildly suggested dynamite. Annabel turned to Jimmy, her large eyes full of anguish, but not yet despairing. To a woman nothing seems quite impossible to the powers of the man she worships.

"Can't you do something, Ralph—try, won't you?"

He looked at her with a queer, soft smile on his lips and in his keen eyes.

"Annabel," he said, "give me that rose you are wearing, will you?" ▶

Hardly believing that she had heard him aright, she unpinned the bud from the bosom of her dress, and placed it in his hand. Jimmy stuffed it into his vest pocket, threw off his coat and pulled up his shirt sleeves. With that act Ralph D. Spencer passed away and Jimmy Valentine took his place.

"Get away from the door, all of you," he commanded, shortly.

He set his suitcase on the table, and opened it out flat. From that time on he seemed to be unconscious of the presence of anyone else. He laid out the shining, queer implements swiftly and orderly, whistling softly to himself as he always did when at work. In a deep silence and immovable, the others watched him as if under a spell.

In a minute Jimmy's pet drill was biting smoothly into the steel door. In ten minutes—breaking his own burglarious record—he threw back the bolts and opened the door.

ANALYZE

What choice does Jimmy face at this moment? Tell what is at risk for him.

_____

_____

_____

_____

💡 TestSmart

Jimmy most likely asks Annabel for the rose because

- **A** he is afraid she will leave him when she learns his true identity
- **B** he thinks that this action will distract her
- **C** he believes the rose will bring him luck opening the safe
- **D** he knows he will be arrested soon

TIP When a question includes a qualifier, such as *most likely* or *probably*, you will often be required to **make an inference** in order to answer. To guess at something the author doesn't state directly, combine clues from the story with your own knowledge and experience. Jimmy is about to reveal skills from his criminal past in front of Annabel's family. What would he be most concerned about?

A RETRIEVED REFORMATION   45

EVALUATE

Is Ben Price a **dynamic character** or a **static character**? Explain why you think as you do.

_____
_____
_____
_____

Big Question

Look back at the Big Question on page 35. Do you think Jimmy deserves the second chance Ben Price gave him? Why or why not? MAKE JUDGMENTS

_____
_____
_____
_____

Agatha, almost collapsed, but safe, was gathered into her mother's arms.

280 Jimmy Valentine put on his coat, and walked outside the railings toward the front door. As he went he thought he heard a faraway voice that he once knew call "Ralph!" But he never hesitated. At the door a big man stood somewhat in his way.

"Hello, Ben!" said Jimmy, still with his strange smile. "Got around at last, have you? Well, let's go. I don't know that it makes much difference, now."

And then Ben Price acted rather strangely.

"Guess you're mistaken, Mr. Spencer," he said. "Don't
290 believe I recognize you. Your buggy's waiting for you, ain't it?"

And Ben Price turned and strolled down the street. ◀

46 UNIT 2: ANALYZING CHARACTER AND POINT OF VIEW

Reading Comprehension

DIRECTIONS Answer these questions about "A Retrieved Reformation" by filling in the correct ovals.

1. How can you tell that "A Retrieved Reformation" is told from the third-person omniscient point of view?
    - A The narrator tells what Jimmy Valentine intends.
    - B The narrator knows what Ben Price wants.
    - C The narrator observes the two main characters' actions.
    - D The narrator tells what all the characters think and feel.

2. From his statement to Mike Dolan in lines 72–74, you can tell that Jimmy
    - A is smart and sincere
    - B plans to go straight
    - C has not been rehabilitated
    - D means well, but makes a lot of mistakes

3. How are Jimmy's emotions revealed in lines 111–114?
    - A through the narrator's explanation
    - B through what another character tells Jimmy
    - C through what Jimmy says
    - D through what another character says about Jimmy

4. In Jimmy's letter to his friend, which of the following is *not* part of his plans?
    - A moving West
    - B robbing a bank
    - C marrying Annabel
    - D selling the shoe store

5. Based on Ben Price's comments in lines 191–192, what does he probably think Jimmy has planned?
    - A an honest business venture
    - B a career as a banker
    - C a second marriage
    - D a bank robbery

6. You can tell that Annabel Adams is a static character because she
    - A is not changed by her experiences
    - B narrates the story
    - C experiences an important change
    - D is omniscient

7. What does the word *stir* mean in line 9?
    - A mix with a spoon
    - B a prison
    - C move slightly
    - D make trouble

8. What does the word *straight* mean in line 12?
    - A in a line
    - B not curved
    - C without stopping
    - D in an honest way

Assessment Practice I

GO ON

A RETRIEVED REFORMATION 47

Assessment Practice I

Responding in Writing

9. Short Response Write a character sketch of Jimmy Valentine.

___

Test-Taker's Toolkit

ACADEMIC VOCABULARY When you're asked to write a **character sketch,** you need to write a brief but detailed description of a character. Include information about his or her appearance, background, and **character traits.**

GRAPHIC ORGANIZER Use the graphic organizer below to help you gather the details you'll need to write a successful character sketch.

- JIMMY VALENTINE
  - How others react to him
  - How he looks
  - Who he is
  - What his personality is like

UNIT 2: ANALYZING CHARACTER AND POINT OF VIEW

Related Nonfiction

What's the Connection?

Second chances aren't reserved for stories, songs, and movies. Like Jimmy Valentine, real-life judge Greg Mathis and movie subject Frank Abagnale turned away from lives of crime to become responsible citizens. The magazine article "When the Curtain Comes Up on a Second Act" traces their journeys from juvenile offenders to respected personalities. Should more kids with criminal backgrounds be given a second chance? The newspaper editorial "Juvenile Justice on Trial" makes the case that they should.

THINK AHEAD What determines whether a troubled teenager can successfully change course? Explore your opinions on the topic of teens and rehabilitation by answering the questions in the anticipation guide. After you've read both selections, return to this page and indicate whether your thinking has changed.

- **When the Curtain Comes Up on a Second Act**
  MAGAZINE ARTICLE
- **Juvenile Justice on Trial**
  EDITORIAL

Use with "A Retrieved Reformation," p. 34

	BEFORE READING	AFTER READING
1. Who has the most control over whether someone gets a second chance? A. parents and other family members B. law enforcement officials C. the individual himself or herself	A B C	A B C
2. Should teenagers and adults who commit the same crime receive the same treatment from the justice system? A. yes, if the crime is the same, the punishment should be also B. no, teens should be treated with more compassion C. maybe, depending on the nature of the crime	A B C	A B C

LEARN THE SKILL: IDENTIFY AUTHOR'S PURPOSE

Every author has a **purpose**, or reason, for writing a text. An author may write for one or more of the following reasons:

- to inform readers about a topic or to explain something
- to persuade readers to do or believe something
- to express thoughts and feelings
- to entertain readers

If you can identify why an author is writing, it will help you to understand what you reading.

For more on author's purpose, see *Nonfiction Handbook* page R5.

RELATED NONFICTION **49**

CLOSE READ

SET A PURPOSE
My purpose for reading is
_____
_____
_____

When the Curtain Comes Up on a Second Act

by Molly Landek

Whether it's breaking the rules or breaking the law, ruining a friendship or committing an act of betrayal, most of us eventually recognize when we've made a terrible mistake. In fact, that recognition, along with the shame, embarrassment, and dread that it inspires, can become self-defeating, making it even harder to make amends. But the truth is, one mistake—or even a series of mistakes—doesn't have to mean the end of hope. In time, the curtain of life will rise on a second act. It's how we respond to this new opportunity that says the most about what kind of person we are. As actress Mary Pickford once said, "If you have made mistakes, even serious ones, there is always another chance for you. What we call failure is not the falling down but the staying down." Two well-known and upstanding citizens have learned this lesson for themselves. Perhaps their stories can inspire those of us who are tempted to wallow in our failures.

TOUGH LOVE FOR A TOUGH TEEN

Greg Mathis, star of TV's popular courtroom show "Judge Mathis," got the second chance he needed when his mother made a dying wish. As a teenager in Detroit, Mathis had frequent run-ins with the law. By the time he was 17, Mathis was a high school drop-out with an extensive rap sheet of charges, including larceny,[1] purse snatching, and car theft. When he was arrested on a weapons charge and prosecuted as an adult, Mathis's mother Alice decided it was time to teach him a lesson. She refused to bail him out of jail for three weeks. Tragically, Alice became sick with cancer. She visited Mathis in jail and told him she had only a year to live, and that she wanted to see him lead a productive life. Mathis promised his mother that he would turn his life around once and for all. After his release from jail, Mathis earned his high school equivalency diploma (GED). But he didn't stop there. Mathis went on to college and then to law school. He became a lawyer. When he decided to campaign for judge, Mathis faced a difficult challenge. His opponents in the election dredged up his spotty past, even going so far as to leak sealed juvenile court documents to the press. But Mathis's determination paid off. He chose to fight the allegations that his criminal past made him a poor candidate—and he won. Mathis became the youngest judge in Michigan history. Today, Mathis presides over litigants[2] in his TV courtroom with the same "tough love" attitude that Alice showed him all those years ago. ▶

A CON ARTIST GETS AN OFFER HE CAN'T REFUSE

Frank Abagnale Jr. found his second chance after years of running. Abagnale left home when he was just 16 years old. To get a job, Abagnale, a tall youth with graying hair, changed the age on his ID card, making himself 10 years older. But his deceits didn't stop there. Over the next five years, Abagnale became an adept

---

> **TestSmart**
>
> What is the main reason Greg Mathis pursued his education after dropping out of school?
>
> A) He didn't want to disappoint the judge who offered him a second chance.
> B) His mother refused to bail him out of jail.
> C) His dying mother asked him to make a positive change in his life.
> D) He wanted to go to college.
>
> **TIP** When a question asks why something occurred, it is asking you to identify a **cause-and-effect relationship**. Remember, just because one event occurs after another doesn't mean the first event was the cause of the second. Think carefully about the relationships between events before choosing your answer.

---

1. **larceny** (lär′sə-nē): theft of personal property.
2. **litigants** (lĭt′ĭ-gəntz): people engaged in lawsuits.

con-artist, passing himself off as an airline pilot, an attorney, and even a doctor. He created elaborate check-cashing scams, and, as "Pilot Frank Williams," traveled the world on money he stole.

Abagnale's free ride came to a screeching halt when he was 21. He was arrested by French police and **incarcerated** for five years on forgery charges. He was then transferred to a U.S. penitentiary to begin a 12-year sentence for multiple counts of forgery. Abagnale was released after four years, on the condition that he help the FBI fight white-collar crime—without pay. Hoping to get a fresh start, Abagnale seized the opportunity.

After his release from prison, Abagnale found it nearly impossible to obtain a legitimate job because of his criminal record. These conditions might have led others to give up trying, and perhaps even to go back to a life of crime. But Abagnale found the courage to approach a bank and offer to train its employees on how to recognize various check-cashing schemes. He told the bank managers that if they didn't like his training, they owed him nothing; if they found it useful, they would pay him $50 and tell other banks about his program. Luckily, the plan worked, and Frank Abagnale Jr. began a legitimate and profitable career as a security consultant. His story became the subject of the Steven Spielberg movie "Catch Me if You Can."

KNOWING WHEN TO ACT

Most of us will make mistakes in our lives, and most of us will be given second chances. What sets people like Mathis and Abagnale apart from the rest is their ability to recognize an opportunity when it's offered to them, and their determination to see the opportunity through, despite the hurdles they encounter along the way. Bouncing back from a big mistake is not easy, but if you're given the opportunity to do so, summon your courage, set aside your fears, and act on your best instincts. If you do that, you can never be a failure.

Juvenile Justice on Trial

by Sheri Steinberg

It seems that every month, there's another sensational story about adolescents who are being tried for committing serious crimes. When these teenagers face the court, should the justice system be more concerned with gaining retribution[1] for society or with aiding the rehabilitation of the offenders? Different states and legal professionals answer that question differently. It is crucial, however, that we look carefully at how justice is administered to juveniles in this country and work toward a system that best serves both the offenders and society as a whole.

The teenage years can be difficult, as both neurological[2] and physical changes take place rapidly. No longer children, but not yet adults, teenagers sometimes get shipwrecked while trying to navigate this challenging decade. Those who end up breaking the law don't fit neatly into the justice system. Although juvenile courts were established to deal with these youths, increasing numbers of young criminals are being transferred into the criminal justice system and tried as adults.

Underage in Adult Court

Violent crimes committed by young people rose dramatically in the late 1980s and early 1990s. The number of murders, for example, tripled between 1984 and 1993. In response, most states have passed laws enabling the courts to try juveniles as adults. As a result, in some states, juveniles who commit serious crimes automatically funnel into the adult system.

---

1. **retribution** (rĕt′rə-byoo′shən): punishment for wrongdoing.
2. **neurological** (noo-rŏl′ə-jē-ĭ-kəl): having to do with the body's nervous system.

CLOSE READ

PREVIEW
Read the title and headings. Based on these, what do you think you think the purpose of this article is?

EXAMINE PERSPECTIVES
The first paragraph of the article states two different perspectives about what the purpose of the justice system should be. Underline those perspectives, and label them 1 and 2.

On the lines below, restate the perspectives in your own words.

Some people believe that

while others think that

RELATED NONFICTION 53

TestSmart

Which statement is one the author gives in support of juvenile courts?

- **A** Teens do not have the maturity, control, or awareness of consequences of adults.
- **B** Teens benefit from more severe punishment than adults.
- **C** Treating teens is less costly than treating adults.
- **D** Teens are less likely than adults to be treated successfully.

TIP When a question asks you to choose a statement from the author, you know the answer can be found in the text. First, skim the text for a word or phrase that suggests where you will find the answer. To answer this question for example, you would **locate** the section titled "The Case for the Juvenile Courts." Then **reread** that section and look for a statement that matches one of the answer choices.

Unfortunately, teens who have committed less-serious crimes also get transferred to the criminal courts. In fact, "The majority of kids being tried as adults are being tried for nonviolent crimes," says Vincent Schiraldi, president of the Center for Juvenile and Criminal Justice. These teens often end up being held not in juvenile homes with others their own age but in prisons with violent adults. As a result of these procedures, the number of new underage inmates in adult prisons more than doubled—from 3,400 to 7,400—between 1985 and 1997.

This approach to juvenile crime has benefited neither the offenders nor society, however. According to Mark Soler of the Youth Law Center in Washington, D.C., "Prosecuting kids as adults is counterproductive.[3] It creates more crime." Statistics show that juveniles prosecuted as adults are 30% more likely to commit new—and more violent—crimes than those prosecuted as juveniles.

The Case for the Juvenile Courts

These statistics support the case for treating juvenile offenders differently from adults. Many judges and other law enforcement officials who work with juvenile offenders strongly agree. They point out that teens do not have the maturity, control, or awareness of consequences of adults and should not be held as rigidly accountable for their actions. If given a second chance, they are more able than adults to respond to treatment and change the direction of their lives. ◀

Where the adult courts tend to dispense a more or less one-size-fits-all justice, the juvenile system is far more flexible and responsive to the needs of individual offenders. It is also geared to provide rehabilitation rather than retribution. Although no approach works for every teen, studies show that treatment can be extremely effective. In one program that focused on prevention and early intervention, 78%

---

3. **counterproductive** (koun′tər-prə-dŭk′tĭv): interfering with the accomplishment of a desired outcome.

of the offenders stayed out of further trouble.

Professionals connected with the justice system would be the first to admit that the juvenile courts are far from perfect. But, like the young people they serve, they can be rehabilitated. Suggested changes include increasing

- training for judges
- legal representation for offenders
- standardization of procedures
- community involvement
- education
- funding

These changes may seem like a stiff sentence for society, but don't we owe it to our young people—and to ourselves—to give these measures a fair trial?

THE VERDICT: SEPARATE TREATMENT

". . . very generally, the 14-year-old does not have the level of maturity, thought process, decision-making, experience, or wisdom that a 24-year-old presumably has. Secondly, a 14-year-old is still growing, may not appreciate the consequences of that type of behavior, and is susceptible to change, at least to a higher degree than a 24-year-old is."

Thomas Edwards, Presiding Judge, Juvenile Court of Santa Clara County, CA

"If the 14-year-old engages in criminal conduct, and it's the same kind of conduct that the 24-year-old engages in, I don't think the response of society . . . should be to look only at the fact that they engaged in the same behavior, so treat them both the same as adults. . . . They have different life experiences that got them to that point. If the 14-year-old . . . can still benefit from having some kind of services . . . we ought to do it."

LaDoris Cordell, Trial Judge, CA State Court

"I think the community understands, or should understand, that the younger a person is, the more likely it is that they can change . . . And the younger they are, the more likely it is that they are going to come back into our community. So I guess as a community we have to decide what is it we're willing to get back in the long run."

Bridgett Jones, Former Supervisor, Juvenile Division, Santa Clara County Public Defender's Office

---

INTERPRET

Read the quotations in the sidebar "The Verdict: Separate Treatment." Do you think the people who are quoted here agree or disagree with the author's views on juvenile courts?

☐ agree
☐ disagree

List three reasons they give to support this view.

1. _____
   _____

2. _____
   _____

3. _____
   _____

RELATED NONFICTION 55

Assessment Practice II

Reading Comprehension

DIRECTIONS *Answer these questions by filling in the correct ovals.*

1. Which statement *best* sums up the last two paragraphs of "When the Curtain Comes Up"?
   - (A) When given an opportunity for a second chance, you must act on it.
   - (B) It is better to avoid making mistakes than to correct them later on.
   - (C) The second act is limited to those who have been incarcerated.
   - (D) Mathis and others like him are praised for their metamorphosis.

2. In "When the Curtain Comes Up," Abagnale created an opportunity for himself when he
   - (A) joined the FBI
   - (B) he entered college
   - (C) was charged as an adult
   - (D) offered to train bank employees

3. In "Juvenile Justice," which statement does a legal expert give in support of different treatment for juvenile offenders?
   - (A) "Studies show that treatment can be extremely effective."
   - (B) "The majority of kids being tried as adults are being tried for nonviolent crimes."
   - (C) "A 14-year-old is . . . susceptible to change, at least to a higher degree than a 24-year old is."
   - (D) "The juvenile system is far more flexible and responsive to the needs of individual offenders."

4. What is the author's main purpose for writing "Juvenile Justice on Trial"?
   - (A) to inform readers about the system
   - (B) to tell entertaining courtroom stories
   - (C) to inspire readers to vote for judges sympathetic to juveniles
   - (D) to persuade readers that juvenile offenders need special treatment

5. According to "Juvenile Justice," why are more teens now tried in adult courts?
   - (A) Trying juveniles as adults decreased the rate of juvenile crime.
   - (B) The number of violent crimes committed by young people increased.
   - (C) The justice system became less concerned with rehabilitation.
   - (D) Juvenile courts became too crowded.

6. What topic do all three selections address?
   - (A) punishment for wrongdoing
   - (B) the prevention of crime
   - (C) the possibility of transformation
   - (D) statistical evidence about crime

7. In line 48 of "When the Curtain Comes Up" *adept* means
   - (A) adaptable
   - (B) skilled
   - (C) anxious
   - (D) famous

8. In line 21 of "Juvenile Justice on Trial," the word *neurological* refers to
   - (A) what happens in court
   - (B) what happens inside the body
   - (C) what happens during an interview
   - (D) what happens in society

56 UNIT 2: ANALYZING CHARACTER AND POINT OF VIEW

Timed Writing Practice

PROMPT

Does everyone deserve a second chance? Write an (opinion essay) in which you answer this question. Support your opinion with details from the selections you have read and your own experiences.

BUDGET YOUR TIME

You have 30 minutes to respond. Decide how much time to spend on each step.

Analyze _____
Plan _____
Write _____
Review _____

Test-Taker's Toolkit

1. ANALYZE THE PROMPT

A. **Read the prompt** slowly to get a general idea of what you are being asked to do. Circle key words that tell you what you must do to get a good score. One example has been circled for you.

B. **List Key Ideas** Based on the circled words, jot down a list of the key elements you need to include in your essay.

> Paragraph 1: Opener and statement of opinion
> Paragraph 2: Supporting ideas from the selections I have read
> Paragraph 3: Supporting ideas from my own experience
> Paragraph 4: Restatement of opinion and conclusion

2. PLAN YOUR RESPONSE

A. **Make notes** Start by clarifying your opinion. You might want to do some quick freewriting to make sure you know what you think and why. Then find and note details and examples that support your opinion.

B. **Organize your information** Use your notes to help you structure your essay. You may want to organize it as shown here:

3. WRITE AND REVIEW

A. **Draft an opening** In your very first sentence or two, you should demonstrate that you understand the prompt. For this prompt, you'll want to summarize the issue and make your opinion clear right away. Write a draft of your opening below.

B. **Write your full response** on a second sheet of paper. Be sure to leave time to check your spelling and grammar.

RELATED NONFICTION

UNIT 3
UNDERSTANDING THEME

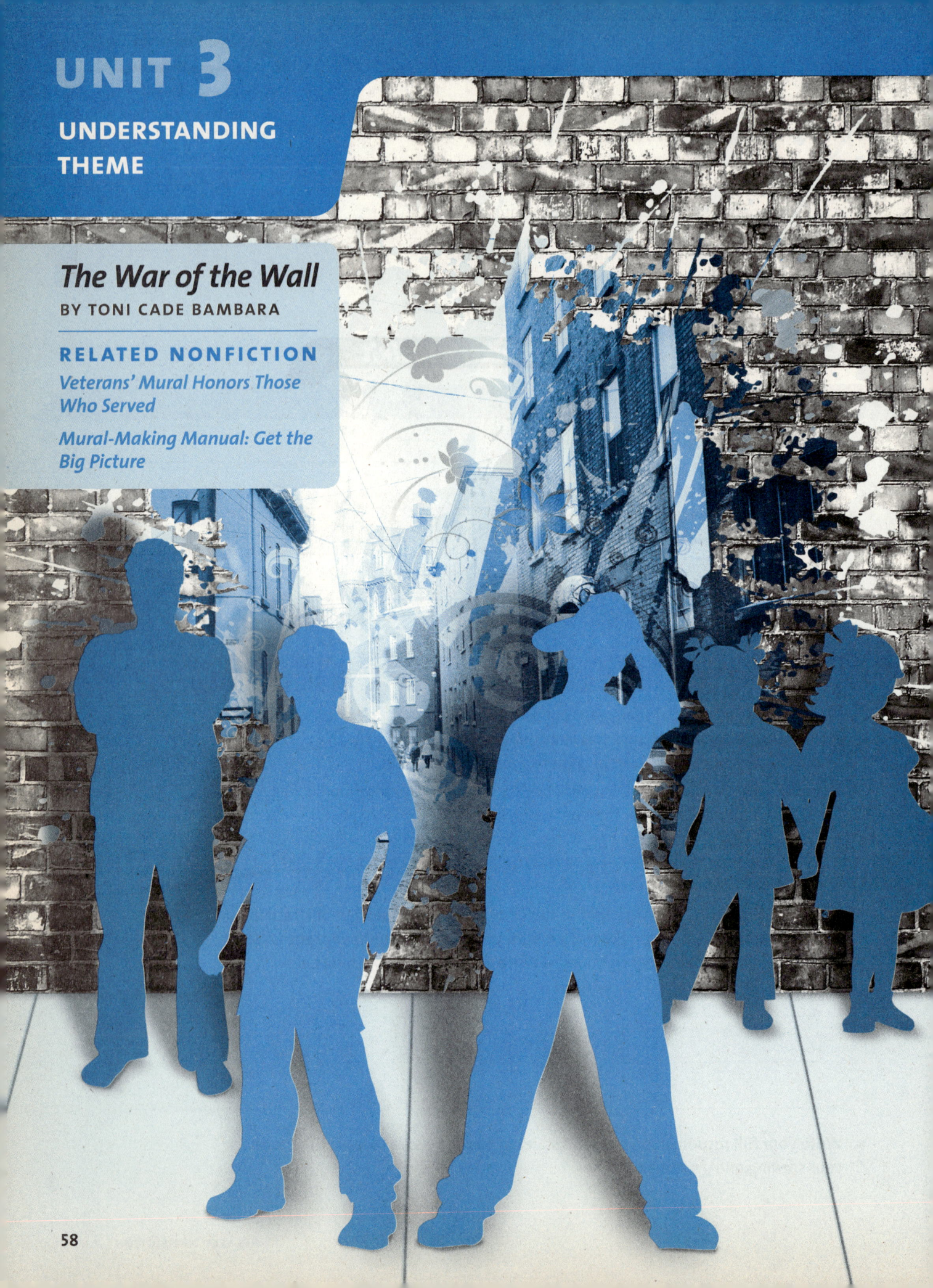

The War of the Wall
BY TONI CADE BAMBARA

RELATED NONFICTION
Veterans' Mural Honors Those Who Served

Mural-Making Manual: Get the Big Picture

What makes a COMMUNITY?

Belonging to a community can give people a sense of identity and security. What places and things in a community help contribute to those feelings? In "The War of the Wall," an outsider comes into town and starts making changes to a spot that means a great deal to the people who live there.

SKETCH IT Most people have a place in their neighborhood that they feel a personal connection to. In the notebook shown, draw a simple sketch of a local spot that has special meaning to you. Then complete the sentences. Share your work with a partner.

The place I feel connected to is _____

This place is special to me because _____

If someone tried to change this place, I would feel _____

ASSESSMENT GOALS

By the end of this lesson, you will be able to . . .
- analyze theme in a work of fiction
- apply critical thinking skills to analyze text
- identify the characteristics of nonfiction forms
- analyze a writing prompt and write a personal response to literature

LEARN THE TERMS: ACADEMIC VOCABULARY

Theme

"The War of the Wall" is a story about two friends who try to stop an outsider from changing something in their neighborhood. But like many stories, this one communicates something more than details about characters and events. "The War of the Wall" has a deeper meaning, or theme.

THEME is a message about life or human nature that a writer wants you to understand. This message can often be summed up in a sentence, such as "Hardship can bring friends closer." Sometimes the theme of a story is stated directly by the author. Other times, you must figure out the theme on your own. The theme is usually revealed near or at the end of the story. The chart below provides clues that can help you recognize a story's theme:

CLUES TO A STORY'S THEME

TITLE
The title may reflect a story's theme.
Ask yourself
- What ideas does the title emphasize?

PLOT
A story's plot often revolves around a conflict that is important to the theme. Ask yourself
- What conflicts do the characters face?
- How are the conflicts resolved?

CHARACTERS
What characters do and learn can reflect a theme. Ask yourself
- How do the characters respond to the conflicts?
- How and why do the characters change?
- What lessons do the characters learn?

SETTING
A setting can suggest a theme because of what it means to the characters. Ask yourself
- How does the setting influence the characters?
- How does the setting affect the conflicts?
- What might the setting represent?

ADDITIONAL TERMS FOR CRITICAL ANALYSIS

An author develops a theme throughout a story. To recognize how, you often have to review the selection. Notice ways Toni Cade Bambara develops the **theme** using devices such as these:

- **IRONY** is a special kind of contrast between appearance and reality. A contrast between what a character or reader thinks and what actually exists is one kind of irony.

- **A SYMBOL** is a person, place, object, or activity that stands for something beyond itself. For example, a white dove is a symbol of peace.

THE WAR OF THE WALL

TONI CADE BAMBARA

BACKGROUND A mural is a large picture painted on a wall of a building. Many murals illustrate scenes from history or depict typical people in a community. In the 1960s, African-American artists started a "wall of respect" movement. They painted murals that deal with the struggle for freedom and equality. Such murals appeared in big cities such as New York, Chicago, and Los Angeles and in small Southern towns, such as the one in which this story takes place.

Me and Lou had no time for courtesies. We were late for school. So we just flat out told the painter lady to quit messing with the wall. It was our wall, and she had no right coming into our neighborhood painting on it. Stirring in the paint bucket and not even looking at us, she mumbled something about Mr. Eubanks, the barber, giving her permission. That had nothing to do with it as far as we were concerned. We've been pitching pennies against that wall since we were little kids. Old folks have been dragging their chairs out to sit in the shade of the wall for years. Big kids have been playing handball against the wall since so-called integration[1] when the crazies 'cross town poured cement in

---

1. **since so-called integration:** from the time in the 1960s when segregation, the separation of the races in public places, was outlawed. The narrator is being sarcastic, suggesting that integration has not been successful.

ANALYZE

Underline a detail in the boxed text that doesn't seem important now but becomes significant at the end of the story.

How does this detail help to reveal the story's **theme**?

_____
_____
_____
_____

INTERPRET

What might the wall be a **symbol** of at this point in the story?

_____
_____
_____

aroma (ə-rō′mə) *n.*
a smell; odor

our pool so we couldn't use it. I'd sprained my neck one time boosting my cousin Lou up to chisel Jimmy Lyons's name into the wall when we found out he was never coming home from the war in Vietnam to take us fishing. ◀

"If you lean close," Lou said, leaning hipshot against her beat-up car, "you'll get a whiff of bubble gum and kids' sweat. And that'll tell you something—that this wall belongs to the kids of 20 Taliaferro Street." I thought Lou sounded very convincing. But the painter lady paid us no mind. She just snapped the brim of her straw hat down and hauled her bucket up the ladder.

"You're not even from around here," I hollered up after her. The license plates on her old piece of car said "New York." Lou dragged me away because I was about to grab hold of that ladder and shake it. And then we'd really be late for school.

When we came from school, the wall was slick with white. The painter lady was running string across the wall and taping it here and there. Me and Lou leaned against the 30 gumball machine outside the pool hall and watched. She had strings up and down and back and forth. Then she began chalking them with a hunk of blue chalk.

The Morris twins crossed the street, hanging back at the curb next to the beat-up car. The twin with the red ribbons was hugging a jug of cloudy lemonade. The one with yellow ribbons was holding a plate of dinner away from her dress. The painter lady began snapping the strings. The blue chalk dust measured off halves and quarters up and down and sideways too. Lou was about to say how hip it all was, but I dropped my book satchel 40 on his toes to remind him we were at war. ◀

Some good **aromas** were drifting our way from the plate leaking pot likker[2] onto the Morris girl's white socks. I could tell from where I stood that under the tinfoil was baked ham, collard greens, and candied yams. And knowing Mrs. Morris, who sometimes bakes for my mama's restaurant, a

---

2. **pot likker:** the broth or liquid in which meat or vegetables have been cooked.

slab of buttered cornbread was probably up under there too, sopping up some of the pot likker. Me and Lou rolled our eyes, wishing somebody would send us some dinner. But the painter lady didn't even turn around. She was pulling the strings down and prying bits of tape loose.

Side Pocket came strolling out of the pool hall to see what Lou and me were studying so hard. He gave the painter lady the once-over, checking out her paint-spattered jeans, her chalky T-shirt, her floppy-brimmed straw hat. He hitched up his pants and glided over toward the painter lady, who kept right on with what she was doing.

"Whatcha got there, sweetheart?" he asked the twin with the plate.

"Suppah," she said all soft and countrylike.

"For her," the one with the jug added, jerking her chin toward the painter lady's back. ▶

Still she didn't turn around. She was rearing back on her heels, her hands jammed into her back pockets, her face squinched up like the **masterpiece** she had in mind was taking shape on the wall by magic. We could have been gophers crawled up into a rotten hollow for all she cared. She didn't even say hello to anybody. Lou was muttering something about how great her concentration was. I butt him with my hip, and his elbow slid off the gum machine.

"Good evening," Side Pocket said in his best ain't-I-fine voice. But the painter lady was moving from the milk crate to the step stool to the ladder, moving up and down fast, scribbling all over the wall like a crazy person. We looked at Side Pocket. He looked at the twins. The twins looked at us. The painter lady was giving a show. It was like those old-timey music movies where the dancer taps on the tabletop and then starts jumping all over the furniture, kicking chairs over and not skipping a beat. She didn't even look where she was stepping. And for a minute there, hanging on the ladder to reach a far spot, she looked like she was going to tip right over. ▶

DRAW CONCLUSIONS
What conclusions can you draw about a community in which strangers are brought home-cooked meals?

masterpiece (măs′tər-pēs′) *n.* a great work of art

ANALYZE
The narrator believes the painter lady is unaware of the people in the community. Underline details in the boxed text that show his view.

What is **ironic** about the narrator's perception?

trance (trăns) *n.* a condition of daydreaming or being unconscious of one's surroundings

MAKE JUDGMENTS
Underline details in the boxed text that reveal how Side Pocket and the narrator regard the painter lady's response.

Given what you later learn about her diet, explain whether you think the painter lady handled the situation well.

_____
_____
_____
_____
_____

"Ahh," Side Pocket cleared his throat and moved fast to catch the ladder. "These young ladies here have brought you some supper."

"Ma'am?" The twins stepped forward. Finally the painter turned around, her eyes "full of sky," as my grandmama would say. Then she stepped down like she was in a **trance**. She wiped her hands on her jeans as the Morris twins offered up the plate and the jug. She rolled back the tinfoil, then wagged her head as though something terrible was on the plate.

"Thank your mother very much," she said, sounding like her mouth was full of sky too. "I've brought my own dinner along." And then, without even excusing herself, she went back up the ladder, drawing on the wall in a wild way. Side Pocket whistled one of those oh-brother breathy whistles and went back into the pool hall. The Morris twins shifted their weight from one foot to the other, then crossed the street and went home. Lou had to drag me away, I was so mad. We couldn't wait to get to the firehouse to tell my daddy all about this rude woman who'd stolen our wall. ◄

All the way back to the block to help my mama out at the restaurant, me and Lou kept asking my daddy for ways to run the painter lady out of town. But my daddy was busy talking about the trip to the country and telling Lou he could come too because Grandmama can always use an extra pair of hands on the farm.

Later that night, while me and Lou were in the back doing our chores, we found out that the painter lady was a liar. She came into the restaurant and leaned against the glass of the steam table, talking about how starved she was. I was scrubbing pots and Lou was chopping onions, but we could hear her through the service window. She was asking Mama was that a ham hock in the greens, and was that a neck bone in the pole beans, and were there any vegetables cooked without meat, especially pork.

64 UNIT 3: UNDERSTANDING THEME

"I don't care who your spiritual leader is," Mama said in that way of hers. "If you eat in the community, sistuh, you gonna eat pig by-and-by, one way or t'other."

Me and Lou were cracking up in the kitchen, and several customers at the counter were clearing their throats, waiting for Mama to really fix her wagon[3] for not speaking to the elders when she came in. The painter lady took a stool at the counter and went right on with her questions. Was there cheese in the baked macaroni, she wanted to know? Were there eggs in the salad? Was it honey or sugar in the iced tea? Mama was fixing Pop Johnson's plate. And every time the painter lady asked a fool question, Mama would dump another spoonful of rice on the pile. She was tapping her foot and heating up in a dangerous way. But Pop Johnson was happy as he could be. Me and Lou peeked through the service window, wondering what planet the painter lady came from. Who ever heard of baked macaroni without cheese, or potato salad without eggs?

"Do you have any bread made with unbleached flour?" the painter lady asked Mama. There was a long pause, as though everybody in the restaurant was holding their breath, wondering if Mama would dump the next spoonful on the painter lady's head. She didn't. But when she set Pop Johnson's plate down, it came down with a bang.

When Mama finally took her order, the starving lady all of a sudden couldn't make up her mind whether she wanted a vegetable plate or fish and a salad. She finally settled on the broiled trout and a tossed salad. But just when Mama reached for a plate to serve her, the painter lady leaned over the counter with her finger all up in the air.

"Excuse me," she said. "One more thing." Mama was holding the plate like a Frisbee, tapping that foot, one hand on her hip. "Can I get raw beets in that tossed salad?"

---

3. **fix her wagon:** a slang expression meaning "put her in her place; bring about her downfall."

ANALYZE

In the underlined sentence, the narrator is asking a rhetorical question, which means he doesn't really want an answer. Based on what is revealed at the end of the story, why is this question an example of **irony**?

_____
_____
_____
_____

Tell how this question relates to the story's **theme**.

_____
_____
_____
_____
_____

DRAW CONCLUSIONS

Underline details on this page that suggest the narrator's family's attitude toward the North. 🔵

What impression do they have of that region?

_____
_____
_____

"You will get," Mama said, leaning her face close to the painter lady's, "whatever Lou back there tossed. Now sit down." And the painter lady sat back down on her stool and shut right up.

All the way to the country, me and Lou tried to get Mama to open fire on the painter lady. But Mama said that seeing as how she was from the North, you couldn't expect her to have any manners. Then Mama said she was sorry she'd been so impatient with the woman because she seemed like a decent person and was simply trying to stick to a very strict diet. Me and Lou didn't want to hear that. <u>Who did that lady think she was, coming into our neighborhood and taking over our wall?</u> ◀

"Welllllll," Mama drawled, pulling into the filling station so Daddy could take the wheel, "it's hard on an artist, ya know. They can't always get people to look at their work. So she's just doing her work in the open, that's all."

Me and Lou definitely did not want to hear that. Why couldn't she set up an easel downtown or draw on the sidewalk in her own neighborhood? Mama told us to quit fussing so much; she was tired and wanted to rest. She climbed into the back seat and dropped down into the warm hollow Daddy had made in the pillow.

All weekend long, me and Lou tried to scheme up ways to recapture our wall. Daddy and Mama said they were sick of hearing about it. Grandmama turned up the TV to drown us out. On the late news was a story about the New York subways. When a train came roaring into the station all covered from top to bottom, windows too, with writings and drawings done with spray paint, me and Lou slapped five. Mama said it was too bad kids in New York had nothing better to do than spray paint all over the trains. Daddy said that in the cities, even grown-ups wrote all over the trains and buildings too. Daddy called it "graffiti." Grandmama called it a shame. ◀

66   UNIT 3: UNDERSTANDING THEME

We couldn't wait to get out of school on Monday. We couldn't find any black spray paint anywhere. But in a junky hardware store downtown we found a can of white epoxy[4] paint, the kind you touch up old refrigerators with when they get splotchy and peely. We spent our whole allowance on it. And because it was too late to use our bus passes, we had to walk all the way home lugging our book satchels and gym shoes, and the bag with the epoxy. ▶

When we reached the corner of Taliaferro and Fifth, it looked like a block party or something. Half the neighborhood was gathered on the sidewalk in front of the wall. I looked at Lou, he looked at me. We both looked at the bag with the epoxy and wondered how we were going to work our scheme. The painter lady's car was nowhere in sight. But there were too many people standing around to do anything. Side Pocket and his buddies were leaning on their cue sticks, hunching each other. Daddy was there with a lineman[5] he catches a ride with on Mondays. Mrs. Morris had her arms flung around the shoulders of the twins on either side of her. Mama was talking with some of her customers, many of them with napkins still at the throat. Mr. Eubanks came out of the barbershop, followed by a man in a striped poncho, half his face shaved, the other half full of foam.

"She really did it, didn't she?" Mr. Eubanks huffed out his chest. Lots of folks answered right quick that she surely did when they saw the straight razor in his hand.

Mama **beckoned** us over. And then we saw it. The wall. Reds, greens, figures outlined in black. Swirls of purple and orange. Storms of blues and yellows. It was something. I recognized some of the faces right off. There was Martin Luther King, Jr. And there was a man with glasses on and his mouth open like he was laying down a heavy rap. Daddy came up alongside and reminded us that that was Minister Malcolm X. The serious woman with a rifle I knew was

---

4. **epoxy** (ĭ-pŏk′sē): a plastic used in glues and paints.
5. **lineman:** a person who repairs telephone or power lines.

TestSmart

VOCABULARY
What does the word *lugging* mean in line 189?

- A leaving something behind
- B carrying something heavy
- C struggling up a hill
- D dropping something

TIP When a test question asks you to identify the meaning of an unfamiliar word, look for **context clues** in the same sentence or in a nearby sentence. Context clues for *lugging* appear in the same sentence as the word. To find the correct answer, substitute each possible answer for the word *lugging* and decide which one makes the most sense.

beckon (bĕk′ən) *v.* to summon or call, usually by a gesture or nod

INTERPRET

On pages 67 and 68, circle the names of the famous people the painter included in the mural.

What do you think these people **symbolize** for the narrator's community?

_____
_____
_____
_____

MAKE INFERENCES

What does the mural suggest that the painter lady understands about the people in this community?

_____
_____
_____
_____
_____

Harriet Tubman because my grandmama has pictures of her all over the house. And I knew Mrs. Fannie Lou Hamer 'cause a signed photograph of her hangs in the restaurant next to the calendar. ◄

Then I let my eyes follow what looked like a vine. It trailed past a man with a horn, a woman with a big white flower in her hair, a handsome dude in a tuxedo seated at a piano, and a man with a goatee holding a book. When I looked more closely, I realized that what had looked like flowers were really faces. One face with yellow petals looked just like Frieda Morris. One with red petals looked just like Hattie Morris. I could hardly believe my eyes.

"Notice," Side Pocket said, stepping close to the wall with his cue stick like a classroom pointer. "These are the flags of liberation," he said in a voice I'd never heard him use before. We all stepped closer while he pointed and spoke. "Red, black and green," he said, his pointer falling on the leaflike flags of the vine. "Our liberation flag.[6] And here Ghana, there Tanzania. Guinea-Bissau, Angola, Mozambique."[7] Side Pocket sounded very tall, as though he'd been waiting all his life to give this lesson.

Mama tapped us on the shoulder and pointed to a high section of the wall. There was a fierce-looking man with his arms crossed against his chest guarding a bunch of children. His muscles bulged, and he looked a lot like my daddy. One kid was looking at a row of books. Lou hunched me 'cause the kid looked like me. The one that looked like Lou was spinning a globe on the tip of his finger like a basketball. There were other kids there with microscopes and compasses. And the more I looked, the more it looked like the fierce man was not so much guarding the kids as defending their right to do what they were doing. ◄

---

6. **Red, black and green . . . liberation flag:** a banner of red, black, and green horizontal stripes has been used in the United States as well as Africa to stand for the liberation, or freedom, sought by people of African heritage.

7. **Ghana . . . Tanzania. Guinea-Bissau, Angola, Mozambique** (mō'zəm-bēk'): countries in southern and western Africa.

Then Lou gasped and dropped the paint bag and ran forward, running his hands over a rainbow. He had to tiptoe and stretch to do it, it was so high. I couldn't breathe either. The painter lady had found the chisel marks and had painted Jimmy Lyons's name in a rainbow.

"Read the **inscription**, honey," Mrs. Morris said, urging little Frieda forward. She didn't have to urge much. Frieda marched right up, bent down, and in a loud voice that made everybody quit oohing and ahhing and listen, she read,

> *To the People of Taliaferro Street*
> *I Dedicate This Wall of Respect*
> *Painted in Memory of My Cousin*
> *Jimmy Lyons* ▶

inscription (ĭn-skrĭp'shən) *n.* something written, carved, or engraved on a surface

INTERPRET

What do you think the **theme** of this story is? (Remember that there can be more than one way to interpret a story's theme.)

Big Question

In your opinion, is the painter lady a part of the town's community? Why or why not? MAKE JUDGMENTS

Assessment Practice I

Reading Comprehension

DIRECTIONS Answer these questions about "The War of the Wall" by filling in the correct ovals.

1. Which aspect of the setting is *most* important to the conflict in "The War of the Wall"?
   - Ⓐ It has a hardware store, a restaurant, a barbershop, and a school.
   - Ⓑ It is a small Southern town with its own culture and customs.
   - Ⓒ It is located near farms, far away from a city.
   - Ⓓ It has a place where the local kids hang out.

2. How does Lou feel about the painter lady?
   - Ⓐ He likes the painter lady as soon as he meets her.
   - Ⓑ He dislikes her even more than the narrator does.
   - Ⓒ He feels some admiration for her and her work.
   - Ⓓ He is glad that she is painting their wall.

3. Which story detail is an example of irony?
   - Ⓐ The stranger in town is from New York.
   - Ⓑ The stranger in town is related to Jimmy Lyons.
   - Ⓒ The stranger in town knows Mr. Eubanks.
   - Ⓓ The stranger in town doesn't like the local food.

4. What are the flags in the mural a symbol of?
   - Ⓐ the arts
   - Ⓒ education
   - Ⓑ freedom
   - Ⓓ trustworthiness

5. What makes the narrator change his mind about the mural?
   - Ⓐ He realizes that the mural honors people he cares about and respects.
   - Ⓑ He understands that the painter lady is trying her best to fit in.
   - Ⓒ He decides that the wall isn't that important to him after all.
   - Ⓓ He notices that everyone else likes it.

6. Which sentence below *best* describes a theme of this story?
   - Ⓐ Public art is for all to enjoy.
   - Ⓑ Don't resort to illegal acts to get your way.
   - Ⓒ Trusting people you don't know can get you in trouble.
   - Ⓓ People who are very different can be connected to the same community.

7. What does the word *courtesies* mean in line 1?
   - Ⓐ actions
   - Ⓒ politeness
   - Ⓑ artists
   - Ⓓ rudeness

8. What does the word *chisel* mean in line 14?
   - Ⓐ cut with a tool
   - Ⓒ pick with an axe
   - Ⓑ grab
   - Ⓓ stick

Responding in Writing

9. Short Response In a paragraph, explain how the narrator's view of the painter lady's work changes from the beginning of the story to the end. Tell what lesson you think the narrator learns.

For help, use the **Test-Taker's Toolkit** below.

Test-Taker's Toolkit

GRAPHIC ORGANIZER Use the graphic organizer below to help you plan your response. As you fill out the chart, look back at the story to find details that support your explanations.

VIEW AT BEGINNING OF STORY	VIEW AT END OF STORY	LESSON LEARNED
SUPPORTING DETAIL	SUPPORTING DETAIL	SUPPORTING DETAIL

THE WAR OF THE WALL

Related Nonfiction

- **Veterans' Mural Honors Those Who Served**
  NEWSPAPER ARTICLE

- **Mural-Making Manual: Get the Big Picture**
  HOW-TO MANUAL

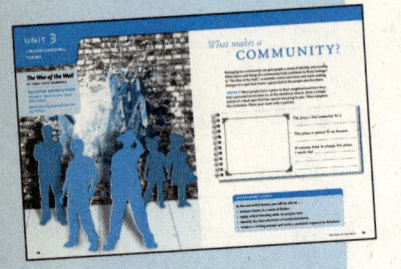

Use with "The War of the Wall," p. 58

What's the Connection?

Of all art forms, murals are perhaps the best at celebrating community. The projects can be huge—the newspaper article "Veterans' Mural Honors Those Who Served" describes a mural that stretches half a city block—or they can be simple. But they always involve people making and viewing art publicly. "Mural-Making Manual: Get the Big Picture" provides instruction on how to get an image up on a wall.

CREATE A MURAL PROPOSAL On the form below, plan a mural you might like to create for your school or community. Then present your mural idea to a group.

MURAL PROPOSAL

Location of Mural: _____

Who or what the mural will honor: _____
_____

Images the mural will include: _____
_____

Who will participate in the project: _____
_____

LEARN THE SKILL: IDENTIFY CHARACTERISTICS OF FORMS

Knowing what to expect from nonfiction will increase your comprehension. Before you begin reading something, take a moment to think about the form of the material. Two common **forms** of nonfiction are listed below:

1. **Feature articles** appear in newspapers and magazines. They usually
   - focus on a person or topic of human interest
   - include language and imagery that appeals to emotions
2. **Instructions** can be found in books, manuals, or accompanying products. They often include
   - text features to make information easily identifiable
   - diagrams or other graphic aids
   - numbered steps

For more information about forms of nonfiction, see *Nonfiction Handbook*, page R13.

MONDAY, AUGUST 15, 2005

Veterans' Mural Honors Those Who Served

by Rick Olivio

For over a century, Chequamegon Bay communities have sent their young men and women to the armed forces, defending the United States from foreign foes. Hundreds have gone; not all of them have come back.

The sacrifices of those young men and women in uniform, living and dead, are now recognized and recalled in perhaps the most ambitious work to date in the Ashland Mural Walk Project. ▶

The product of two years of work by artists Kelly Meredith and Sue Martinsen, the Veterans' mural recalls the soldiers, sailors, airmen and marines of all eras, in a painting that stretches half a city block on the west brick wall of the Bay Theater on Vaughn Avenue. The project was formally dedicated Saturday amid the applause of surviving veterans, their families, and others at the event.

"It's a big day, not so much for me, but for the community," said Martinsen.

Martinsen said the project required a huge amount of time, not just in painting under the hot summer sun, but in getting the project organized.

"It's a lot of days that people don't see, days of research, of time and energy," she said.

She said many people had taken the time to send in photographs to be considered for the project, along with the stories behind the photos.

"It's been a wonderful experience. It makes all the days in the hot sun worth it," she said.

The mural is the seventh in the Ashland Mural Walk series, which has covered topics from aviation to lighthouse keepers, pioneers to lumberjacks, Ashland's historic build-

CHARACTERISTICS OF FORMS

Reread the boxed text. Underline images and details in this anecdote that appeal to the emotions.

What do these details suggest about the mural's impact?

_____
_____
_____
_____

CONNECT

Feature articles often invite readers to make personal connections. Reread lines 91–105. Recall a person or group that made a sacrifice for which you feel grateful. What does your own experience help you understand about the artist's feelings?

_____
_____
_____
_____

ings to a turn-of-the-century grocery. . . .

At the ribbon cutting ceremony, Meredith and Martinsen were both praised for their efforts to capture Ashland's history.

"We are so proud of these two women," said Ashland Mural Walk Project spokeswoman Tina Miller. "They have captured the essence of Ashland in so many ways. Their work is timeless, and we are so proud of the work they have done on this Veterans' mural."

In her comments, Martinsen recalled that early in the painting of the project she became aware of a presence behind her.

"I turned to see a large, burley man on a motorcycle, wearing much leather and having every appearance of being able to eat nails and spit them out. He stared me in the eye for a few moments, and then I noticed he had tears streaming down from his eyes. I was stunned, and was forever humbled, when he said a simple 'Thank you for what you are doing,' and drove off," she said.

Martinsen said that scene was played out time and again during the painting of the mural.

"I came to see the whole gamut of human emotion, she said. "The pride of service, the pain of service, the pride and pain of sacrifice. The true paradoxes[1] of life were reflected in their eyes," she said. "It was as though their laughter, tears, loss of innocence, deep pain, as well as deep pride and honor became mixed into my paints," she said. "This mural is simply my way of answering back, for generations to come, thank you all for what you have done."

Ashland Area Chamber of Commerce Representative Maribeth Monroe called the veterans who were portrayed in the mural "Ashland's best."

"This mural represents sacrifice, bravery, courage, and pride in the United States of America, and in a city that is small in size, but large in heart, Ashland, Wisconsin," she said. "How proud we should all be."

A number of veterans portrayed on the mural attended the dedication ceremony. One was Lawrence "Ozzy" Gregoire.

---

1. **paradoxes** (păr'ə-dŏks-əs): seemingly contradictory ideas that are true nonetheless.

74   UNIT 3: UNDERSTANDING THEME

"I think it is a tribute to the surrounding area of Ashland," he said. "I am very proud of it."

Gregoire said his wife submitted the picture of him, taken in his youth in a sailor's uniform.

130 He said when he saw the mural, he was "quite proud, you bet I was, and quite humbled."

"I think it's great, really something," said fellow vet Art Bertheaume. "I had only turned 19 and I was in the South Pacific. I never thought I would be on a wall in Ashland at age 80."

140 Ashland resident Stan Bebeau said he was "amazed" by the mural.

"I was 20 years old in Saigon, Vietnam, when that picture was taken. I knew there would be a lot of pictures submitted, I never thought that I would get on the wall. But I'm there, and I appreciate it, and I thank 150 the artists and all the people who are gathered here today. It's very heartwarming." ▶

Family members of veterans were also honored by the inclusion of their relatives in the mural. Silvia Cloud of Odanah was among a sizable contingent of family members attending the event. Her grandfather, 160 John M. Cloud, a member of the Bad River Band of Lake Superior Chippewa Indians, is in the mural. According to Silvia, her grandfather was among the first in the Ashland area to volunteer for service during World War I.

"He went in as soon as the war started and he was in for 170 three years," she said. "Our people didn't have the right to vote until 1924, but he served, and he wasn't the only one. His brother Frank Cloud also served. There were quite a few men from Odanah who served during World War I."

Cloud said the enshrinement[2] of her grandfather in 180 the mural was recognition of the worth and honor of his service.

"It's hard to express this, but it shows that our men, our warriors, were there no matter what, that even though he couldn't vote in this country, this was our land, the land the creator put us on. He rose up 190 and he went when he was very young and he protected the land." ▶

---

2. **enshrinement** (ĕn-shrīn′ mənt): to be preserved and cherished as sacred.

TestSmart

The veterans whose pictures appear in the mural share a feeling of

- Ⓐ pride at being included
- Ⓑ gratitude for their families
- Ⓒ appreciation for the artists
- Ⓓ sadness about revisiting old memories

TIP When a question asks you what people have in common, you often have to make a **generalization**, or a broad statement about a specific category of people based on a study of some of its members. In this case, although some of the answer choices might accurately describe an individual, the correct choice is the one that can apply to all the veterans mentioned. Underline the quotations in lines 123–152. Which of the choices above is the most accurate generalization?

CLARIFY

Why did John M. Cloud's family think it was especially significant that he was represented in the mural?

_____
_____
_____

RELATED NONFICTION 75

CLOSE READ

MURAL-MAKING MANUAL
GET THE *Big Picture*

You've already done the hard work. You've decided that you want to show your community support by creating a mural; you've gotten together with friends and neighbors to discuss the project; and you've sketched out on paper what the finished product will look like, collecting any photographs or other materials you want to reproduce. You've even gotten permission to paint on a suitable public wall. Now it's time to get the big picture—to enlarge your design and get it up where the world can see it. What's the best way to transfer the artistry demonstrated in your plan to the "big screen"? You've got three choices: draw it directly, project it, or create a grid.

No matter which method—or combination of methods—you use, you'll need to make sure the wall is clean and dry before getting started. If the top of the wall is too high to reach standing on the ground, set up several ladders for the artists to use. Make sure the legs are positioned securely and resting on level ground.

Draw It Directly
In this method of transferring your design, you draw it freehand directly on the wall. Do just what you did in making your original sketch, only on a larger scale. This process works well for landscapes and other sweeping images. If several artists will be transferring the design, you might want to have one person outline the whole image first to give it a consistent overall style. Then the other artists can use their creativity in filling in the outline.

Project It
Projecting your drawing is an accurate way to transfer and enlarge it, especially if it's very complicated or detailed. If your mural wall is outdoors, you should do the projection at night for the best visibility. First, make a transparency or slide of your

---

CLARIFY

Underline the sentence in the first paragraph that tells what these **instructions** will explain.

drawing or your photograph. Then project it onto the wall with an overhead or slide projector. Make sure the image hits the wall head-on, and not at an angle. You may need to put the projector on a ladder to get the position right. Finally, trace the outlines of the design with charcoal or thin acrylic paint.

Create a Grid ▶

Both professional and amateur artists have used grids for centuries to enlarge their designs easily and accurately.

1. Draw a 1-inch-by-1-inch grid over your design using <u>acetate</u> or tracing paper.
2. Letter the squares across the top of the grid and number the ones along the side.
3. Create a grid 1-foot-by-1-foot on the wall using a yardstick, a chalk line, chalk, and a level to make sure your lines are straight. This job requires at least three people.
4. Fill in the details of the design, working square by square.

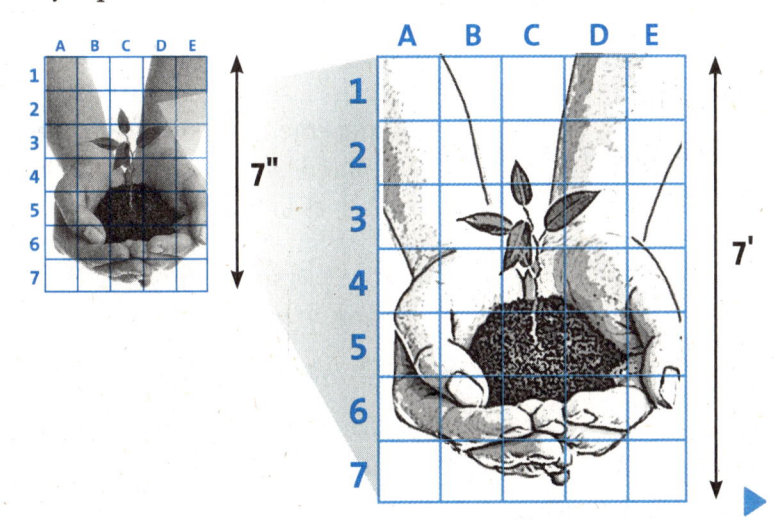

Make Your Choice

You can use any of these methods alone or in combination to create your mural. For example, you might want to project the drawing onto the wall and then use a grid and freehand drawing to fill in the details. Experiment to see which method works best to help you get the big picture across to your community.

CHARACTERISTICS OF FORMS

Instructions often contain text features such as **subheadings** that help readers find information easily. Put a check next to what the first three subheadings all describe.

☐ methods of creating a grid
☐ ways of enlarging an image to fit a wall
☐ tips for choosing a method of enlarging an image
☐ things to do before beginning a mural project

SPECIALIZED Vocabulary

If the word *acetate* in line 39 is new to you, use context clues to figure out its meaning. Underline a phrase in the sentence that might mean nearly the same thing as *acetate*.

Then read on to see what the acetate is to be used for. What do you think the word means? **WORD ANALYSIS**

_____
_____
_____

RELATED NONFICTION 77

Assessment Practice II

Reading Comprehension

DIRECTIONS *Answer these questions about "Veterans' Mural Honors Those Who Serve" and "Mural-Making Manual: Get the Big Picture" by filling in the correct ovals.*

1. In "Veterans' Mural," what do the people in the mural have in common?

   Ⓐ They served in the armed forces.
   Ⓑ They received military honors.
   Ⓒ They gave their lives in a war.
   Ⓓ They fought in Vietnam.

2. In "Veterans' Mural," what aspect of John Cloud's military service was different from that of the other veterans?

   Ⓐ He served as an older man.
   Ⓑ He gained fame as a soldier.
   Ⓒ He made sacrifices during the war.
   Ⓓ He defended a country that didn't let him vote.

3. What does the diagram in "Mural-Making Manual" help to explain?

   Ⓐ How to use a chalk line to make sure the lines are straight.
   Ⓑ How to use a grid to enlarge an image onto a wall.
   Ⓒ How to outline an image for others to fill in.
   Ⓓ How to use a transparency.

4. According to the manual, what is the best method to use if you want to transfer a complex drawing onto a wall?

   Ⓐ the grid method
   Ⓑ the tracing method
   Ⓒ the freehand method
   Ⓓ the projection method

5. Which section of the manual helps explain how the mural in "The War of the Wall" was enlarged?

   Ⓐ "Project It"
   Ⓑ "Create a Grid"
   Ⓒ "Draw It Directly"
   Ⓓ "Make Your Choice"

6. What characteristic appears in the feature article that you would not expect to find in a set of instructions?

   Ⓐ language that appeals to emotions
   Ⓑ explanation of a process
   Ⓒ images and captions
   Ⓓ numbered steps

7. Read this sentence from "Veteran's Mural"

   > Family members of veterans were also honored by the inclusion of their relatives in the mural.

   From this sentence, you can tell that *inclusion* means

   Ⓐ way of deciding
   Ⓑ act of concluding
   Ⓒ way of beginning
   Ⓓ act of including

8. What does the word *transparency* mean in line 29 of the manual?

   Ⓐ photographic slide
   Ⓑ large window
   Ⓒ scale model
   Ⓓ exact image

78 UNIT 3: UNDERSTANDING THEME

Timed Writing Practice

PROMPT

Write an essay that shows your understanding of the theme in "The War of the Wall." Sum up what the characters learn, then state the theme in your own words. End your essay by telling why the theme is important for people to understand. Support your ideas with examples from the story and from your own experience.

BUDGET YOUR TIME

You have 40 minutes to complete this assignment. Decide how much time to spend on each step.

Analyze _____
Plan _____
Write _____
Review _____

Test-Taker's Toolkit

1. ANALYZE THE PROMPT

A. **Read the prompt** carefully. Circle the key words that tell you what you must include to get a good score.

B. **Make a list** of the elements you must include in your response.

2. PLAN YOUR RESPONSE

A. **Make notes** Jot down your interpretation of the story's theme. Then note details and examples that show you understand the theme and why it is important.

B. **Organize your information** Use your notes to help you structure your essay. You may want to organize it as shown in the outline here.

A. Paragraph 1
introduction and statement of theme

B. Paragraph 2
summary of what happened in the story and what the characters learn

C. Paragraph 3
why the theme is important, plus examples

D. Paragraph 4
conclusion

3. WRITE AND REVIEW

A. **Write an opener** A strong opener can help your essay get a good score. Make sure you show your understanding of the theme in the first few sentences.

B. **Write your full response** Don't forget to leave time to check your spelling and grammar.

RELATED NONFICTION 79

UNIT 4

MOOD, TONE, AND STYLE

Dark They Were, and Golden-Eyed
BY RAY BRADBURY

RELATED NONFICTION
How Terraforming Mars Will Work

Can where you are CHANGE who you are?

Your hobbies, interests, and habits often depend on the climate you are used to and the people and places you encounter every day. If you were to move away from everything you know, how much of who you are would change? How much would stay the same?

DISCUSS IT With a group, discuss the question at the top of the page. Take turns answering the question and explaining your reasons. Record your group's responses in the notebook.

Can Where You Are Change Who You Are?		
Name	Yes or No?	Why or Why Not?

ASSESSMENT GOALS

By the end of this lesson, you will be able to...

- analyze mood, tone, and style
- apply critical thinking skills to analyze text
- identify text clues in nonfiction texts
- analyze a writing prompt and plan a fictional narrative

DARK THEY WERE, AND GOLDEN-EYED

LEARN THE TERMS: ACADEMIC VOCABULARY

Mood, Tone, and Style

Think of a story as a homemade meal. You've learned about the basic ingredients: plot, characters, setting, and theme. What gives a writer's work a unique flavor? What makes you tear hungrily through one story, while another is hard to digest? The answer is the blend of spices known as mood, tone, and style.

MOOD

MOOD is the feeling that a writer creates for a reader.

Words to describe mood
- eerie
- peaceful
- frightning
- romantic
- wondrous
- anxious

A writer creates mood through
- descriptions of setting
- characters' speech or feelings
- imagery, or words and phrases that appeal to the readers' five senses

TONE

TONE is a writer's attitude toward his or her subject.

Words to describe tone
- humorous
- sarcastic
- sympathetic
- angry
- serious
- admiring

A writer creates tone through
- words that let the reader "hear" the author's attitude
- details that make a subject appear a certain way

STYLE

STYLE is the unique way a writer puts words together. Style is not *what* is said but *how* it's said.

Words to describe style
- conversational
- economical
- lively
- flowery

Writer's create their unique style through the use of
- word choice
- sentence structure
- imagery

ADDITIONAL TERMS FOR CRITICAL ANALYSIS

Ray Bradbury is one of the world's most famous science fiction writers, but he writes other kinds of stories as well. The following terms can help you discuss both the selection you're about to read and Bradbury's general style:

- **SCIENCE FICTION** is fiction in which a writer imagines unexpected possibilities of the past or the future, using known scientific data and theories as well as his or her own creative ideas.

- **SYNTAX** is the way in which words are put together to form phrases and sentences. Syntax includes the order of words in a sentence.

DARK THEY WERE, AND Golden-Eyed

RAY BRADBURY

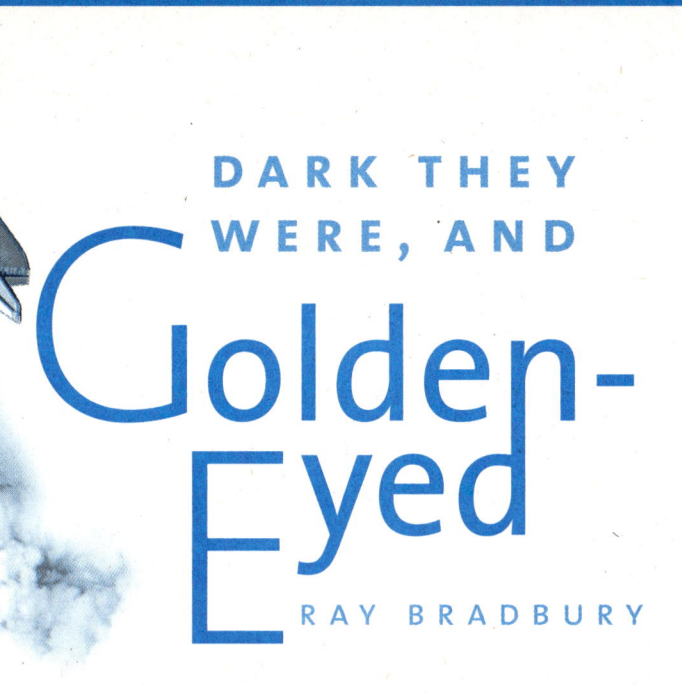

BACKGROUND The setting for this story is Mars. The Red Planet (nicknamed for its rust-colored atmosphere) has some things in common with our blue planet. As on Earth, a day on Mars lasts about twenty-four hours, and Mars has four seasons. Some scientists—and many writers—are interested in the idea that some form of life once existed on Mars.

The rocket metal cooled in the meadow winds. Its lid gave a bulging *pop*. From its clock interior stepped a man, a woman, and three children. The other passengers whispered away across the Martian meadow, leaving the man alone among his family.

The man felt his hair flutter and the tissues of his body draw tight as if he were standing at the center of a vacuum. His wife, before him, seemed almost to whirl away in smoke. The children, small seeds, might at any instant be sown to all the Martian climes.

The children looked up at him, as people look to the sun to tell what time of their life it is. His face was cold.

"What's wrong?" asked his wife.

"Let's get back on the rocket."

ANALYZE

Reread the boxed text. What later events are foreshadowed, or hinted at, in this passage?

_____
_____
_____
_____

TestSmart

Which word *best* describes the overall mood created by the characters' speech and feelings in lines 34–45?

Ⓐ peaceful
Ⓑ lively
Ⓒ anxious
Ⓓ weary

TIP When a question asks you to define a story's **mood**, think about your own emotional response. What feeling do you have at this point in the story? Decide which answer choice is closest to your feeling. Then make sure you can support your answer with evidence from the text. For this question, underline the words that help create a distinct mood in lines 34–45.

"Go back to Earth?"

"Yes! Listen!"

◆ The wind blew as if to flake away their identities. At any moment the Martian air might draw his soul from him, as marrow comes from a white bone. He felt submerged in a chemical that 20 could dissolve his intellect and burn away his past. ◀

They looked at Martian hills that time had worn with a crushing pressure of years. They saw the old cities, lost in their meadows, lying like children's delicate bones among the blowing lakes of grass.

"Chin up, Harry," said his wife. "It's too late. We've come over sixty million miles."

The children with their yellow hair hollered at the deep dome of Martian sky. There was no answer but the racing hiss of wind through the stiff grass.

30 He picked up the luggage in his cold hands. "Here we go," he said—a man standing on the edge of a sea, ready to wade in and be drowned.

They walked into town.

Their name was Bittering. Harry and his wife Cora; Dan, Laura, and David. They built a small white cottage and ate good breakfasts there, but the fear was never gone. It lay with Mr. Bittering and Mrs. Bittering, a third unbidden partner at every midnight talk, at every dawn awakening.

"I feel like a salt crystal," he said, "in a mountain stream, 40 being washed away. We don't belong here. We're Earth people. This is Mars. It was meant for Martians. For heaven's sake, Cora, let's buy tickets for home!"

But she only shook her head. "One day the atom bomb will fix Earth. Then we'll be safe here."

"Safe and insane!" ◀

Tick-tock, seven o'clock sang the voice-clock; *time to get up.* And they did.

Something made him check everything each morning— warm hearth, potted blood-geraniums—precisely as if he 50 expected something to be amiss. The morning paper was

---

84   UNIT 4: MOOD, TONE, AND STYLE

toast-warm from the 6 A.M. Earth rocket. He broke its seal and tilted it at his breakfast place. He forced himself to be **convivial**.

"Colonial days all over again," he declared. "Why, in ten years there'll be a million Earthmen on Mars. Big cities, everything! They said we'd fail. Said the Martians would resent our invasion. But did we find any Martians? Not a living soul! Oh, we found their empty cities, but no one in them. Right?"

A river of wind submerged the house. When the windows ceased rattling Mr. Bittering swallowed and looked at the children. ▶

"I don't know," said David. "Maybe there're Martians around we don't see. Sometimes nights I think I hear 'em. I hear the wind. The sand hits my window. I get scared. And I see those towns way up in the mountains where the Martians lived a long time ago. And I think I see things moving around those towns, Papa. And I wonder if those Martians *mind* us living here. I wonder if they won't do something to us for coming here." ▶

"Nonsense!" Mr. Bittering looked out the windows. "We're clean, decent people." He looked at his children. "All dead cities have some kind of ghosts in them. Memories, I mean." He stared at the hills. "You see a staircase and you wonder what Martians looked like climbing it. You see Martian paintings and you wonder what the painter was like. You make a little ghost in your mind, a memory. It's quite natural. Imagination." He stopped. "You haven't been prowling up in those ruins, have you?"

"No, Papa." David looked at his shoes.

"See that you stay away from them. Pass the jam."

"Just the same," said little David, "I bet something happens."

---

convivial (kən-vĭv′ē-əl) *adj.* enjoying the company of others; sociable

TestSmart

VOCABULARY
The word *submerged* means "covered in water." What is the most likely meaning of the prefix *sub-*, which is used to form *submerged* in line 59?

- Ⓐ over
- Ⓑ under
- Ⓒ beside
- Ⓓ between

TIP When a test question asks you about the meaning of a **prefix**, the definition of a word that includes the prefix can help you find the answer. In this case, think about the definition of *submerged*. If you know that to submerge something is to place it under water, what does that tell you about the meaning of *sub-*?

INTERPRET

Bradbury uses wind **imagery** throughout this story. Underline two examples of this kind of imagery in lines 59–69.

Look for other examples as you continue your second read. What do you think the wind might represent?

_____
_____
_____
_____

DARK THEY WERE, AND GOLDEN-EYED

Something happened that afternoon. Laura stumbled through the settlement, crying. She dashed blindly onto the porch.

"Mother, Father—the war, Earth!" she sobbed. "A radio flash just came. Atom bombs[1] hit New York! All the space rockets blown up. No more rockets to Mars, ever!"

"Oh, Harry!" The mother held onto her husband and daughter.

"Are you sure, Laura?" asked the father quietly.

Laura wept. "We're stranded on Mars, forever and ever!"

For a long time there was only the sound of the wind in the late afternoon.

Alone, thought Bittering. Only a thousand of us here. No way back. No way. No way. Sweat poured from his face and his hands and his body; he was drenched in the hotness of his fear. He wanted to strike Laura, cry, "No, you're lying! The rockets will come back!" Instead, he stroked Laura's head against him and said, "The rockets will get through someday."

"Father, what will we do?"

"Go about our business, of course. Raise crops and children. Wait. Keep things going until the war ends and the rockets come again."

The two boys stepped out onto the porch.

"Children," he said, sitting there, looking beyond them, "I've something to tell you."

"We know," they said.

In the following days, Bittering wandered often through the garden to stand alone in his fear. As long as the rockets had spun a silver web across space, he had been able to accept Mars. For he had always told himself: Tomorrow, if I want, I can buy a ticket and go back to Earth. ◀

But now: The web gone, the rockets lying in jigsaw heaps of molten girder and unsnaked wire. Earth people left to the

---

1. **atom bombs:** In 1945, the United States dropped atomic bombs over the cities of Hiroshima and Nagasaki, in Japan, killing over 100,000 people and injuring many thousands more.

ANALYZE

Underline an image on this page that appeals to the sense of touch. Circle an image that appeals to the sense of sight.

What **mood** does this **imagery** help to create?

_____
_____
_____

strangeness of Mars, the cinnamon dusts and wine airs, to be baked like gingerbread shapes in Martian summers, put into harvested storage by Martian winters. What would happen to him, the others? This was the moment Mars had waited for. Now it would eat them.

He got down on his knees in the flower bed, a spade in his nervous hands. Work, he thought, work and forget.

He glanced up from the garden to the Martian mountains. He thought of the proud old Martian names that had once been on those peaks. Earthmen, dropping from the sky, had gazed upon hills, rivers, Martian seats left nameless in spite of names. Once Martians had built cities, named cities; climbed mountains, named mountains; sailed seas, named seas. Mountains melted, seas drained, cities tumbled. In spite of this, the Earthmen had felt a silent guilt at putting new names to these ancient hills and valleys.

Nevertheless, man lives by symbol and label. The names were given.

Mr. Bittering felt very alone in his garden under the Martian sun, anachronism[2] bent here, planting Earth flowers in a wild soil.

Think. Keep thinking. Different things. Keep your mind free of Earth, the atom war, the lost rockets.

He perspired. He glanced about. No one watching. He removed his tie. Pretty bold, he thought. First your coat off, now your tie. He hung it neatly on a peach tree he had imported as a sapling from Massachusetts.

He returned to his philosophy of names and mountains. The Earthmen had changed names. Now there were Hormel Valleys, Roosevelt[3] Seas, Ford Hills, Vanderbilt Plateaus, Rockefeller[4] Rivers, on Mars. It wasn't right. The American settlers had shown wisdom, using old Indian prairie names:

---

2. **anachronism** (ə-năk'rə-nĭz'əm): something placed outside of its proper time period.
3. **Roosevelt:** most likely refers to Franklin Delano Roosevelt, the 32nd president of the United States.
4. **Hormel . . . Ford . . . Vanderbilt . . . Rockefeller:** names of industrial and financial "giants" in American history.

ANALYZE

Reread the boxed text, paying attention to the **sentence structure.** Notice how Bradbury uses a verb-noun pattern in the underlined sentence. Write the verb-noun phrases below. One has been done for you.

built   cities

___   ___

___   ___

___   ___

___   ___

Now notice how the author reverses the position of the verbs and nouns in the shaded text. What does the **syntax** in the boxed text suggest? Check one answer below.

☐ It suggests creation and destruction.

☐ It suggests a steady increase.

Wisconsin, Minnesota, Idaho, Ohio, Utah, Milwaukee, Waukegan, Osseo. The old names, the old meanings.

150 Staring at the mountains wildly, he thought: Are you up there? All the dead ones, you Martians? Well, here we are, alone, cut off! Come down, move us out! We're helpless!

The wind blew a shower of peach blossoms.

He put out his sun-browned hand and gave a small cry. He touched the blossoms and picked them up. He turned them, he touched them again and again. Then he shouted for his wife.

"Cora!"

She appeared at a window. He ran to her.

"Cora, these blossoms!"

160 She handled them.

"Do you see? They're different. They've changed! They're not peach blossoms any more!"

"Look all right to me," she said.

"They're not. They're wrong! I can't tell how. An extra petal, a leaf, something, the color, the smell!"

The children ran out in time to see their father hurrying about the garden, pulling up radishes, onions, and carrots from their beds.

"Cora, come look!"

170 They handled the onions, the radishes, the carrots among them.

"Do they look like carrots?"

"Yes . . . no." She hesitated. "I don't know."

"They're changed."

"Perhaps." ◀

"You know they have! Onions but not onions, carrots but not carrots. Taste: the same but different. Smell: not like it used to be." He felt his heart pounding, and he was afraid. He dug his fingers into the earth. "Cora, what's happening?

180 What is it? We've got to get away from this." He ran across

---

COMPARE AND CONTRAST

Underline dialogue on this page that shows Harry's feelings of alarm. Double underline dialogue that shows Cora's feelings of calm.

What effect do Harry's and Cora's contrasting feelings have on the **mood** of the story?

_____
_____
_____
_____
_____

the garden. Each tree felt his touch. "The roses. The roses. They're turning green!"

And they stood looking at the green roses.

And two days later Dan came running. "Come see the cow. I was milking her and I saw it. Come on!"

They stood in the shed and looked at their one cow.

It was growing a third horn.

And the lawn in front of their house very quietly and slowly was coloring itself like spring violets. Seed from Earth but growing up a soft purple. ▶

"We must get away," said Bittering. "We'll eat this stuff and then we'll change—who knows to what? I can't let it happen. There's only one thing to do. Burn this food!"

"It's not poisoned."

"But it is. **Subtly**, very subtly. A little bit. A very little bit. We mustn't touch it."

He looked with dismay at their house. "Even the house. The wind's done something to it. The air's burned it. The fog at night. The boards, all warped out of shape. It's not an Earthman's house any more."

"Oh, your imagination!"

He put on his coat and tie. "I'm going into town. We've got to do something now. I'll be back."

"Wait, Harry!" his wife cried. But he was gone.

In town, on the shadowy step of the grocery store, the men sat with their hands on their knees, conversing with great leisure and ease.

Mr. Bittering wanted to fire a pistol in the air.

What are you doing, you fools! he thought. *Sitting here! You've heard the news—we're stranded on this planet. Well, move! Aren't you frightened? Aren't you afraid? What are you going to do?*

"Hello, Harry," said everyone.

ANALYZE

Repeating certain words and sentence patterns is part of Bradbury's **style**. Reread the boxed text. Underline sentences that begin with the word *and*.

What does this **sentence structure** help to convey? Check one answer below.

☐ The word *and* creates an image in readers' minds.

☐ The use of *and* emphasizes a whole sequence of changes.

subtly (sŭt′lē) *adv.* not obviously; in a manner hard to notice or perceive

"Look," he said to them. "You did hear the news, the other day, didn't you?"

They nodded and laughed. "Sure. Sure, Harry."

"What are you going to do about it?"

"Do, Harry, do? What *can* we do?"

"Build a rocket, that's what!"

"A rocket, Harry? To go back to all that trouble? Oh, Harry!"

"But you *must* want to go back. Have you noticed the peach blossoms, the onions, the grass?"

"Why, yes, Harry, seems we did," said one of the men.

"Doesn't it scare you?"

"Can't recall that it did much, Harry."

"Idiots!"

"Now, Harry."

Bittering wanted to cry. "You've got to work with me. If we stay here, we'll all change. The air. Don't you smell it? Something in the air. A Martian virus, maybe; some seed, or a pollen. Listen to me!" ◀

They stared at him.

"Sam," he said to one of them.

"Yes, Harry?"

"Will you help me build a rocket?"

"Harry, I got a whole load of metal and some blueprints. You want to work in my metal shop on a rocket, you're welcome. I'll sell you that metal for five hundred dollars. You should be able to construct a right pretty rocket, if you work alone, in about thirty years."

Everyone laughed.

"Don't laugh."

Sam looked at him with quiet good humor.

"Sam," Bittering said. "Your eyes—"

"What about them, Harry?"

"Didn't they used to be gray?"

"Well now, I don't remember."

"They were, weren't they?"

MAKE JUDGEMENTS

Based on the story's outcome as well as the situation on Earth, do you think Harry is right to try to alarm the others about the changes that are taking place? Circle your answer.

Yes   No

Explain why you think as you do.

_____

_____

_____

_____

---

90   UNIT 4: MOOD, TONE, AND STYLE

"Why do you ask, Harry?"

"Because now they're kind of yellow-colored."

"Is that so, Harry?" Sam said, casually.

"And you're taller and thinner—"

"You might be right, Harry."

"Sam, you shouldn't have yellow eyes."

"Harry, what color eyes have *you* got?" Sam said.

"My eyes? They're blue, of course."

"Here you are, Harry." Sam handed him a pocket mirror. "Take a look at yourself."

Mr. Bittering hesitated, and then raised the mirror to his face.

There were little, very dim flecks of new gold captured in the blue of his eyes. ▶

"Now look what you've done," said Sam a moment later. "You've broken my mirror."

Harry Bittering moved into the metal shop and began to build the rocket. Men stood in the open door and talked and joked without raising their voices. Once in a while they gave him a hand on lifting something. But mostly they just idled and watched him with their yellowing eyes.

"It's suppertime, Harry," they said.

His wife appeared with his supper in a wicker basket.

"I won't touch it," he said. "I'll eat only food from our Deepfreeze. Food that came from Earth. Nothing from our garden."

His wife stood watching him. "You can't build a rocket."

"I worked in a shop once, when I was twenty. I know metal. Once I get it started, the others will help," he said, not looking at her, laying out the blueprints.

"Harry, Harry," she said, helplessly.

"We've got to get away, Cora. We've got to!" ▶

EVALUATE

Are the changes in Sam's appearance realistic according to the laws of science, or are they changes that would only appear in a work of **science fiction**? Explain.

MAKE JUDGEMENTS

Knowing the outcome of the story, do you think Harry is right to fight against his transformation? Or do you think the other men are wiser to accept it? Explain.

forlorn (fər-lôrn′) *adj.*
appearing lonely or sad

TestSmart

Which element of Bradbury's style is most obvious in lines 286–292?

Ⓐ his characters' realistic dialogue

Ⓑ his detailed description of setting

Ⓒ his use of short sentences and sentence fragments

Ⓓ his use of imagery that appeals to readers' senses

TIP Test questions about **style** require you to reread the lines in question and figure out what makes them special. To answer this question, try rereading lines 286–292, drawing lines between the sentences so that you think about each one. Which answer choice best describes the elements of style found here?

COMPARE

Harry suddenly says the Martian word *Iorrt*. What similar events occur with other characters later in the story?

_____

_____

_____

The nights were full of wind that blew down the empty moonlit sea meadows past the little white chess cities lying for their twelve-thousandth year in the shallows. In the Earthmen's settlement, the Bittering house shook with a feeling of change.

Lying abed, Mr. Bittering felt his bones shifted, shaped, melted like gold. His wife, lying beside him, was dark from many sunny afternoons. Dark she was, and golden-eyed, burnt almost black by the sun, sleeping, and the children
290 metallic in their beds, and the wind roaring **forlorn** and changing through the old peach trees, the violet grass, shaking out green rose petals. ◀

The fear would not be stopped. It had his throat and heart. It dripped in a wetness of the arm and the temple and the trembling palm.

A green star rose in the east.

A strange word emerged from Mr. Bittering's lips.

"*Iorrt. Iorrt.*" He repeated it. ◀

It was a Martian word. He knew no Martian.

300 In the middle of the night he arose and dialed a call through to Simpson, the archaeologist.

"Simpson, what does the word *Iorrt* mean?"

"Why that's the old Martian word for our planet Earth. Why?"

"No special reason."

The telephone slipped from his hand.

"Hello, hello, hello, hello," it kept saying while he sat gazing out at the green star. "Bittering? Harry, are you there?"

The days were full of metal sound. He laid the frame of the rocket with the reluctant help of three indifferent men. He
310 grew very tired in an hour or so and had to sit down.

"The altitude," laughed a man.

"Are you *eating*, Harry?" asked another.

"I'm eating," he said, angrily.

"From your Deepfreeze?"

"Yes!"

"You're getting thinner, Harry."

---

92   UNIT 4: MOOD, TONE, AND STYLE

"I'm not!"

"And taller."

"Liar!"

His wife took him aside a few days later. "Harry, I've used up all the food in the Deepfreeze. There's nothing left. I'll have to make sandwiches using food grown on Mars."

He sat down heavily.

"You must eat," she said. "You're weak."

"Yes," he said.

He took a sandwich, opened it, looked at it, and began to nibble at it.

"And take the rest of the day off," she said. "It's hot. The children want to swim in the canals and hike. Please come along."

"I can't waste time. This is a crisis!"

"Just for an hour," she urged. "A swim'll do you good."

He rose, sweating. "All right, all right. Leave me alone. I'll come."

"Good for you, Harry."

The sun was hot, the day quiet. There was only an immense staring burn upon the land. They moved along the canal, the father, the mother, the racing children in their swimsuits. They stopped and ate meat sandwiches. He saw their skin baking brown. And he saw the yellow eyes of his wife and his children, their eyes that were never yellow before. A few tremblings shook him, but were carried off in waves of pleasant heat as he lay in the sun. He was too tired to be afraid.

"Cora, how long have your eyes been yellow?"

She was bewildered. "Always, I guess."

"They didn't change from brown in the last three months?"

She bit her lips. "No. Why do you ask?"

"Never mind." ▶

They sat there.

"The children's eyes," he said. "They're yellow, too."

"Sometimes growing children's eyes change color."

DRAW CONCLUSIONS

Reread the boxed text. Underline the phrases that show that Harry is beginning to accept the changes.

Why do you think he is beginning to accept the changes?

_____
_____
_____
_____

"Maybe *we're* children, too. At least to Mars. That's a thought." He laughed. "Think I'll swim."

They leaped into the canal water, and he let himself sink down and down to the bottom like a golden statue and lie there in green silence. All was water-quiet and deep, all was peace. He felt the steady, slow current drift him easily.

If I lie here long enough, he thought, the water will work and eat away my flesh until the bones show like coral. Just my skeleton left. And then the water can build on that skeleton—green things, deep water things, red things, yellow things. Change. Change. Slow, deep, silent change. And isn't that what it is up *there*?

He saw the sky submerged above him, the sun made Martian by atmosphere and time and space.

Up there, a big river, he thought, a Martian river; all of us lying deep in it, in our pebble houses, in our sunken boulder houses, like crayfish hidden, and the water washing away our old bodies and lengthening the bones and—

He let himself drift up through the soft light.

Dan sat on the edge of the canal, regarding his father seriously.

"*Utha,*" he said.

"What?" asked his father.

The boy smiled. "You know. *Utha's* the Martian word for 'father.'"

"Where did you learn it?"

"I don't know. Around. *Utha!*"

"What do you want?"

The boy hesitated. "I—I want to change my name."

"Change it?"

"Yes."

His mother swam over. "What's wrong with Dan for a name?"

ANALYZE

Reread the underlined sentence. Notice how the author's unusual **syntax** suggests a dreamy, unfocused state of mind. Underline another sentence in the boxed passage that contains unusual syntax.

In your opinion, what atmosphere does the syntax in the sentence you underlined help to create?

Dan fidgeted. "The other day you called Dan, Dan, Dan. I didn't even hear. I said to myself, That's not my name. I've a new name I want to use."

Mr. Bittering held to the side of the canal, his body cold and his heart pounding slowly. "What is this new name?"

"Linnl. Isn't that a good name? Can I use it? Can't I, please?"

Mr. Bittering put his hand to his head. He thought of the silly rocket, himself working alone, himself alone even among his family, so alone. ▶

He heard his wife say, "Why not?"

He heard himself say, "Yes, you can use it."

"Yaaa!" screamed the boy. "I'm Linnl, Linnl!"

Racing down the meadowlands, he danced and shouted.

Mr. Bittering looked at his wife. "Why did we do that?"

"I don't know," she said. "It just seemed like a good idea."

They walked into the hills. They strolled on old mosaic paths, beside still pumping fountains. The paths were covered with a thin film of cool water all summer long. You kept your bare feet cool all the day, splashing as in a creek, wading.

They came to a small deserted Martian villa with a good view of the valley. It was on top of a hill. Blue marble halls, large murals, a swimming pool. It was refreshing in this hot summertime. The Martians hadn't believed in large cities.

"How nice," said Mrs. Bittering, "if we could move up here to this villa for the summer."

"Come on," he said. "We're going back to town. There's work to be done on the rocket."

But as he worked that night, the thought of the cool blue marble villa entered his mind. As the hours passed, the rocket seemed less important.

In the flow of days and weeks, the rocket **receded** and **dwindled**. The old fever was gone. It frightened him to think he had let it slip this way. But somehow the heat, the air, the working conditions—

MAKE INFERENCES
Did anyone teach Dan the Martian names *Utha* and *Linnl*? Support your response with events that happen earlier and later in the story.

_____
_____
_____
_____
_____

recede (rĭ-sēd') *v.* to become fainter or more distant

dwindle (dwĭn'dl) *v.* to become less, until little remains

He heard the men murmuring on the porch of his metal shop.

"Everyone's going. You heard?"

"All going. That's right."

Bittering came out. "Going where?" He saw a couple of trucks, loaded with children and furniture, drive down the dusty street.

"Up to the villas," said the man.

"Yeah, Harry. I'm going. So is Sam. Aren't you Sam?"

"That's right, Harry. What about you?"

430 "I've got work to do here."

"Work! You can finish that rocket in the autumn, when it's cooler."

He took a breath. "I got the frame all set up."

"In the autumn is better." Their voices were lazy in the heat.

"Got to work," he said.

"Autumn," they reasoned. And they sounded so sensible, so right.

"Autumn would be best," he thought. "Plenty of time, then."

No! cried part of himself, deep down, put away, locked
440 tight, suffocating. No! No!

"In the autumn," he said.

"Come on, Harry," they all said.

"Yes," he said, feeling his flesh melt in the hot liquid air. "Yes, in the autumn. I'll begin work again then." ◀

"I got a villa near the Tirra Canal," said someone.

"You mean the Roosevelt Canal, don't you?"

"Tirra. The old Martian name."

"But on the map—"

"Forget the map. It's Tirra now. Now I found a place in the
450 Pillan Mountains—"

"You mean the Rockefeller Range," said Bittering.

"I mean the Pillan Mountains," said Sam.

"Yes," said Bittering, buried in the hot, swarming air. "The Pillan Mountains."

INTERPRET

Reread the boxed text. What part of Harry is being "locked up tight?" Check one answer below:

☐ his yellowing eyes
☐ his human past
☐ his fear of Mars

How does the story's outcome support your answer to this question?

_____
_____
_____
_____

96   UNIT 4: MOOD, TONE, AND STYLE

Everyone worked at loading the truck in the hot, still afternoon of the next day.

Laura, Dan, and David carried packages. Or, as they preferred to be known, Ttil, Linnl, and Werr carried packages.

The furniture was abandoned in the little white cottage.

"It looked just fine in Boston," said the mother. "And here in the cottage. But up at the villa? No. We'll get it when we come back in the autumn."

Bittering himself was quiet.

"I've some ideas on furniture for the villa," he said after a time. "Big, lazy furniture."

"What about your encyclopedia? You're taking it along, surely?"

Mr. Bittering glanced away. "I'll come and get it next week."

They turned to their daughter. "What about your New York dresses?"

The bewildered girl stared. "Why, I don't want them any more."

They shut off the gas, the water, they locked the doors and walked away. Father peered into the truck.

"Gosh, we're not taking much," he said. "Considering all we brought to Mars, this is only a handful!"

He started the truck.

Looking at the small white cottage for a long moment, he was filled with a desire to rush to it, touch it, say good-bye to it, for he felt as if he were going away on a long journey, leaving something to which he could never quite return, never understand again.

Just then Sam and his family drove by in another truck.

"Hi, Bittering! Here we go!"

The truck swung down the ancient highway out of town. There were sixty others traveling in the same direction. The town filled with a silent, heavy dust from their passage. The canal waters lay blue in the sun, and a quiet wind moved in the strange trees. ▶

ANALYZE

On this page, underline characters' words or feelings that contribute to the strange and eerie **mood**. Put a star by **imagery** or descriptions of setting that contribute to this mood.

pendulum (pĕn′jə-ləm) *n.* a weight hung so that it can swing freely, sometimes used in timing the workings of certain clocks

> **ANALYZE**
>
> Reread lines 493–497. Think about how the author uses **imagery** to help you imagine the abandoned settlement. Write an *S* next to details that appeal to sight. Write a *T* next to details that appeal to touch.
>
> What does this description of the setting contribute to the **mood** of the story?
>
> _____
> _____
> _____
> _____

muse (myōōz) *v.* to say thoughtfully

> **EVALUATE**
>
> In your opinion, are the Bitterings still human at this point in the story? Explain your answer.
>
> _____
> _____
> _____
> _____

490 "Good-bye, town!" said Mr. Bittering.

"Good-bye, good-bye," said the family, waving to it.

They did not look back again.

Summer burned the canals dry. Summer moved like flame upon the meadows. In the empty Earth settlement, the painted houses flaked and peeled. Rubber tires upon which children had swung in back yards hung suspended like stopped clock **pendulums** in the blazing air. ◀

At the metal shop, the rocket frame began to rust.

In the quiet autumn Mr. Bittering stood, very dark now, 500 very golden-eyed, upon the slope above his villa, looking at the valley.

"It's time to go back," said Cora.

"Yes, but we're not going," he said quietly. "There's nothing there any more."

"Your books," she said. "Your fine clothes."

"Your *llles* and your fine *ior uele rre*," she said.

"The town's empty. No one's going back," he said. "There's no reason to, none at all."

The daughter wove tapestries and the sons played songs 510 on ancient flutes and pipes, their laughter echoing in the marble villa.

Mr. Bittering gazed at the Earth settlement far away in the low valley. "Such odd, such ridiculous houses the Earth people built."

"They didn't know any better," his wife **mused**. "Such ugly people. I'm glad they've gone."

They both looked at each other, startled by all they had just finished saying. They laughed.

"Where did they go?" he wondered. He glanced at his wife. 520 She was golden and slender as his daughter. She looked at him, and he seemed almost as young as their eldest son. ◀

"I don't know," she said.

"We'll go back to town maybe next year, or the year after, or the year after that," he said, calmly. "Now—I'm warm. How about taking a swim?"

98 UNIT 4: MOOD, TONE, AND STYLE

They turned their backs to the valley. Arm in arm they walked silently down a path of clear-running spring water.

Five years later a rocket fell out of the sky. It lay steaming in the valley. Men leaped out of it, shouting.

"We won the war on Earth! We're here to rescue you! Hey!"

But the American-built town of cottages, peach trees, and theaters was silent. They found a **flimsy** rocket frame rusting in an empty shop.

The rocket men searched the hills. The captain established headquarters in an abandoned bar. His lieutenant came back to report.

"The town's empty, but we found native life in the hills, sir. Dark people. Yellow eyes. Martians. Very friendly. We talked a bit, not much. They learn English fast. I'm sure our relations will be most friendly with them, sir."

"Dark, eh?" mused the captain. "How many?"

"Six, eight hundred, I'd say, living in those marble ruins in the hills, sir. Tall, healthy. Beautiful women."

"Did they tell you what became of the men and women who built this Earth settlement, Lieutenant?"

"They hadn't the foggiest notion of what happened to this town or its people."

"Strange. You think those Martians killed them?"

"They look surprisingly peaceful. Chances are a plague did this town in, sir."

"Perhaps. I suppose this is one of those mysteries we'll never solve. One of those mysteries you read about."

The captain looked at the room, the dusty windows, the blue mountains rising beyond, the canals moving in the light, and he heard the soft wind in the air. He shivered. Then, recovering, he tapped a large fresh map he had thumbtacked to the top of an empty table. ▶

---

flimsy (flĭm′zē) *adj.* not solid or strong

ANALYZE

It is part of Bradbury's **style** to use both very short and very long sentences. Underline the long sentence in lines 554–558. Box the short sentence.

What **mood** do these sentences help to create?

DARK THEY WERE, AND GOLDEN-EYED 99

ANALYZE

Reread the boxed text. What are the rocket men doing that has been done before?

_____

_____

The authors of **science fiction** stories sometimes include a message or comment about human civilization. What comment do you think Bradbury is making about civilization in this story?

_____

_____

_____

_____

Big Question

Look back at the question on page 81. Which answer does this story support? Why?

_____

_____

_____

_____

"Lots to be done, Lieutenant." His voice droned on and
560 quietly on as the sun sank behind the blue hills. "New settlements. Mining sites, minerals to be looked for. Bacteriological specimens[5] taken. The work, all the work. And the old records were lost. We'll have a job of remapping to do, renaming the mountains and rivers and such. Calls for a little imagination.

"What do you think of naming those mountains the Lincoln Mountains, this canal the Washington Canal, those hills—we can name those hills for you, Lieutenant. Diplomacy. And you, for a favor, might name a town for me.
570 Polishing the apple.[6] And why not make this the Einstein Valley, and farther over . . . are you _listening_, Lieutenant?" ◀

The lieutenant snapped his gaze from the blue color and the quiet mist of the hills far beyond the town.

"What? Oh, _yes_, sir!" ◀

---

5. **bacteriological specimens:** samples of different kinds of single-celled living things.
6. **polishing the apple:** acting in a way to get on the good side of another person.

Reading Comprehension

DIRECTIONS *Answer these questions by filling in the correct ovals.*

1. Which element of Bradbury's style is most obvious in lines 6–7?
   - (A) his use of vivid imagery
   - (B) his choice of unusual words
   - (C) his description of the story's setting
   - (D) his short sentences and sentence fragments

2. Which pair of words *best* describes the mood created in lines 59–69?
   - (A) pleasant, happy
   - (B) eerie, fearful
   - (C) bitter, angry
   - (D) sad, lonely

3. Which element most contributes to the mood in lines 532–534?
   - (A) the description of the setting
   - (B) the conversation between the rocket men
   - (C) the attitude of the Martians
   - (D) the imagery used to describe the spacecraft

4. Which sentence from the story uses unusual syntax?
   - (A) "He looked at his children."
   - (B) "Nevertheless, man lives by symbol and label."
   - (C) "The paths were covered with a thin film of cool water all summer long."
   - (D) "They moved along in the canal, the father, the mother, the racing children in their swimsuits."

5. Which event below could only happen in a science fiction story?
   - (A) Humans build space rockets.
   - (B) Atom bombs cause destruction on Earth.
   - (C) Food can be stored in a deep freeze.
   - (D) Humans learn the Martian language.

6. At the end of the story, why do the Martians learn English so quickly?
   - (A) Martian and English are very similar.
   - (B) The rocket men are good teachers.
   - (C) The Martians used to be humans.
   - (D) They had met Earthlings before.

7. The word *bidden* means "invited or asked to come." What is the most likely meaning of the prefix *un-*, which is used to form *unbidden* in line 37?
   - (A) the opposite of
   - (B) not finished
   - (C) always
   - (D) again

8. Read this sentence from the story:

   > Rubber tires upon which children had swung in back yards hung suspended like stopped clock pendulums in the blazing air.

   In this sentence, *suspended* means
   - (A) sent away
   - (B) full of suspense
   - (C) delayed
   - (D) hung from above

Assessment Practice I

Responding in Writing

9. Short Response In a paragraph, analyze how the imagery in "Dark They Were, and Golden-Eyed" adds to the story's mood.

___

Test-Taker's Toolkit

ACADEMIC VOCABULARY When you're asked to **analyze** how an element in a story works, you first need to look at specific examples of that element. Then you need to explain how those examples affect the whole selection. To complete this response, start by identifying the story's **mood**. Then find three specific images that help to create that mood.

GRAPHIC ORGANIZER Use the chart below to help you plan your response.

WORDS THAT DESCRIBE THE MOOD OF THIS STORY:

IMAGES THAT HELP CREATE THIS MOOD:

UNIT 4: MOOD, TONE, AND STYLE

What's the Connection?

"Dark They Were, and Golden-Eyed" is a purely fictional account of a human settlement on Mars. The science article "How Terraforming Mars Will Work" describes what it would actually take to make the Red Planet suitable for human habitation.

PLAN IT? To support human life, Mars would need to be much warmer and much wetter. Which two of the following ideas seem like the most reasonable ways to make this happen? Check them. Then draw a simple sketch of how one of the plans might work.

- ☐ Use giant mirrors to reflect sunlight toward Mars to melt its polar ice caps.
- ☐ Send rockets full of water to Mars and fill the empty seas.
- ☐ Hurl asteroids at Mars to raise its temperature and melt the ice caps.
- ☐ Use hydrogen bombs to interrupt Mars's orbit and move it closer to the sun.

Related Nonfiction

- **How Terraforming Mars Will Work**
  SCIENCE ARTICLE

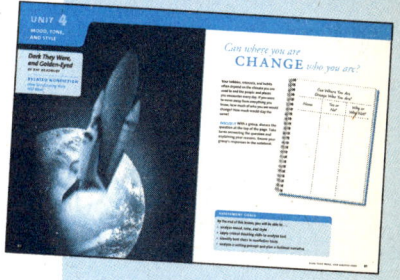

Use with "Dark They Were, and Golden-Eyed," p. 80

LEARN THE SKILL: IDENTIFY TEXT CLUES

Authors of nonfiction try to organize their writing so that readers can easily keep track of the flow of ideas. Here are three **text clues** you can look for to help you follow along as new ideas are introduced.

- **Transitions** are words or phrases that signal a change in idea. A new idea may be introduced using transition phrase such as *Another option for*. Headings also signal a change in idea.
- **Signal words** help you understand how ideas relate to each other. For example, the word *but* can signal that a contrasting idea is coming up. Words such as *if* signal a cause-effect relationship.
- **Demonstrative pronouns** such as *this, these,* and *those* are often used to make relationships between topics and ideas clear. Notice the people, places, or ideas to which these words refer.

For more on transitions and other text clues, see *Nonfiction Handbook* page R24.

RELATED NONFICTION 103

How Terraforming Mars Will Work

by Kevin Bonsor

Why would we ever want to go to Mars? It has a very thin atmosphere and no signs of existing life—but Mars does hold some promise for the continuation of the human race. <u>There are more than six billion people on Earth, and that number continues to grow unabated. This overcrowding, or the possibility of planetary disaster, will force us to eventually consider new homes in our solar system, and Mars may have more to offer us than the photos of its barren landscape now show.</u>

Recently, NASA probes[1] have discovered hints to a warmer past on Mars, one in which water may have flowed and life might have existed. . . . [A]n effort to colonize Mars would begin with altering the current climate and atmosphere to more closely resemble that of Earth. The process of transforming the Martian atmosphere to create a more habitable living environment is called terraforming. . . .

WHY MARS?

Mars is the next closest planet to us. And although it is a cold, dry planet today, it holds all of the elements that are needed for life to exist, including

- Water, which may be frozen at the polar ice caps
- Carbon and oxygen in the form of carbon dioxide (CO_2)
- Nitrogen

There are amazing similarities between the Martian atmosphere that exists today and the atmosphere that existed on Earth billions of years ago. . . . [T]he similarity [between] the early Earth and modern

---

1. **probes:** small, unmanned spacecraft that gather and send back information.

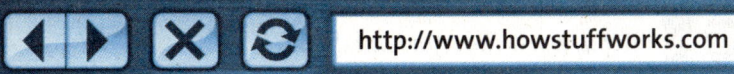

Mars atmospheres has led some scientists to speculate [that] the same process that turned the Earth's atmosphere from mostly carbon dioxide into breathable air could be repeated on Mars. [This process] would thicken the atmosphere and create a greenhouse effect[2] that would heat the planet and provide a suitable living environment for plants and animals. . . .

Other worlds have been considered as possible candidates for terraforming, including Venus, Europa (a Jupiter moon), and Titan (a Saturn moon). However, Europa and Titan are too far from the sun, and Venus is too close (the average temperature on Venus is about 900 degrees Fahrenheit [482.22 Celsius]). Mars stands alone as the one planet in our solar system, not including Earth, that might be able to support life. In the next section, learn how scientists plan to transform the dry, cold landscape of Mars into warm, livable habitat. ▶

This photograph of Mars was taken by the rover *Spirit* in 2007.

CREATING A MARTIAN GREENHOUSE

Terraforming Mars will be a huge undertaking, if it is ever done at all. Initial stages of terraforming Mars could take several decades or centuries. Terraforming the entire planet into an Earth-like habitat would have to be done over several millennia.[3] Some have even

---

2. **greenhouse effect:** the warming of the lower atmosphere of a planet due to gases in the upper atmosphere that trap heat from the sun.
3. **millennia** (mə-lĕn'ē-ə): plural form of millennium, meaning "one thousand years."

TestSmart

What is the purpose of the bulleted list on page 106?

Ⓐ It names the three methods of terraforming Mars that are going to be described.

Ⓑ It sums up three topics that have already been discussed.

Ⓒ It reveals the author's purpose and perspective.

Ⓓ It summarizes the entire article.

TIP To answer a question about the purpose of a list, start by **rereading** the sentence that introduces it. (Underline the sentence that introduces the list on this page.) Then reread the items in the list itself. The correct answer will be the one that restates the introductory sentence and describes the relationship between the items.

SPECIALIZED Vocabulary

The word **propulsion** in line 61 is related to the word *propel* in line 63. *Propel* is a verb that means "to push forward." *Propulsion* is a noun that means "the act of propelling or pushing forward." The word *propulsion* is used to describe the forward momentum of jets, rockets, and other aircraft. What do you think a propulsion system would do?

WORD ANALYSIS

_____

_____

---

http://www.howstuffworks.com

◀ 1 | 2 | 3 | 4 ▶

suggested that such a project would last thousands of millennia. So, how are we supposed to transform a dry, desert-like land into a lush environment, where people, plants and other animals can survive? Here are three terraforming methods that have been proposed:

- Large orbital mirrors that will reflect sunlight and heat the Mars surface
- Greenhouse gas-producing factories to trap solar radiation
- Smashing ammonia-heavy asteroids[4] into the planet to raise the greenhouse gas level ◀

NASA is currently working on a solar sail **propulsion system** that would use large reflective mirrors to harness the sun's radiation to propel spacecraft through space. Another use for these large mirrors would be to place them a couple hundred thousand miles from Mars and use the mirrors to reflect the sun's radiation and heat the Martian surface. Scientists have proposed building Mylar[5] mirrors that would have a diameter of 250 km (155.34 miles) and cover an area larger than Lake Michigan. . . . ◀

If a mirror this size were to be directed at Mars, it could raise the surface temperature of a small area by a few degrees. The idea would be to concentrate the mirrors on the polar caps to melt the ice and release the carbon dioxide that [is] believed to be trapped inside the ice. Over a period of many years, the rise in temperature would release greenhouse gases, such as chlorofluorocarbons (CFCs), which you can find in your air conditioner or refrigerator.

Another option for thickening the atmosphere of Mars, and, in turn, raising the temperature of the planet, would be to set up solar-powered, greenhouse-gas producing factories. Humans have had a lot of experience with this over the last century, as we have inadvertently[6] released tons of greenhouse gases into our own atmosphere, which

---

4. **asteroids** (ăs'tə-roids): large pieces of rock that exist between the orbits of the planets.
5. **Mylar** (mī'lär): a strong, flexible, stable plastic material.
6. **inadvertently** (ĭn'əd-vûr'tnt-lē): accidentally.

UNIT 4: MOOD, TONE, AND STYLE

some believe is raising the Earth's temperature. The same heating effect could be reproduced on Mars by setting up hundreds of these factories. Their sole purpose would be to pump out CFCs, methane, carbon dioxide and other greenhouse gases into the atmosphere. . . .

Space scientist Christopher McKay and Robert Zubrin, author of *The Case For Mars*, have also proposed a more extreme method for greenhousing Mars. They believe that hurling large, icy asteroids containing ammonia at the red planet would produce tons of greenhouse gases and water. For this to be done, nuclear thermal rocket engines would have to be somehow attached to asteroids from the outer solar system. . . .

If it is possible to smash an asteroid of such enormous size into Mars, the energy of one impact would raise the temperature of the planet by three degrees Celsius. The sudden rise in temperature would melt about a trillion tons of water, which is enough water to form a lake, . . . Several of these missions over 50 years would create a temperate climate and enough water to cover 25 percent of the planet's surface. However, the bombardment by asteroids, each releasing energy equivalent to 70,000 one-megaton[7] hydrogen bombs, would delay human settlement of the planet for centuries. ▶

While we may reach Mars this century, it could take several millennia for the idea of terraforming to be fully realized. It took the Earth billions of years to transform into a planet on which plants and animals could flourish. To transform the Mars landscape into one that resembles Earth is not a simple project. It will take many centuries of human ingenuity and labor to develop a habitable environment and bring life to the cold, dry world of Mars. ▶

---

7. **megaton:** a unit of explosive power that is equal to the explosive power of one million tons of TNT (a common explosive).

MAKE JUDGEMENTS

On the lines below, list the positive and negative results of blasting Mars with asteroids.

Positive: _____
_____
_____
_____

Negative: _____
_____
_____
_____
_____

Do you think blasting Mars with asteroids is a good idea? Why or why not?

_____
_____
_____

ANALYZE

Remember that **tone** is a writer's attitude toward his or her subject. Circle two words below that describe the **tone** of the article.

humorous   sincere
sarcastic   angry
skeptical   serious

Underline at least two phrases in the article that support your choices.

Assessment Practice II

Reading Comprehension

DIRECTIONS *Answer these questions by filling in the correct ovals.*

1. What must be done to colonize Mars?
   - A) discover life on that planet
   - B) send a probe to learn about Mars
   - C) alter the climate and atmosphere
   - D) learn to grown crops in terra firma

2. What is the purpose of the bulleted list on page 104?
   - A) It notes why Mars is cold and dry.
   - B) It tells what we must add to Mars.
   - C) It cites the elements needed for life.
   - D) It states the similarities between Mars's atmosphere and Earth's.

3. According to the article, what positive result would greenhouse gases have on Mars?
   - A) They would trap the sun's radiation and make Mars cooler.
   - B) They would make the atmosphere thinner.
   - C) They would trap the sun's radiation and make Mars warmer.
   - D) They would take the place of poisonous gases.

4. What text clue in lines 76–79 signals the introduction of a new idea?
   - A) the signal words "in turn"
   - B) the demonstrative pronoun "this"
   - C) the synonyms "Mars" and "the planet"
   - D) the transitional phrase "another option"

5. The main purpose of the section "Creating a Martian Greenhouse" is to explain
   - A) how to build factories on Mars
   - B) why we should hurl asteroids at Mars
   - C) how mirrors can warm Mars
   - D) various ideas for making Mars livable

6. According to the facts presented in "Terraforming Mars," what problems have the humans solved in "Dark They Were"?
   - A) They sent a rocket to Mars and back.
   - B) They heated Mars, located water, and thickened the atmosphere.
   - C) They added ammonia, carbon dioxide, and nitrogen to Mars.
   - D) They got rid of the old Martian civilization and renamed the hills.

7. Read the following sentence from the text:

   > It will take many centuries of human ingenuity and labor to develop a habitable environment and bring life to the cold, dry world of Mars.

   In this sentence, the word *ingenuity* means
   - A) geniuses
   - B) rockets
   - C) needs
   - D) creativity

8. What does *unabated* mean in line 4?
   - A) illegally
   - B) naturally
   - C) without control
   - D) without worry

108 UNIT 4: MOOD, TONE, AND STYLE

Timed Writing Practice

PROMPT

Write a (fictional narrative) about an imaginary event that happens on Mars. Create characters, a plot, and details with your imagination. Also include facts about Mars and space exploration that you learned from the Related Nonfiction.

BUDGET YOUR TIME

You have 45 minutes to complete this assignment. Decide how much time to spend on each step.

Analyze _____
Plan _____
Write _____
Review _____

Test-Taker's Toolkit

1. ANALYZE THE PROMPT

- **A. Read the prompt** carefully. Draw lines between the sentences to help you focus on each one.
- **B. Note key words** that tell you exactly what you must do. The writing form has been circled for you. Circle the topic, and underline the sources you need to consult to find relevant details.

2. PLAN YOUR RESPONSE

- **A. Plan your story** Use a story map like the one shown to help you plan your story.
- **B. Gather facts** Look back through the nonfiction selections you read. Find some facts you might include to make your story details seem realistic. List these facts below. They might provide inspiration.

_____
_____
_____
_____

SETTING:

CHARACTERS:

PROBLEM:

PLOT/EVENTS:

RESOLUTION:

3. WRITE AND REVIEW

- **A. Write an interest-grabbing opening** Try to reveal your story's setting in the first paragraph.
- **B. Write out your story** Leave enough time to read through it. Make sure you have met all the requirements. Also check your spelling and grammar.

RELATED NONFICTION 109

UNIT 5
APPRECIATING POETRY

LESSON 5A

the earth is a living thing
BY LUCILLE CLIFTON

Sleeping in the Forest
BY MARY OLIVER

Gold
BY PAT MORA

RELATED NONFICTION
What's Your Ecological Footprint?

Cool School

What is our place in NATURE?

When you left the house to go to school this morning, what was the weather like? Was it sunny or cloudy? Was it cool or warm? Did you hear birds singing or see an insect darting by? The natural world surrounds us, but sometimes we forget to notice.

SURVEY People have different ideas about how we fit in with the natural world. Some people see human beings as an important part of nature. Others believe that we're not very connected to what's around us. Talk to three classmates. Ask each one whether they think people are part of nature or separate from it, and why. Record each person's response in the notebook. Add your own response, too.

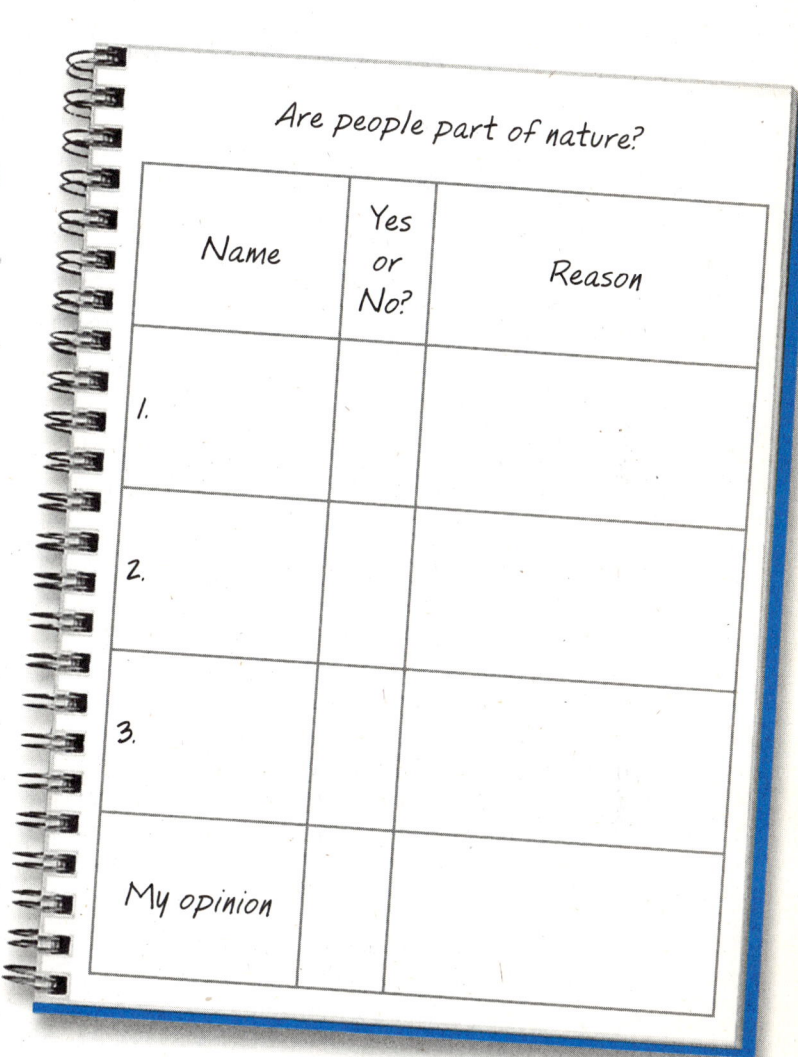

Are people part of nature?

Name	Yes or No?	Reason
1.		
2.		
3.		
My opinion		

ASSESSMENT GOALS

By the end of this unit, you will be able to . . .
- analyze imagery and figurative language in poetry
- apply critical thinking skills to analyze text
- evaluate information in nonfiction texts
- analyze a writing prompt and plan an expository essay

THE EARTH IS A LIVING THING

LEARN THE TERMS: ACADEMIC VOCABULARY

Imagery and Figurative Language

The three poems you are about to read describe different experiences with nature. The poets make these experiences vivid for the reader by using **IMAGERY,** or language that appeals to the five senses.

One way poets create imagery is through the use of **FIGURATIVE LANGUAGE.** Figurative language uses creative comparisons to help readers imagine ordinary things in new ways. The chart below describes three types of figurative language.

TYPE	EXAMPLES
SIMILE a comparison between two unlike things, using the word *like* or *as*	The strong wind made the trees sway like dancers.
METAPHOR a comparison between two unlike things that does not contain the word *like* or *as*	The ring of trees was a fortress where we took refuge.
PERSONIFICATION a description that gives human qualities to an animal, object, or idea	The tree welcomed me with a sigh.

ADDITIONAL TERMS FOR CRITICAL ANALYSIS

Imagery and figurative language are not the only ways a poem communicates its message to the reader. A poem's form helps convey its meaning, as well.

- **FORM** is the way a poem's words and lines are laid out on the page. Form includes the length of lines; the placement of lines; and the grouping of lines into stanzas.

- A **STANZA** is a group of two or more lines that form a unit in a poem. Stanzas may have the same number of lines or a different number of lines.

- Poetry that does not follow traditional rules about lines, rhythm, or rhyme is called **FREE VERSE.** The three poems you are about to read are examples of this type of poetry. The lines in free verse often flow more naturally than those in poems with strict patterns of rhyme, so they sound more like everyday speech.

the earth is a living thing
Lucille Clifton

is a black shuffling bear
ruffling its wild back and tossing
mountains into the sea

is a black hawk circling
5   the burying ground circling the bones
picked clean and discarded[1]

is a fish black blind in the belly of water
is a diamond blind in the black belly of coal

is a black and living thing
10   is a favorite child
of the universe
feel her rolling her hand
in its kinky hair
feel her brushing it clean

---

1. **discarded** (dĭ-skärd′ĕd): thrown away; gotten rid of.

SECOND READ: CRITICAL ANALYSIS

ANALYZE

In this poem, the poet compares the earth to six different things. Put a check mark next to each comparison.

What is the term for this type of **figurative language**?

_____

INTERPRET

Identify the type of **figurative language** Clifton uses in the boxed lines.

_____

What relationship between the earth and the universe is suggested by the poet's use of this technique?

_____

THE EARTH IS A LIVING THING

TestSmart

The description of the earth in lines 1–5 is an example of which type of figurative language?

- (A) metaphor
- (B) simile
- (C) personification
- (D) rhyme

TIP When a test item includes **academic vocabulary**, first recall the definitions of the terms. In this case, look over the definitions in the chart on page 112. Then, as you reread lines 1–5, notice that Oliver refers to the earth using the pronouns *her* and *she*. Think about which type of **figurative language** this might point toward.

ANALYZE

To what senses does the **imagery** in this poem appeal? Next to each image that appeals to the sense of sight, write an *S*; hearing, an *H*; and touch, a *T*.

Sleeping in the FOREST
Mary Oliver

I thought the earth
remembered me, she
took me back so tenderly, arranging
her dark skirts, her pockets
full of lichens[1] and seeds. I slept
as never before, a stone
on the riverbed, nothing
between me and the white fire of the stars
but my thoughts, and they floated
light as moths among the branches
of the perfect trees. All night
I heard the small kingdoms breathing
around me, the insects, and the birds
who do their work in the darkness. All night
I rose and fell, as if in water, grappling[2]
with a luminous doom. By morning
I had vanished at least a dozen times
into something better.

---

1. **lichens** (līʹkəns): fungi that grow together with algae and form crustlike growths on rocks or tree trunks.
2. **grappling**: struggling.

UNIT 5A: APPRECIATING POETRY

GOLD
Pat Mora

When Sun paints the desert
with its gold,
I climb the hills.
Wind runs round boulders, ruffles
5   my hair. I sit on my favorite rock,
lizards for company, a rabbit,
ears stiff in the shade
of a saguaro.¹
In the wind, we're all
10 eye to eye.

Sparrow on saguaro watches
rabbit watch us in the gold
of sun setting.
Hawk sails on waves of light, sees
15 sparrow, rabbit, lizards, me,
our eyes shining,
watching red and purple
sand rivers stream down the hills.

I stretch my arms wide as the sky
20 like hawk extends her wings
in all the gold light of this, home.

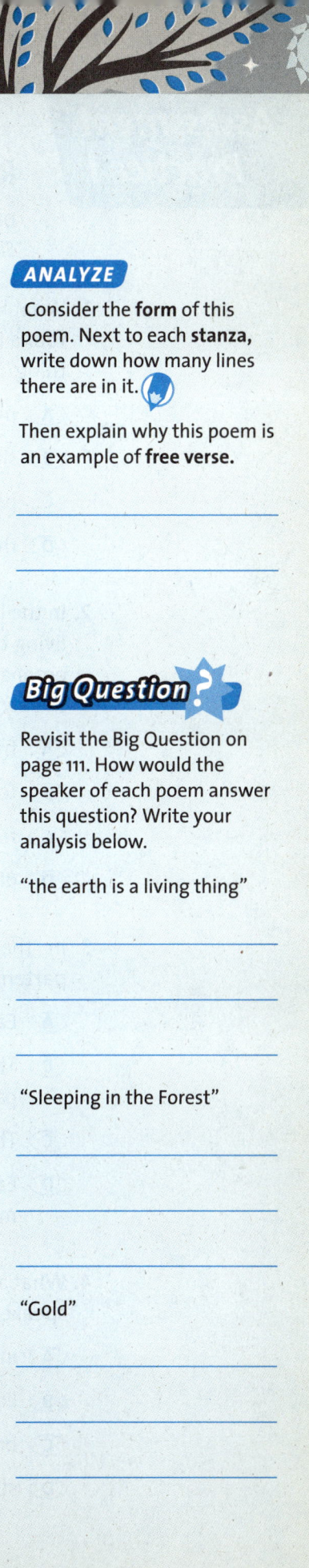

---

1. **saguaro** (sə-gwär'ō): a tall, branching cactus found in the southwestern United States and northern Mexico.

Assessment Practice I

Reading Comprehension

DIRECTIONS *Answer these questions about "the earth is a living thing," "Sleeping in the Forest," and "Gold" by filling in the correct ovals.*

1. What kind of figurative language is found in line 7 of "the earth is a living thing"?
   - Ⓐ metaphor
   - Ⓑ simile
   - Ⓒ personification
   - Ⓓ rhyme

2. In the last stanza of "the earth is a living thing," figurative language helps emphasize that the relationship between the earth and the universe is one of
   - Ⓐ frustration
   - Ⓑ tenderness
   - Ⓒ forcefulness
   - Ⓓ dissatisfaction

3. In "the earth is a living thing," what pattern do you see in the stanzas?
   - Ⓐ Each stanza has three lines.
   - Ⓑ The stanzas have the same rhyme pattern.
   - Ⓒ The stanzas all personify the sea.
   - Ⓓ Each stanza begins with a metaphor.

4. What are the "small kingdoms" that the speaker hears in "Sleeping in the Forest"?
   - Ⓐ insects and birds
   - Ⓑ lichens and seeds
   - Ⓒ branches and trees
   - Ⓓ stones and riverbeds

5. In "Sleeping in the Forest," the imagery "All night I rose and fell, as if in water" appeals to which sense?
   - Ⓐ hearing
   - Ⓒ sight
   - Ⓑ touch
   - Ⓓ taste

6. Which line from "Gold" contains an example of a simile?
   - Ⓐ "When Sun paints the desert..." (line 1)
   - Ⓑ "Wind runs round boulders..." (line 4)
   - Ⓒ "Hawk sails on waves of light..." (line 14)
   - Ⓓ "I stretch my arms wide as the sky..." (line 19)

7. How can you tell "Gold" is written in free verse?
   - Ⓐ It does not rhyme.
   - Ⓑ It includes stanzas.
   - Ⓒ It has a strong rhythm.
   - Ⓓ It contains figurative language.

8. Which *best* describes the form of "Gold"?
   - Ⓐ three stanzas; lines of different lengths
   - Ⓑ one stanza; lines of different lengths
   - Ⓒ three stanzas; 10 lines in each
   - Ⓓ no stanzas; 21 lines in all

Responding in Writing

9. Short Response Which poem's figurative language did you like best? What did this language make you feel or imagine as you read? Write a paragraph about one of the three poems in this lesson, focusing on why you enjoyed the figurative language it contains. Be sure to include examples from the poem to support your opinion.

For help, use the **Test-Taker's Toolkit** below.

Test-Taker's Toolkit

GRAPHIC ORGANIZER Use the graphic organizer below to help you plan your response. You don't necessarily need to fill in all three rows. Look back at the poem to help you recall examples of figurative language.

POEM: _____

TYPE OF FIGURATIVE LANGUAGE	EXAMPLE FROM POEM	WHAT THIS MADE ME FEEL OR IMAGINE

EARTH . . . / SLEEPING . . . / GOLD   117

Related Nonfiction

- **What's Your Ecological Footprint?**
  TEXTBOOK
- **Cool School**
  MAGAZINE ARTICLE

Use with "the earth is a living thing," "Sleeping in the Forest," and "Gold," p. 110

What's the Connection?

The poems you just read explore the effects that nature can have on humans. But what about the effects we humans have on nature? The nonfiction you're about to read investigates this topic. "What's Your Ecological Footprint?" is a textbook excerpt from *McDougal Littell Life Science*. It discusses the impact different populations have on Earth's resources. The magazine article "Cool School" describes an environmentally friendly school in Hawaii.

CHART IT In the first column of the chart below, write what you know about conserving Earth's energy and resources. You could list ways to save electricity or to keep trash out of landfills, for example, or just jot down what you know about the state of the environment. In the second column, write some questions you have about this topic. After reading the two articles, write what you learned about conservation in the third column.

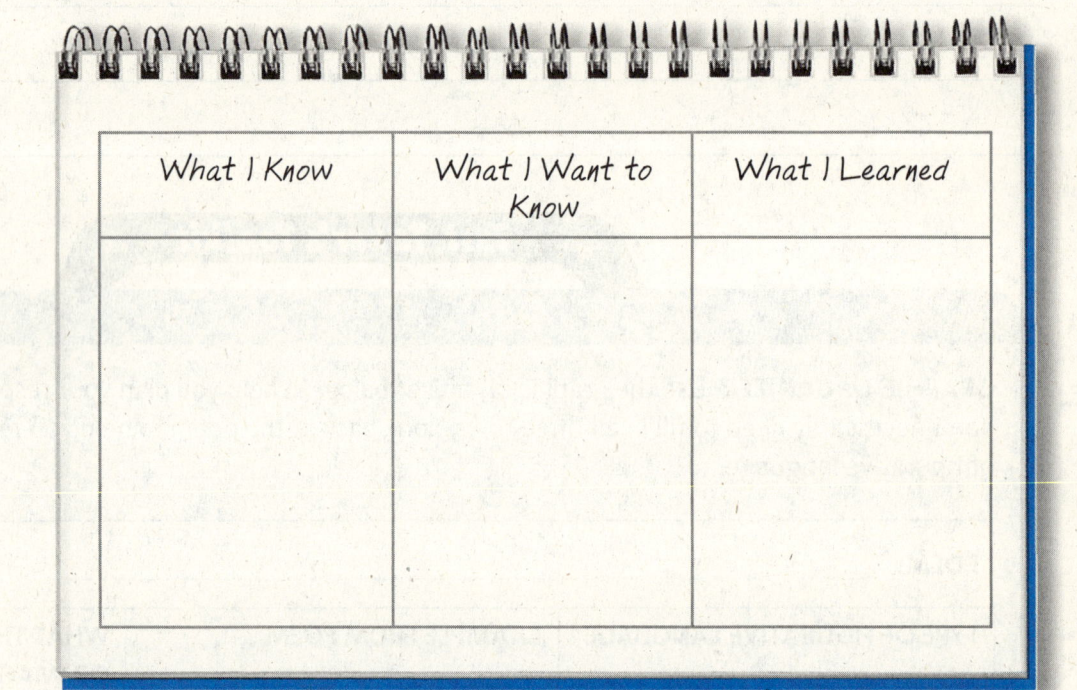

What I Know	What I Want to Know	What I Learned

LEARN THE SKILL: EVALUATE INFORMATION

When you **evaluate information,** you examine and judge the details that are offered to support a main idea. It is important to have a set of standards by which to make these critical judgments. The following questions can help:

- Is the evidence thorough enough to support the main idea?
- Are the examples relevant to the topic?
- Are the facts presented verifiable? That is, can they be proved by eyewitness accounts, encyclopedias, or experts' opinions?

For more on evaluating support, see *Nonfiction Handbook* page R11.

What's Your Ecological Footprint?

Humans need natural resources to survive, but the way resources are used threatens the welfare of the human population. Earth's carrying capacity depends on how much land is needed to support each person on Earth. The amount of land necessary to produce and maintain enough food and water, shelter, energy, and waste is called an **ecological footprint.** The size of an ecological footprint depends on a number of factors. These include the amount and efficiency of resource use, and the amount and toxicity of waste produced.

10   Individuals and populations vary in their use of resources and production of waste, and therefore in the size of their ecological footprints. The average U.S. citizen's ecological footprint covers an area larger than 24 football fields (9.7 hectares) and is one of the largest in the world. But the ecological footprint of individuals in developing nations is growing, and nations such as China and India have populations that are more than three times the size of the U.S. population. Individuals in the United States may have a large footprint, but other nations have a lot more "feet."

As the world population continues to grow, we face many
20   challenging decisions. Waste production and management is an issue that will become more important as we move into the future. Our welfare, and the welfare of future generations, depends on sustainable management of Earth's resources.

AVERAGE ECOLOGICAL FOOTPRINT OF INDIVIDUALS AROUND THE WORLD

Source: Global Footprint Network

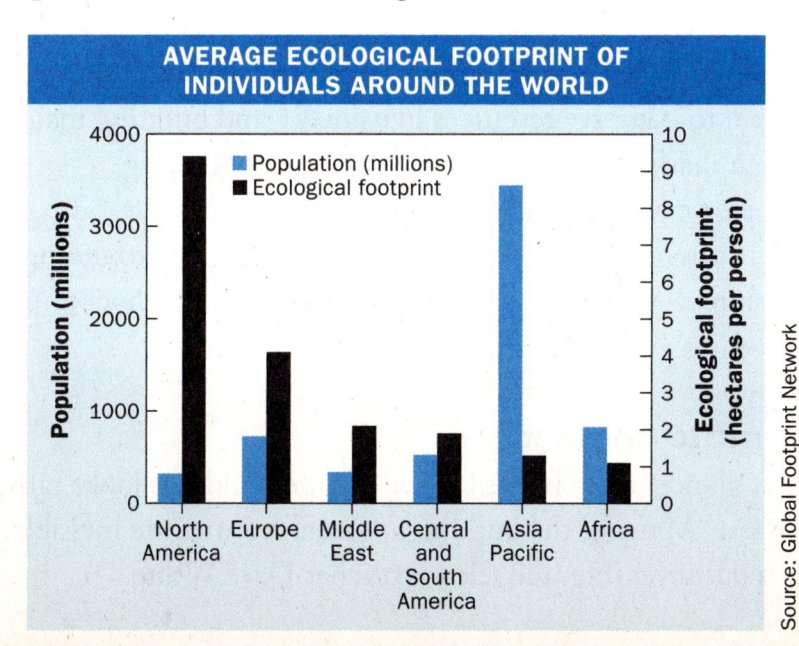

CLOSE READ

SET A PURPOSE
My purpose for reading is
_____
_____
_____

TestSmart

The bar graph supports the idea that a region's population is

A caused by many factors

B equal to its ecological footprint

C unequal to its ecological footprint

D dependent on access to natural resources

TIP To answer a question about a **graphic aid,** you must understand its purpose. Use the features of the graphic aid, such as the title, labels, and color key, to figure out what it is showing. When you look at the bar graph referred to by this question, pay special attention to the comparison between each region's population and its ecological footprint.

RELATED NONFICTION   119

CLOSE READ

Cool SCHOOL

Check out the most Earth-friendly middle school in the country
by Emily Costello

Seventh-grader Lauren Haruno considers herself passionate about protecting the environment. The 13-year-old may be drawing inspiration from her school: Case Middle School in Honolulu, Hawaii.

When the school opened in 2004, building-industry experts applauded it as one of the most Earth-friendly schools in the United States. Everything from the school's lights to the lockers is designed to conserve resources like energy and building materials. That emphasis is what makes Case a "green" building.

"When we learn about environmental issues in class, our teachers often refer to examples in the buildings surrounding us," says Lauren. *Science World* gives you a tour of the school to reveal some of its "green" features. ◀

Invisible Impact

At first glance, the school's cluster of nine buildings looks rather ordinary. "Many of the buildings' 'green' features are invisible," points out seventh-grade science teacher Dave White.

ANALYZE

Reread the boxed text. Underline the sentence that explains why Case Middle School is a "green" school.

Would you expect that buildings like this one would help to increase or decrease the size of a region's ecological footprint? Explain your thinking.

_____

_____

_____

120 UNIT 5A: APPRECIATING POETRY

For example, you can't tell that approximately 25 percent of the school was built using recycled materials. If you could peek inside
20 the school's walls, you would find supporting steel rods made from recycled metals such as melted-down cans and automobile parts. And while the students' lockers at Case may look like the metal ones that line most schools' hallways, they are made of plastic. This plastic comes from thousands of recycled milk containers.

By using recycled products, the school's builders helped to keep tons of useful materials from becoming landfill-clogging trash.

Be Cool

Perched on a hillside with views of Waikiki Beach, Case Middle School's location provides more than just stunning scenery.
30 The school is situated to take maximum advantage of natural ventilation.

The buildings are staggered and angled in a way to allow trade winds—or a natural wind pattern that sends cool winds blowing from east to west while moving toward Earth's equator—to flow between the structures. That way, when classrooms heat up in the afternoon sun, students can open the windows to let in the cooling winds. ▶

Ice Maker

Although the average temperature in Honolulu is a mild 25°C
40 (77°F), there are days when students need more than a breeze to keep cool. But air-conditioning systems require a lot of electricity to run, says Steve Piper, Case Middle School's physical-plant manager. Furthermore, traditional air conditioners are usually switched on during the hottest hours of the day—a time when electricity is in the greatest demand, and therefore costs the most money. That's why the school installed an energy-and-cost-saving air-conditioning system. ▶

To cool a building, a traditional air-conditioning system blows air past metal coils filled with supercold chemical fluids. The coils
50 chill the gush of air before it blasts out of the air-conditioning vents. What keeps the fluids cool is an energy-guzzling machine

EVALUATE SUPPORT

Underline the text that explains how Case Middle School takes advantage of Hawaii's trade winds.

Why is this detail **relevant** to the article's main idea?

_____
_____
_____

SUMMARIZE

Summarize the reasons why traditional air conditioners are costly.

_____
_____
_____

EVALUATE SUPPORT

What have you learned so far about this middle school's "green" features? On the lines below, sum up the main points the author makes in each section. Then, next to each subheading, write a plus sign (+) or a minus sign (–) to show whether you think that section presents relevant facts that can be verified.

"Invisible Impact"

_____

_____

_____

"Be Cool"

_____

_____

_____

"Ice Maker"

_____

_____

_____

"Likeable Lighting"

_____

_____

_____

---

called a chiller. Case did away with the chiller. Its replacement is a cheaper, more natural cooler: ice.

Eight enormous tanks located under the parking lot freeze ice at night when people are asleep and the demand for energy is low. At night, the cost of electricity is roughly half the daytime rate. When the air conditioner is switched on during the school day, a liquid refrigerant is pumped through the ice. This cools the refrigerant, which is then pumped through the machine's metal 60 coils. Then, energy-efficient fans blow air past the frigid coils and send the cooled air through the school.

Likeable Lighting

The school also reduces its dependency on the electric company by powering one building entirely with solar energy. This type of energy comes from converting the photons (particles of light energy) from sunlight into electricity.

On the rooftop of the eighth-grade creative-learning center are large panels filled with photovoltaic[1] cells. Each of these thin cells is made up of layers of the element silicon (Si)[2] and other materials. 70 When sunlight hits the panel, electrons (negatively charged particles) flow through the cell. The electrical energy created by these moving electrons can be stored in a battery until it is needed to turn on the center's lights or computers. ◂

Great Outdoors

Like many of Case's 1,024 students, seventh-grader Elise Minkin's favorite part of the four-acre campus is the group of "team spaces." During a break, students can gather in one of these spacious open-air verandas. One reason why students are drawn to these areas: They look out over a beautiful, lush landscape. 80 But maintaining these grounds requires thousands of gallons of water. Case avoids wasting water by taking advantage of Hawaii's frequent bouts of rain.

---

1. **photovoltaic** (fō′tō-vŏl-tā′ĭc): relating to the electrical voltage produced when light strikes two different materials that are in close contact.
2. **(Si)** (sē): The chemical symbol for silicon on the periodic table of the elements.

Every day, the school's storm drains—as well as a stream that's connected to an onsite lily pond—send approximately 132,000 liters (35,000 gallons) of rainwater into the ocean. So the school installed an underground tank to capture this overflowing rainwater, which is then used to keep the campus grounds lush. This method scores an "A" in teaching students about water conservation. "Our class is always trying to find ways to save water," says seventh-grader Adrian Yee. ▶

Hawaii's Environmentally Friendly Punahou School[3]

Case Middle School includes dozens of "green" features never before used in a project this size in Hawaii. In addition to saving energy with solar panels and a special air-conditioning system, the school reduces energy use with lights that automatically dim when the last person exits a room. Lockers, countertops, and flooring are made from recycled materials. These Earth-friendly features added cost to the school's construction, but will ultimately save money by decreasing the school's energy needs.

Big Lessons

Case's eco-friendly design helps save energy and natural resources every day. But school officials say the real job of the $62 million new school is to educate. That's why every "green" design element in the school is labeled with a sign explaining the technology and how it works. "At Punahou, every day is Earth Day," says teacher Dave White. The students agree. "Going to school in 'green' buildings has shown us that there are many ways to help the environment," says Elise.

TestSmart

The sections titled "Great Outdoors" and "Be Cool" both support the idea that Case Middle School makes good use of

- A natural resources
- B recycled materials
- C electrical power
- D solar energy

TIP Subheadings alone do not provide enough information to answer most test questions. To answer this question, **locate** each subheading and **skim** the text beneath it. "Be Cool" describes how the school uses trade winds. "Great Outdoors" describes how it uses rainwater. Which answer choice names the category wind and water are part of?

---

3. **Punahou School:** Chase Middle School is a part of the larger Punahou School, a college preparatory school that encompasses kindergarten through grade 12.

Assessment Practice II

Reading Comprehension

DIRECTIONS *Answer these questions about "What's Your Ecological Footprint?" and "Cool School" by filling in the correct ovals.*

1. An individual's ecological footprint refers to the amount of
   - (A) fuel required to transport the person
   - (B) land required to sustain the person
   - (C) impact the person has on others
   - (D) region in which the person lives

2. According to the bar graph in "What's Your Ecological Footprint?" which region has the largest ecological footprint, after North America?
   - (A) South America
   - (B) Europe
   - (C) Africa
   - (D) Asia

3. You can evaluate the information in "What's Your Ecological Footprint?" by
   - (A) deciding whether you agree with the author
   - (B) studying the bar graph
   - (C) checking the information in another source
   - (D) identifying each main idea

4. According to "Cool School," using recycled milk containers to make the school's lockers reduced
   - (A) landfill use
   - (B) electricity use
   - (C) "green" features
   - (D) water consumption

5. Which feature of Case Middle School addresses the importance of conserving water?
   - (A) a storm drain that sends water into the ocean
   - (B) the location of its nine buildings
   - (C) a tank that catches rainwater
   - (D) eight ice-freezing tanks

6. Which of the following concerns mentioned in "What's Your Ecological Footprint?" is *not* addressed in "Cool School"?
   - (A) sustainable management of resources
   - (B) waste production and management
   - (C) world population growth
   - (D) efficient resource use

7. Which word from "What's Your Ecological Footprint?" is related to the Latin word *populus*, meaning "people"?
   - (A) production
   - (B) population
   - (C) important
   - (D) footprint

8. Which word from "Cool School" is related to the Latin word *tradere*, meaning "to hand down"?
   - (A) conditioning
   - (B) technology
   - (C) traditional
   - (D) trash

124   UNIT 5A: APPRECIATING POETRY

Timed Writing Practice

PROMPT

Write (an essay) explaining three or four ways nature is important to people. Support your ideas using examples from the poems you have read and from the nonfiction selections.

BUDGET YOUR TIME

You have 30 minutes to complete this assignment. Decide how much time to spend on each step.

Analyze _____
Plan _____
Write _____
Review _____

Test-Taker's Toolkit

1. ANALYZE THE PROMPT

- **A. Read the prompt carefully** Circle key words that tell you exactly what you must do.
- **B. Restate the prompt** so you are sure you understand it. Then reread the prompt against your restatement of it to make sure you have included all the key ideas.

2. PLAN YOUR RESPONSE

- **A. Make notes** Create a planning chart like the one shown. Make sure it reflects all the key ideas.
- **B. Organize your information** Use your planning chart to help you structure your essay. You could begin with an introductory paragraph that lists different ways nature is important to people. Then you could write one paragraph for each of these ideas. Conclude with a paragraph that sums up your ideas.

Different Ways Nature Is Important to People

Idea #1:
  Examples:

Idea #2:
  Examples:

Idea #3:
  Examples:

3. WRITE AND REVIEW

- **A. Write the introductory paragraph** Try to capture your readers' interest as well as suggest how your essay will answer the prompt. Write a draft of your opening sentences below.

- **B. Write your full response** on a second sheet of paper. Be sure to leave time to check your spelling and grammar.

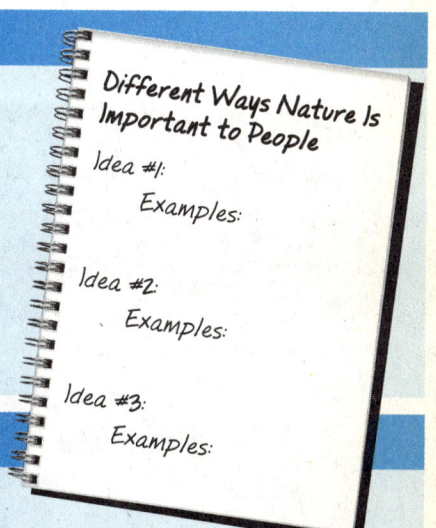

RELATED NONFICTION 125

UNIT 5
APPRECIATING POETRY

LESSON 5B

Scaffolding
BY SEAMUS HEANEY

The World Is Not a Pleasant Place to Be
BY NIKKI GIOVANNI

Annabel Lee
BY EDGAR ALLAN POE

RELATED NONFICTION
Guidelines for Keeping Your Friendships Strong

Whom do you feel CLOSEST TO?

Think about a family member or a friend with whom you are very close. Chances are you've fought with this person. Yet he or she still brings you comfort and happiness. Why do you think this is so? The poems you are about to read explore the mysteries of strong relationships.

WEB IT Fill in the web with qualities that make a relationship strong. It may help to think about the people you are close to and what you like about your relationships with them.

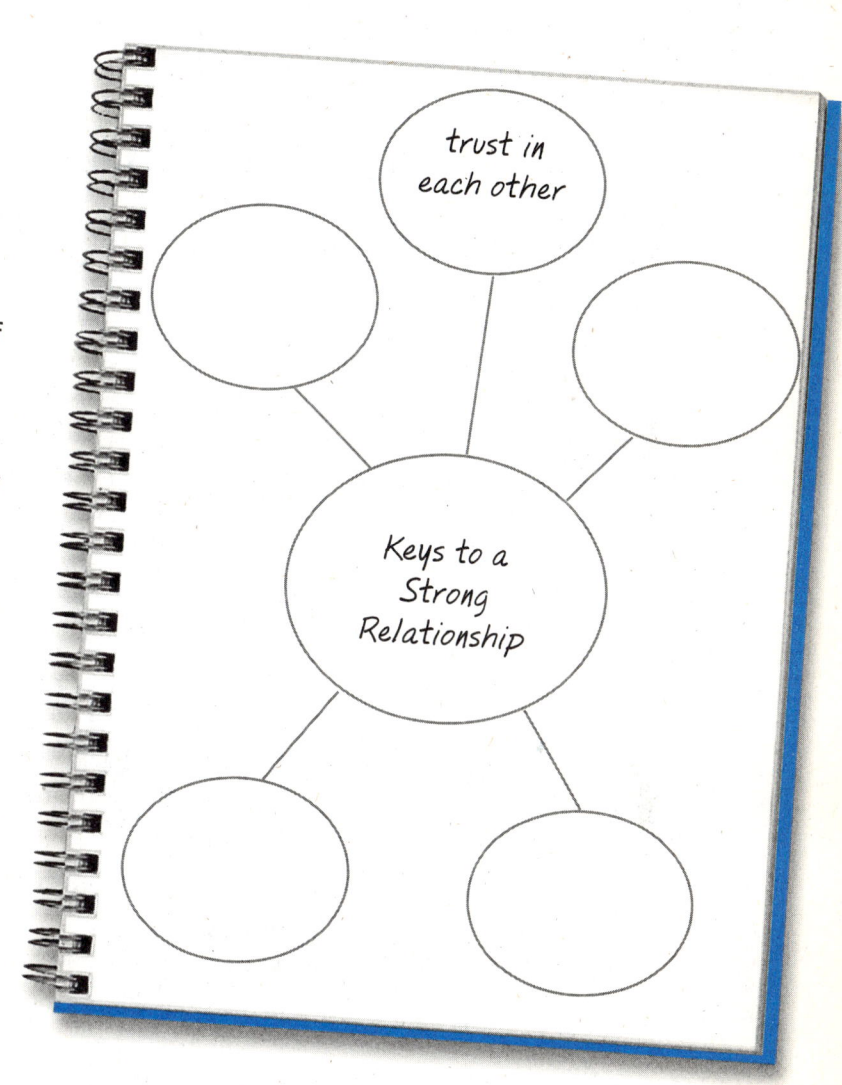

(Web diagram with central circle "Keys to a Strong Relationship" connected to surrounding circles, one labeled "trust in each other")

ASSESSMENT GOALS

By the end of this lesson, you will be able to...
- analyze sound devices in a work of poetry
- apply critical thinking skills to analyze text
- evaluate nonfiction sources for usefulness
- analyze a writing prompt and plan a personal narrative

LEARN THE TERMS: ACADEMIC VOCABULARY

Sound Devices

SOUND DEVICES are the special effects of poetry. Moviemakers use special effects to transport you to their characters' worlds or to keep you on the edge of your seat. Poets use sound devices for similar reasons. Sound devices can make a poem seem as peaceful as ocean waves lapping on the shore or as intense as a hurricane. They can create a mood and emphasize important words or ideas. Here are some of the sound devices used in the poems you're about to read:

SOUND DEVICES	EXAMPLES
RHYME the repetition of sounds at the end of words, as in *me* and *see*	Notice how the rhyme in this poem helps to create a mood that is playful and upbeat, even though the poem addresses a serious subject. They came to tell your faults to me, They named them over one by one; I laughed aloud when they were done, I knew them all so well before,— Oh, they were blind, too blind to see Your faults had made me love you more. ——"Faults" by Sara Teasdale
REPETITION the use of a word, phrase, or line more than once **ALLITERATION** the repetition of consonant sounds at the beginning of words, such as the *c* in *curved crook*	The repeated phrases and the alliteration in the last line help to emphasize the moon's shape. How thin and sharp is the moon tonight! How thin and sharp and ghostly white Is the slim curved crook of the moon tonight! ——"Winter Moon" by Langston Hughes

ADDITIONAL TERMS FOR CRITICAL ANALYSIS

Two of the three poems you are about to read use rhyme in very specific ways. The following terms will help you analyze rhyming poems:

- **RHYME SCHEME** is a pattern of end rhymes in a poem. A rhyme scheme is noted by assigning a letter of the alphabet, beginning with *a*, to each line. Lines that rhyme are given the same letter. For example, the rhyme scheme in the poem "Faults," in the chart above, is *abbcac*.

- A **RHYMING COUPLET** is a type of rhyme scheme—it is a stanza that consists of two rhyming lines. The first stanza in a poem that uses rhyming couplets would have an *aa* rhyme scheme.

SCAFFOLDING
SEAMUS HEANEY

Masons,[1] when they start upon a building,
Are careful to test out the scaffolding;

Make sure that planks won't slip at busy points,
Secure all ladders, tighten bolted joints.[2]

5 And yet all this comes down when the job's done
Showing off walls of sure and solid stone.

So if, my dear, there sometimes seem to be
Old bridges breaking between you and me

Never fear. We may let the scaffolds fall
10 Confident that we have built our wall.

---

1. **masons** (mā'sənz): wallers who build with brick or stone.
2. **joints** (joints): places where two parts or pieces join together.

SECOND READ: CRITICAL ANALYSIS

CLASSIFY

Circle the words in the first three stanzas that **rhyme**. Then note the **rhyme scheme** by lettering the lines with *a*'s, *b*'s, and so on.

What is the name of this type of rhyme scheme?

_____

ANALYZE

Put a ✓ by the stanzas that describe a building. Put an ✗ by the stanzas that describe a relationship.

In your own words, tell how building a wall and establishing a relationship are similar.

_____
_____
_____
_____
_____

THE WORLD IS NOT A PLEASANT PLACE TO BE
Nikki Giovanni

the world is not a pleasant place
to be without
someone to hold and be held by

a river would stop
5   its flow if only
a stream were there
to receive it

an ocean would never laugh
if clouds weren't there
10 to kiss her tears ◀

the world is not
a pleasant place to be without
someone ◀

TestSmart

Which line from the poem contains an example of alliteration?

A line 1
B line 4
C line 9
D line 10

TIP When a test question includes academic vocabulary, start by reminding yourself of the term's definition. To answer this question, recall the meaning of **alliteration**. (See page 128 if you can't remember.) Then reread each line and listen for an example of alliteration.

ANALYZE

Underline words and phrases that are repeated in this poem.

In your own words, tell what message this **repetition** helps to communicate.

_____
_____
_____

Annabel Lee
Edgar Allan Poe

It was many and many a year ago,
    In a kingdom by the sea,
That a maiden there lived whom you may know
    By the name of Annabel Lee;—
5 And this maiden she lived with no other thought
    Than to love and be loved by me.

She was a child and *I* was a child,
    In this kingdom by the sea,
But we loved with a love that was more than love—
10   I and my Annabel Lee—
With a love that the wingéd seraphs[1] of Heaven
    Coveted[2] her and me. ▶

And this was the reason that, long ago,
    In this kingdom by the sea,
15 A wind blew out of a cloud by night
    Chilling my Annabel Lee;
So that her high-born kinsmen came
    And bore her away from me,
To shut her up in a sepulcher[3]
20   In this kingdom by the sea.

The angels, not half so happy in Heaven,
    Went envying her and me;
Yes! that was the reason (as all men know,
    In this kingdom by the sea)
25 That the wind came out of the cloud chilling
    And killing my Annabel Lee. ▶

---

1. **seraphs** (sĕr'əfs): any of the highest order of angels.
2. **coveted** (kŭv'ĭ-tĭd): envied.
3. **sepulcher** (sĕp'əl-kər): a place for burial; tomb.

ANALYZE

This poem is thought to be a tribute to the poet's wife, who died when she was very young. Underline the words that are repeated in line 7 and the word that are repeated in line 9.

What important idea does the **repetition** of these words emphasize?

DRAW CONCLUSIONS

According to the speaker, what did the angels do? Why?

Why might it be important for the speaker to believe this?

ANALYZE

Reread lines 27–33, using letters to mark the **rhyme scheme.** Underline repeated words and phrases.

What feeling is created by the **rhyme, repetition,** and rhythm of these lines?

_____

_____

_____

Big Question

Look back at the web you filled in on page 127. What might the speaker of each poem add to the web? Write your ideas below. **DRAW CONCLUSIONS**

"Scaffolding"

_____

_____

"The World Is Not a Pleasant Place to Be"

_____

_____

"Annabel Lee"

_____

_____

But our love it was stronger by far than the love
    Of those who were older than we—
    Of many far wiser than we—
30 And neither the angels in Heaven above
    Nor the demons down under the sea
Can ever dissever[4] my soul from the soul
    Of the beautiful Annabel Lee:— ◀

For the moon never beams without bringing me dreams
35   Of the beautiful Annabel Lee;
And the stars never rise but I feel the bright eyes
    Of the beautiful Annabel Lee;
And so, all the night-tide, I lie down by the side
Of my darling, my darling, my life and my bride
40   In her sepulcher there by the sea—
    In her tomb by the side of the sea. ◀

---

4. **dissever** (dĭ-sĕv′ər): separate; tear apart.

132 UNIT 5B: APPRECIATING POETRY

Reading Comprehension

Assessment Practice I

DIRECTIONS Answer these questions about "Scaffolding," "The World is Not a Pleasant Place to Be," and "Annabel Lee" by filling in the correct ovals.

1. Whom is the speaker addressing in lines 7–10 of "Scaffolding"?
   - (A) his life-long love
   - (B) a new friend
   - (C) his neighbor
   - (D) a mason

2. Which line from "Scaffolding" contains an example of alliteration?
   - (A) line 1
   - (B) line 2
   - (C) line 4
   - (D) line 6

3. What do you think the speaker of the poem "The World Is Not a Pleasant Place to Be" wants from life?
   - (A) to receive love without having to give it
   - (B) freedom from commitment
   - (C) to love and be loved
   - (D) a lot of friends

4. The rhyme scheme in the first stanza of "Annabel Lee" is
   - (A) aabbcc
   - (B) ababab
   - (C) ababcb
   - (D) abcabc

5. What kind of relationship is described in "Annabel Lee"?
   - (A) close friendship
   - (B) mature love
   - (C) unhappy marriage
   - (D) young love

6. In lines 34–37 of "Annabel Lee," the repetition emphasizes the idea that
   - (A) Annabel Lee will return one day
   - (B) the angels have gotten what they wanted
   - (C) the speaker is always thinking of his love
   - (D) no one is more beautiful than Annabel Lee

7. Which sentence *best* sums up the theme all three poems share?
   - (A) Loving relationships are an important part of life.
   - (B) Close relationships can be made and broken.
   - (C) Loving relationships can lead to sadness.
   - (D) Love is valuable but easily lost.

8. Which poem uses rhyming couplets?
   - (A) "The World Is Not a Pleasant Place to Be"
   - (B) "Scaffolding"
   - (C) "Annabel Lee"
   - (D) none of the above

GO ON

Assessment Practice I

*For help, use the **Test-Taker's Toolkit** below.*

Responding in Writing

9. **Short Response** Choose one of the poems you have just read. Write a paragraph telling how that poem uses two of the three sound devices you learned about in this lesson. Be sure to cite specific examples.

_____
_____
_____
_____
_____
_____
_____
_____

Test-Taker's Toolkit

ACADEMIC VOCABULARY **Sound devices** are ways of using words for the sound qualities they create. **Rhyme, repetition,** and **alliteration** are the three sound devices you learned about in this lesson. To review examples of each device, turn to the chart on page 128.

GRAPHIC ORGANIZER Use the chart below to help you plan your response. You can cross out the row for the sound device you're not describing.

POEM TITLE:		
EXAMPLES OF SOUND DEVICES IN THIS POEM		
RHYME	REPETITION	ALLITERATION

134   UNIT 5B: APPRECIATING POETRY

What's the Connection?

As reflected in the poems you just read, many people find that close relationships are what give meaning to life. "Guidelines for Keeping Your Friendships Strong" is a brochure that tells how you can keep one type of relationship—friendship—alive.

CHART IT In the first column of the chart below, list several things you can do to keep friendships strong. In the second column, list some things you shouldn't do if you want to have a good relationship with your friends. Then compare your chart with the ones other students in your class have completed.

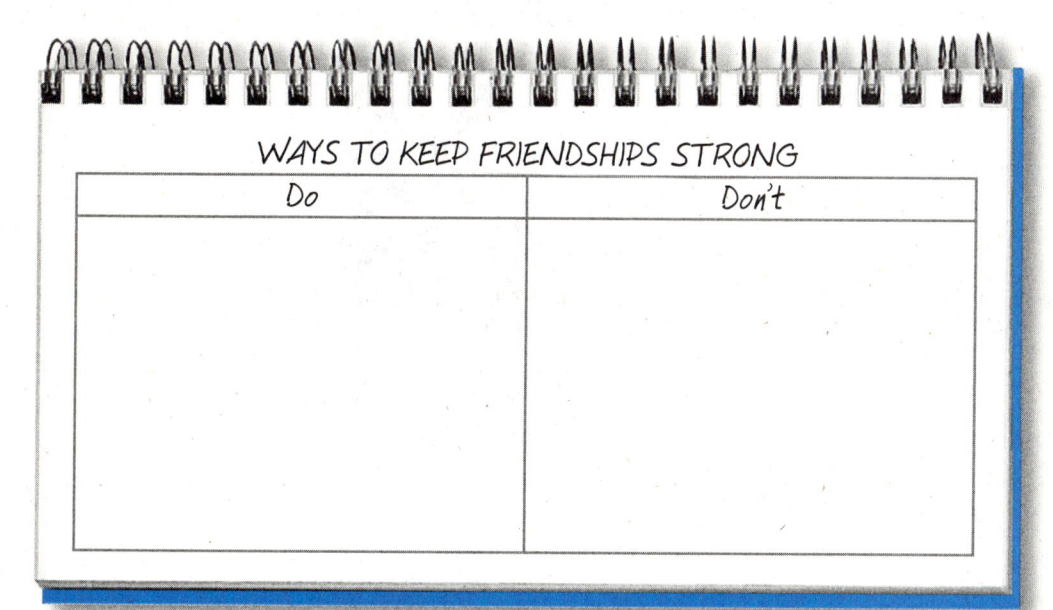

WAYS TO KEEP FRIENDSHIPS STRONG

Do	Don't

Related Nonfiction

Guidelines for Keeping Your Friendships Strong
BROCHURE

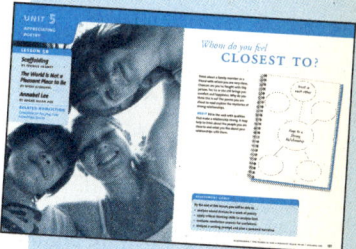

Use with "Scaffolding," "The World Is Not a Pleasant Place to Be," and "Annabel Lee," p. 126

LEARN THE SKILL: EVALUATE SOURCES FOR USEFULNESS

"Don't believe everything you read" is an old saying. It cautions readers not to trust information just because it's in print. How can you know if a source is trustworthy and useful? You establish standards, or criteria, for **evaluating** text. Here are some questions to ask yourself:

- **Is the information substantial and detailed?** Information that is obvious, and is not expanded upon, is not very useful.
- **Is the information accurate?** Does the author giving out the information have the proper education and background? Does research support the author's statements?
- **Are the suggestions realistic and useable?**
- **Is the information complete?** For example, does it contain contact information, or tell you where to go for additional information?

For more on evaluating sources, see *Nonfiction Handbook*, page R11.

CLOSE READ

SET A PURPOSE
My purpose for reading is
_____
_____
_____

PREVIEW
How is this brochure organized? Read the subheadings, scan the text, and look at the boxes labeled *ACTIVITY*. Then describe the purpose of each feature on the lines below.

Subheadings: _____
_____
_____

Activity: _____
_____
_____

EVALUATE SOURCES
What specific suggestions does this brochure offer on how to like yourself? Underline them.

Do you think these suggestions are realistic and usable? Explain.
_____
_____
_____
_____

GUIDELINES FOR
Keeping Your Friendships Strong

◯ *Like yourself.* ◀

If you don't like yourself, don't feel that you have any value, or don't think others will like you, you will have a hard time reaching out to people who may become friends. Work on building your self-esteem by treating yourself well—eating healthy foods, getting plenty of exercise and rest, doing things that you enjoy. Remind yourself over and over that you are a very special and worthwhile person.

> 10 **ACTIVITY** Make a list of at least five things that you do well. Make a sign that says "I am a wonderful person." Hang it in a place where you will see it often—like on your refrigerator door or on the mirror in your bathroom. ◀

136 UNIT 5B: APPRECIATING POETRY

◉ *Have a variety of interests.*

Develop interests in different things. It will open opportunities for connection with others and make you a more interesting person that others enjoy being with. Some interests include music, art, crafts, gardening, watching or participating in sports activities, or fixing cars.

> **ACTIVITY** Make a list of your interests. Hang it on your refrigerator or in another convenient place. It will act as a reminder when you are having a hard time thinking of things to do. ▶

◉ *Take action to make new friends.*

To make new friends, you have to take action. You can do it as slowly or as quickly as you want, taking small steps or big steps. You can also work on improving your relationships with people already in your life by doing things like inviting them to your home to chat, share a meal, play a game, watch a video, or share some other activity, or by doing a favor for them when they are having a hard time.

> **ACTIVITY** Do something that puts you in contact with others. Go to an event in your community. Join a group.

CONNECT

Write down three of your interests. Beside each one, write the name of a friend or person you know who shares that interest.

1. _____
   _____
   _____

2. _____
   _____
   _____

3. _____
   _____
   _____

RELATED NONFICTION   137

INTERPRET

Reread the boxed text. In your own words, what is an "I can top that" story?

_____
_____
_____
_____

EVALUATE SOURCES

Does the section "Take equal responsibility for the friendship" provide you with enough information to make use of the advice?

☐ yes
☐ no

If not, what do you think is needed to make the information more complete?

_____
_____
_____
_____

◯ *Listen and share equally.*

Listen closely to what the other person is saying. Let
40 the other person know you are paying close attention through eye contact, body language, and occasional brief comments like, "I knew you could do it," "That sounds like fun," or "I bet you wish it had happened some other way." Avoid thinking about what your response is going to be while the person is talking. If a person is sharing something intense and personal, give them your full attention. Don't share an "I can top that" story. ◀

Avoid giving others advice unless they ask for it. Just
50 listening is fine! . . . You can be a really good friend by listening to the same story again and again, reassuring that it is OK to do this. Never make fun of what the other person thinks or feels. Avoid judging or criticizing the other person.

◯ *Take equal responsibility for the friendship.*

Both people in a friendship need to take responsibility for the friendship. For instance, you should be making plans for shared activities some of the time and your
60 friend should be making these plans some of the time. If you are taking all of the responsibility for the friendship, talk to your friend about it and figure out a way to make the friendship more equal. ◀

138   UNIT 5B: APPRECIATING POETRY

Keep personal information confidential.

As you feel more and more comfortable with the other person, you will find that you talk more and share more personal information. Have a mutual understanding that anything personal the two of you discuss is absolutely confidential and that you will not share personal information about each other with other people. ▶

> **ACTIVITY** Write, "I will never share any personal information that another person shares with me." Read it over and over to remind yourself.

Have a good time.

Spend most of your time with your friends doing fun, interesting activities, together. Sometimes friendships get "bogged down" if all you ever do is talk about each other's struggles. Go to a movie, walk on the beach, play ball, watch a fun video, work on an art project, cook a meal—whatever would be fun for both of you. Take turns suggesting and initiating these activities.

> **ACTIVITY** call a friend, or someone you know who you hope will become a friend, and ask them to share a fun activity with you—like going to a movie, watching a video, or making supper together. ▶

TestSmart

Which of the following criteria does the brochure *not* fulfill?

- Ⓐ It offers suggestions.
- Ⓑ It provides proof that the author is reliable.
- Ⓒ It explains the reasons behind each suggestion.
- Ⓓ It provides tips for putting suggestions into action.

TIP When asked a question about what a selection does not do, you can use the **process of elimination** to find the right answer. In this case, scan the subheadings, text, and activities. Next to each place in the selection where one of the criteria is met, write the letter of that answer option. The correct answer will be the letter you did not write down.

EVALUATE SOURCES

Did this brochure provide you with useful information? Explain, using examples from the text.

_____

_____

_____

_____

RELATED NONFICTION **139**

Assessment Practice II

Reading Comprehension

DIRECTIONS Answer these questions about "Guidelines for Keeping Your Friendships Strong" by filling in the correct ovals.

1. Which of the following is *not* a suggestion presented in "Guidelines for Keeping Your Friendships Strong"?
   - A Like yourself.
   - B Educate yourself.
   - C Have a good time.
   - D Take equal responsibility.

2. The author of "Guidelines" thinks that people who have a variety of interests are
   - A boring
   - B better listeners
   - C less judgmental
   - D more interesting to others

3. According to "Guidelines," good friends
   - A never give each other advice
   - B share personal information about themselves
   - C spend most of their time discussing problems
   - D think about how they will respond while they are listening

4. Which of the following criteria for usefulness does "Guidelines" fulfill?
   - A It presents the author's qualifications.
   - B It provides research to back up statements.
   - C It tells you where to go to find additional information.
   - D It offers specific recommendations that address the topic.

5. Which statement is supported by both the brochure and the three poems you have read?
   - A Close relationships are an important part of life.
   - B Close relationships take years to develop.
   - C Being with friends makes you confident.
   - D Problems can be dealt with.

6. Which statement is supported *only* by the poem "Annabel Lee"?
   - A People need other people.
   - B Problems can be dealt with successfully.
   - C Young love can be very intense.
   - D Being with friends makes you more confident.

7. In line 5 of "Guidelines" the word *self-esteem* means
   - A liveliness
   - B confidence
   - C individuality
   - D characterization

8. In line 70 of "Guidelines" the word *confidential* means
   - A filled with self-confidence
   - B positive and enthusiastic
   - C private or secret
   - D unique

140   UNIT 5B: APPRECIATING POETRY

Timed Writing Practice

PROMPT

When you look back on your favorite memories, you probably find that many of them involve the people you are closest to. Write a (personal narrative) about a time you spent with someone who is important to you. Include details about what you did together and explain why the experience was meaningful.

BUDGET YOUR TIME

You have 45 minutes to complete this assignment. Decide how much time to spend on each step.

Analyze _____
Plan _____
Write _____ 45
Review _____

Test-Taker's Toolkit

1. ANALYZE THE PROMPT

A. **Read the prompt** carefully. Draw lines between sentences to help you focus on each one.

B. **Note key words** that tell you what you must do. The writing form, a personal narrative, has been circled for you. Underline the words that tell you the two things to be sure you include.

C. **Restate the prompt** in your own words. Then reread the prompt against your restatement to make sure you have included all the key elements.

2. PLAN YOUR RESPONSE

Make notes A personal narrative is an account of an event that happened in your life. This type of writing is usually told in the first-person point of view (you refer to yourself as *I*). Start by jotting down the key information you need for your narrative. A chart like the one shown can help.

Who the person is:
His/her relationship to me:
Where we went:
When we went there:
What we did:
Why the experience was meaningful:

3. WRITE AND REVIEW

A. **Craft an opening** Choose one of the following ways to begin your narrative:
- interesting dialogue that captures the meaning of the day
- a vivid description of the person you're writing about
- in the middle of an exciting action or event

B. **Write the story as it happened**, including all the details you recorded in your notes. Also include dialogue, if it seems appropriate. Leave enough time to read your narrative and make sure you have met all the requirements of the prompt.

RELATED NONFICTION 141

UNIT 6
MYTHS, LEGENDS, AND TALES

Prometheus
RETOLD BY BERNARD EVSLIN

Orpheus and Eurydice
RETOLD BY OLIVIA COOLIDGE

RELATED NONFICTION
An American Prometheus

Discoveries That Changed the World

Do you THINK before you act?

Did you ever make a decision you wished you could take back? If so, then you know that your actions sometimes have consequences, or effects, that you didn't bargain for. You're not the only one to have realized this. From ancient Greek myths to modern best-sellers, there are countless stories based on the very human tendency to act first and think later.

THINK IT THROUGH Examine each potentially risky situation in the notebook. Do you think each decision listed would most likely have positive consequences or negative ones? Check one box for each decision. Then pair up with a classmate to explain your opinions.

DECISION	CONSEQUENCES	
	Positive	Negative
1. You decide to branch out and make friends outside of your group.	☐	☐
2. You choose to try a new sport, though you worry you might not be good at it.	☐	☐
3. You decide to stand up for something you believe in, even though all your friends disagree.	☐	☐

ASSESSMENT GOALS

By the end of this cluster, you will be able to...
- analyze the characteristics of myths
- apply critical thinking skills to analyze text
- recognize cause-and-effect relationships in nonfiction texts
- analyze a writing prompt and write a cause-and-effect composition

LEARN THE TERMS: ACADEMIC VOCABULARY

Myths

From ancient Greece to medieval England, every culture has created its own **MYTHS, LEGENDS,** and **TALES**. These traditional stories were passed down from one generation to the next by word of mouth. The stories were meant to entertain. They were also meant to teach values, explain things, and preserve a group's heritage. They continue to inspire us hundreds or even thousands of years after they were first told.

You are about to read two myths that were first told in Greece over 3,000 years ago. Myths are traditional stories that explain mysteries of the universe. Most share the following characteristics:

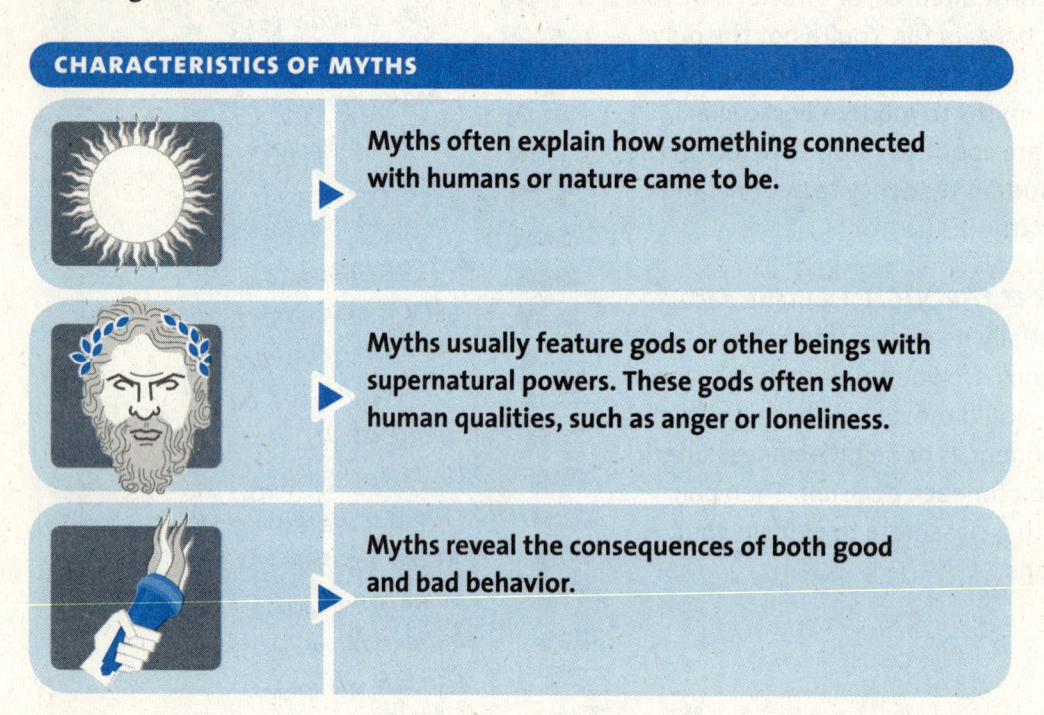

CHARACTERISTICS OF MYTHS

- Myths often explain how something connected with humans or nature came to be.

- Myths usually feature gods or other beings with supernatural powers. These gods often show human qualities, such as anger or loneliness.

- Myths reveal the consequences of both good and bad behavior.

ADDITIONAL TERMS FOR CRITICAL ANALYSIS

Traditional literature often reflects the culture of the people who created it, but it can also speak to the overall human condition. The following terms can help you discuss the ways it does both those things:

- **CULTURAL VALUES** are the ideas or beliefs that a culture holds as important. For example, cultural values may include respect for elders, a love of music, or a belief in hard work. Cultural values often differ from one group of people to the next.

- **UNIVERSAL THEMES** are messages or morals that are found in literature from many different times and places. For example, the message that the journey is more important than the destination is a universal theme, because it appears in stories from different cultures and historical eras.

PROMETHEUS

Retold by Bernard Evslin

BACKGROUND Many Greek myths tell of struggles among the gods and other mythical beings. For example, the god Zeus defeated a family of giants called the Titans to become ruler of all the gods. Zeus then ordered Prometheus, one of the Titans, to create human beings. In this myth, Prometheus challenges Zeus's idea of what humans should be like.

Prometheus was a young Titan, no great admirer of Zeus. Although he knew the great lord of the sky hated explicit questions, he did not hesitate to beard[1] him when there was something he wanted to know.

One morning he came to Zeus and said, "O Thunderer, I do not understand your design. You have caused the race of man[2] to appear on earth, but you keep him in ignorance and darkness."

"Perhaps you had better leave the race of man to me," said Zeus. "What you call ignorance is innocence. What you call darkness is the shadow of my decree. Man is happy now. And he is so framed that he will remain happy unless someone persuades him that he is unhappy. Let us not speak of this again." ▶

---

1. **beard:** to confront or defy.
2. **man:** In older translations, the expression *man* was commonly used to refer to all people.

But Prometheus said, "Look at him. Look below. He crouches in caves. He is at the mercy of beast and weather. He eats his meat raw. If you mean something by this, enlighten me with your wisdom. Tell me why you refuse to give man the gift of fire."

Zeus answered, "Do you not know, Prometheus, that every gift brings a penalty? This is the way the Fates[3] weave destiny—by which gods also must abide. Man does not have fire, true, nor the crafts which fire teaches. On the other hand, he does not know disease, warfare, old age, or that inward pest called worry. He is happy, I say, happy without fire. And so he shall remain."

"Happy as beasts are happy," said Prometheus. "Of what use to make a separate race called man and endow[4] him with little fur, some wit, and a curious charm of unpredictability? If he must live like this, why separate him from the beasts at all?"

"He has another quality," said Zeus, "the capacity for worship. An **aptitude** for admiring our power, being puzzled by our riddles and amazed by our caprice.[5] That is why he was made."

"Would not fire, and the graces he can put on with fire, make him more interesting?"

"More interesting, perhaps, but **infinitely** more dangerous. For there is this in man too: a vaunting pride that needs little sustenance[6] to make it swell to giant size. Improve his lot, and he will forget that which makes him pleasing—his sense of worship, his humility. He will grow big and poisoned with pride and fancy himself a god, and before we know it, we shall see him storming Olympus. Enough, Prometheus! I have been patient with you, but do not try me too far. Go now and trouble me no more with your speculations." ◀

---

3. **the Fates:** in Greek mythology, the three goddesses who decide the course of people's lives.
4. **endow** (ĕn-dou'): to provide with a quality or talent.
5. **caprice** (kə-prēs'): the quality of acting without planning or thinking beforehand.
6. **vaunting pride that needs little sustenance:** boastful pride that needs little support.

---

aptitude (ăp'tĭ-tōōd') n. natural ability

infinitely (ĭn'fə-nĭt-lē) adv. extremely; greatly

TestSmart

Which of the following is *not* one of Zeus's reasons for refusing to give humans fire?

(A) Every gift brings a penalty.
(B) Fire will make humans too proud.
(C) Giving the gift of fire is not within Zeus' power.
(D) Fire may cause humans to rise up and storm Mount Olympus.

TIP When a test question asks about what is *not* in the text, you can use the **process of elimination** to find the answer. Look for each answer choice in the text. If you find it, you can eliminate it, or take it off the list of possible correct answers. This question asks you to identify the one reason Zeus does not give in his argument. Reread Zeus's argument in lines 20–45. Which answer choices are present in the text? The one that is not is the correct answer.

146 UNIT 6: MYTHS, LEGENDS, AND TALES

Prometheus was not satisfied. All that night he lay awake making plans. Then he left his couch at dawn and, standing tiptoe on Olympus, stretched his arm to the eastern horizon where the first faint flames of the sun were flickering. In his hand he held a reed filled with a dry fiber; he thrust it into the sunrise until a spark smoldered. Then he put the reed in his tunic and came down from the mountain.

At first men were frightened by the gift. It was so hot, so quick; it bit sharply when you touched it and for pure spite made the shadows dance. They thanked Prometheus and asked him to take it away. But he took the haunch of a newly killed deer and held it over the fire. And when the meat began to sear and sputter, filling the cave with its rich smells, the people felt themselves melting with hunger and flung themselves on the meat and devoured it greedily, burning their tongues.

"This that I have brought you is called 'fire,'" Prometheus said. "It is an ill-natured spirit, a little brother of the sun, but if you handle it carefully, it can change your whole life. It is very greedy; you must feed it twigs, but only until it becomes a proper size. Then you must stop, or it will eat everything in sight—and you too. If it escapes, use this magic: water. It fears the water spirit, and if you touch it with water, it will fly away until you need it again."

He left the fire burning in the first cave, with children staring at it wide-eyed, and then went to every cave in the land. ▶

Then one day Zeus looked down from the mountain and was amazed. Everything had changed. Man had come out of his cave. Zeus saw woodmen's huts, farmhouses, villages, walled towns, even a castle or two. He saw men cooking their food, carrying torches to light their way at night. He saw forges[7] blazing, men beating out ploughs, keels, swords,

DRAW CONCLUSIONS
What explanation does this **myth** provide?
_____
_____
_____

Tell why people from ancient times might have wanted an explanation for this phenomenon.
_____
_____
_____
_____

---

7. **forges** (fôr′jĭz): places where metal is heated and hammered into shape.

spears. They were making ships and raising white wings of sails and daring to use the fury of the winds for their journeys. They were wearing helmets, riding out in chariots to do battle, like the gods themselves.

Zeus was full of rage. He seized his largest thunderbolt. "So they want fire," he said to himself. "I'll give them fire—more than they can use. I'll turn their miserable little ball of earth into a cinder." But then another thought came to him, and he lowered his arm. "No," he said to himself, "I shall have **vengeance**—and entertainment too. Let them destroy themselves with their new skills. This will make a long, twisted game, interesting to watch. I'll attend to them later. My first business is with Prometheus." ◀

He called his giant guards and had them seize Prometheus, drag him off to the Caucasus,[8] and there bind him to a mountain peak with great chains specially forged by Hephaestus[9]—chains which even a Titan in agony could not break. And when the friend of man was bound to the mountain, Zeus sent two vultures to hover about him forever, tearing at his belly and eating his liver.

Men knew a terrible thing was happening on the mountain, but they did not know what. But the wind shrieked like a giant in torment and sometimes like fierce birds.

Many centuries he lay there—until another hero was born brave enough to defy the gods. He climbed to the peak in the Caucasus and struck the shackles from Prometheus and killed the vultures. His name was Heracles.[10] ◀

---

vengeance (vĕn′jəns) *n.* the infliction of punishment in return for an offense

DRAW CONCLUSIONS
What **cultural values** does "Prometheus" reflect? Circle the qualities that this myth suggests were important to the ancient Greeks:

obedience   humility
creativity   strength
education   curiosity

Big Question
What do you think Prometheus should have considered before giving humans the gift of fire?
MAKE JUDGMENTS

---

8. **Caucasus** (kô′kə-səs): a mountainous region in southeastern Europe.
9. **Hephaestus** (hĭ-fĕs′təs): the Greek god of fire and metalworking.
10. **Heracles** (hĕr′ə-klēz′): another name for Hercules, a son of Zeus who was famous for his great strength and courage.

Orpheus and Eurydice

Retold by Olivia Coolidge

BACKGROUND This myth features another fearsome Greek god: Hades, ruler of the dead. Hades, like all the gods, answered to Zeus, but he was also powerful in his own right. In this myth, you will learn about the bargain struck by Hades and Orpheus, a mythic musician. Ancient myths tell that when Orpheus was a child, the god Apollo gave him a stringed instrument called a lyre. Orpheus went on to become a celebrated musician, singer, and poet.

In the legend of Orpheus the Greek love of music found its fullest expression. Orpheus, it is said, could make such heavenly songs that when he sat down to sing, the trees would crowd around to shade him. The ivy and vine stretched out their tendrils. Great oaks would bend their spreading branches over his head. The very rocks would edge down the mountainsides. Wild beasts crouched harmless by him, and nymphs[1] and woodland gods would listen to him enchanted.

Orpheus himself, however, had eyes for no one but the nymph, Eurydice.[2] His love for her was his inspiration, and

---

1. **nymphs** (nĭmfs): divine beings represented as beautiful maidens who live in natural places such as trees.
2. **Eurydice** (yŏŏ-rĭd′ĭ-sē).

ANALYZE

Underline the sentence that tells what ancient Greek **cultural value** this myth reveals.

What did the ancient Greeks seem to believe about music?

_____
_____
_____
_____

inconsolable (ĭn′kən-sō′lə-bəl) *adj.* impossible or difficult to comfort

COMPARE

Compare this, Orpheus's first crossing of the Styx into Hades, with his second attempt to cross the river. What explains the difference?

The first attempt: _____
_____
_____

The second attempt: _____
_____
_____

The reason for this difference:
_____
_____

TestSmart

VOCABULARY

Which word below is related to the Latin word *resonare*, meaning "to fill with sound"?

Ⓐ rejoiced
Ⓑ restaged
Ⓒ resounded
Ⓓ reasoning

TIP Tests often include questions about the relationship between a **Latin word** and a vocabulary word. Remember that words that are related in spelling and structure are often related in meaning. In this case, look for the answer choice that has the prefix *re-* and a base word that has to do with sound.

---

his power sprang from the passionate longing that he knew in his own heart. All nature rejoiced with him on his bridal day, but on that very morning, as Eurydice went down to the riverside with her maidens to gather flowers for a bridal garland, she was bitten in the foot by a snake, and she died in spite of all attempts to save her.

Orpheus was **inconsolable**. All day long he mourned his bride, while birds, beasts, and the earth itself sorrowed with him. When at last the shadows of the sun grew long, Orpheus 20 took his lyre and made his way to the yawning cave which leads down into the underworld, where the soul of dead Eurydice had gone.

Even grey Charon, the ferryman of the Styx,[3] forgot to ask his passenger for the price of crossing. The dog, Cerberus, the three-headed monster who guards Hades' gate, stopped full in his tracks and listened motionless until Orpheus had passed. As he entered the land of Hades, the pale ghosts came after him like great, uncounted flocks of silent birds. All the land lay hushed as that marvelous voice resounded across the mud 30 and marshes of its dreadful rivers. In the daffodil fields of Elysium[4] the happy dead sat silent among their flowers. In the farthest corners of the place of punishment, the hissing flames stood still. Accursed Sisyphus,[5] who toils eternally to push a mighty rock uphill, sat down and knew not he was resting. Tantalus,[6] who strains forever after visions of cool water, forgot his thirst and ceased to clutch at the empty air. ◀◀

The pillared hall of Hades opened before the hero's song. The ranks of long-dead heroes who sit at Hades' board looked up and turned their eyes away from the pitiless form of Hades

---

3. **Styx** (stĭks): in Greek mythology, the river across which the souls of the dead are transported.
4. **Elysium** (ĭ-lĭz′ē-əm): the home of the blessed, or those who were judged to have lived well, after death.
5. **Sisyphus** (sĭs′ə-fəs): a cruel king of Corinth condemned forever to roll a huge stone up a hill, only to have it fall down again.
6. **Tantalus** (tăn′tə-ləs): a king who, for his crimes, was condemned to stand in water that receded when he tried to drink.

150 UNIT 6: MYTHS, LEGENDS, AND TALES

and his pale, unhappy queen. Grim and unmoving sat the dark king of the dead on his ebony throne, yet the tears shone on his rigid cheeks in the light of his ghastly torches. Even his hard heart, which knew all misery and cared nothing for it, was touched by the love and longing of the music. ▶

At last the minstrel came to an end, and a long sigh like wind in pine trees was heard from the assembled ghosts. Then the king spoke, and his deep voice echoed through his silent land. "Go back to the light of day," he said. "Go quickly while my monsters are stilled by your song. Climb up the steep road to daylight, and never once turn back. The spirit of Eurydice shall follow, but if you look around at her, she will return to me." ▶

Orpheus turned and strode from the hall of Hades, and the flocks of following ghosts made way for him to pass. In vain he searched their ranks for a sight of his lost Eurydice. In vain he listened for the faintest sound behind. The barge of Charon sank to the very gunwales[7] beneath his weight, but no following passenger pressed it lower down. The way from the land of Hades to the upper world is long and hard, far easier to descend than climb. It was dark and misty, full of strange shapes and noises, yet in many places merely black and silent as the tomb. Here Orpheus would stop and listen, but nothing moved behind him. For all he could hear, he was utterly alone. Then he would wonder if the pitiless Hades were deceiving him. Suppose he came up to the light again and Eurydice was not there! Once he had charmed the ferryman and the dreadful monsters, but now they had heard his song. The second time his spell would be less powerful; he could never go again. Perhaps he had lost Eurydice by his readiness to believe.

---

7. **gunwales** (gŭn′əlz): the upper edge of the side of a vessel.

MAKE INFERENCES
What human qualities does Hades display?

_____

_____

TestSmart

What universal theme does "Orpheus and Eurydice" touch upon?

Ⓐ True love continues after death.
Ⓑ Crossing rivers is full of danger.
Ⓒ Music can solve life's problems.
Ⓓ Don't trust those you don't know.

TIP Questions about a **universal theme** require you to **think about the story as a whole** and also to draw on your knowledge of other literature. What conflict or problem does the main character face? In the case of "Orpheus and Eurydice," what message is revealed at the end? Think about other stories that reveal a similar message. If you can think of one or more, you have probably found the universal theme. Choose the answer option that best summarizes it.

ascend (ə-sĕnd´) *v.* to go or move upward; rise

VISUALIZE
Underline details in lines 87–97 that help you imagine the mud bank where Orpheus sits.

Which of your five sense do these details appeal to? Check all that apply.
- ☐ sight
- ☐ hearing
- ☐ taste
- ☐ touch
- ☐ smell

Every step he took, some instinct told him that he was going farther from his bride. He toiled up the path in reluctance and despair, stopping, listening, sighing, taking a few slow steps, until the dark thinned out into greyness. Up ahead a speck of light showed clearly the entrance to the cavern.

At that final moment Orpheus could bear no more. To go out into the light of day without his love seemed to him impossible. Before he had quite **ascended**, there was still a 80 moment in which he could go back. Quick in the greyness he turned and saw a dim shade at his heels, as indistinct as the grey mist behind her. But still he could see the look of sadness on her face as he sprung forward saying, "Eurydice!" and threw his arms about her. The shade dissolved in the circle of his arms like smoke. A little whisper seemed to say, "Farewell," as she scattered into mist and was gone.

The unfortunate lover hastened back again down the steep, dark path. But all was in vain. This time the ghostly ferryman was deaf to his prayers. The very wildness of his 90 mood made it impossible for him to attain the beauty of his former music. At last, his despair was so great that he could not even sing at all. For seven days he sat huddled together on the grey mud banks, listening to the wailing of the terrible river. The flitting ghosts shrank back in a wide circle from the living man, but he paid them no attention. Only he sat with his eyes on Charon, his ears ringing with the dreadful noise of Styx. ◀

Orpheus arose at last and stumbled back along the steep road he knew so well by now. When he came up to earth 100 again, his song was pitiful but more beautiful than ever. Even the nightingale who mourned all night long would hush her voice to listen as Orpheus sat in some hidden place singing of his lost Eurydice. Men and women he could bear no longer,

152 UNIT 6: MYTHS, LEGENDS, AND TALES

and when they came to hear him, he drove them away. At last the women of Thrace, maddened by Dionysus[8] and infuriated by Orpheus' contempt, fell upon him and killed him. It is said that as the body was swept down the river Hebrus, the dead lips still moved faintly and the rocks echoed for the last time, "Eurydice." But the poet's eager spirit was already far down the familiar path. ▶

In the daffodil meadows he met the shade of Eurydice, and there they walk together, or where the path is narrow, the shade of Orpheus goes ahead and looks back at his love. ▶

DRAW CONCLUSIONS

What are two **cultural values** that this **myth** suggests were important to the ancient Greeks?

1. _____

2. _____

Big Question

If Orpheus had trusted Hades and considered the consequences of disobeying him, how might the outcome of this **myth** have been different? *MAKE JUDGMENTS*

_____

---

8. **women of Thrace** (thrās), **maddened by Dionysus** (dĭ'ə-nī'səs): Thrace was a Balkan region colonized by the Greeks; Dionysus was the god of wine.

Assessment Practice I

Reading Comprehension

DIRECTIONS Answer these questions about "Prometheus" and "Orpheus and Eurydice" by filling in the correct ovals.

1. Which summary below *best* describes Prometheus' punishment?
   - (A) In the underworld, he has his liver torn out by crows for eternity.
   - (B) He must live as a human.
   - (C) Shackled to a mountain, he must endure vicious vulture attacks.
   - (D) He is exiled from Greece for all time.

2. Why doesn't Zeus punish humans for accepting fire?
   - (A) He thinks it will be entertaining to watch humans destroy themselves.
   - (B) He knows that Prometheus will protect humankind.
   - (C) He decides not to waste his thunderbolt.
   - (D) He blames Prometheus, not the humans.

3. Why might ancient Greeks have told the myth of Prometheus?
   - (A) to explain the sound of thunder
   - (B) to tell where fire came from
   - (C) to caution against war
   - (D) to celebrate cooking

4. What universal theme is addressed in "Prometheus"?
   - (A) gods know best
   - (B) knowledge has consequences
   - (C) pride causes war
   - (D) helping others never goes unrewarded

5. What human quality does Hades have in "Orpheus and Eurydice"?
   - (A) He can be touched by music.
   - (B) He is jealous of others' love.
   - (C) He cares nothing for misery.
   - (D) His lives in the underworld.

6. Which of the following is a cultural value reflected in both "Prometheus" and "Orpheus and Eurydice"?
   - (A) the importance of obedience to the gods
   - (B) the value of technology and progress
   - (C) the importance of the afterlife
   - (D) the joy of love and music

7. Which word below is related to the Latin root *poena*, meaning "punishment"?
   - (A) poisoned
   - (B) penalty
   - (C) pillared
   - (D) pencil

8. Which word below is related to the Latin word *destinare*, meaning "to determine"?
   - (A) desperate
   - (B) detonate
   - (C) destiny
   - (D) detect

UNIT 6: MYTHS, LEGENDS, AND TALES

Responding in Writing

9. Short Response Greek gods often show human qualities. In a paragraph, describe the traits of one of the gods featured in "Prometheus" or "Orpheus and Eurydice."

Test-Taker's Toolkit

ACADEMIC VOCABULARY **Character traits** refer to the qualities of a character, such as bravery, jealousy, or handsomeness. Similarly, the traits of a Greek god refer to that god's personal characteristics. To support your description of the god's traits, give examples from the myth.

GRAPHIC ORGANIZER Use the graphic organizer below to help you identify the god's traits and gather examples that reveal these traits.

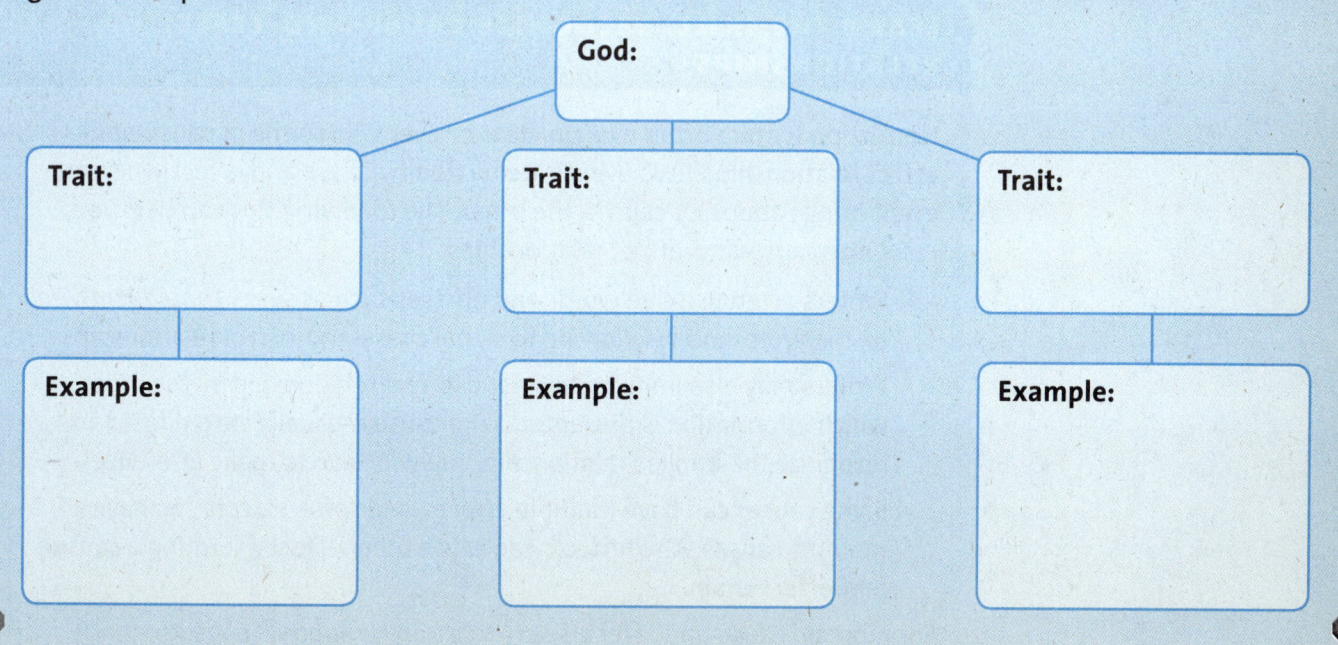

God:

Trait:

Trait:

Trait:

Example:

Example:

Example:

Related Nonfiction

- **An American Prometheus**
  HISTORY ARTICLE
- **Discoveries That Changed the World**
  TIMELINE

Use with "Prometheus" and "Orpheus and Eurydice," p. 142

What's the Connection?

The Greek myths have been popular for so long that some of the gods in them have become cultural symbols. For example, Prometheus represents faith in technology. You are about to read an article that draws a parallel between an American inventor and the god who gave humans fire. The timeline that follows shows technological advances that improved life for humans.

CHART IT Fire affected humans in many ways. How did other technological developments make life better? In the first column of the chart, write the names of three inventions you think were important. In the right-hand column, write how each advancement has helped humankind progress.

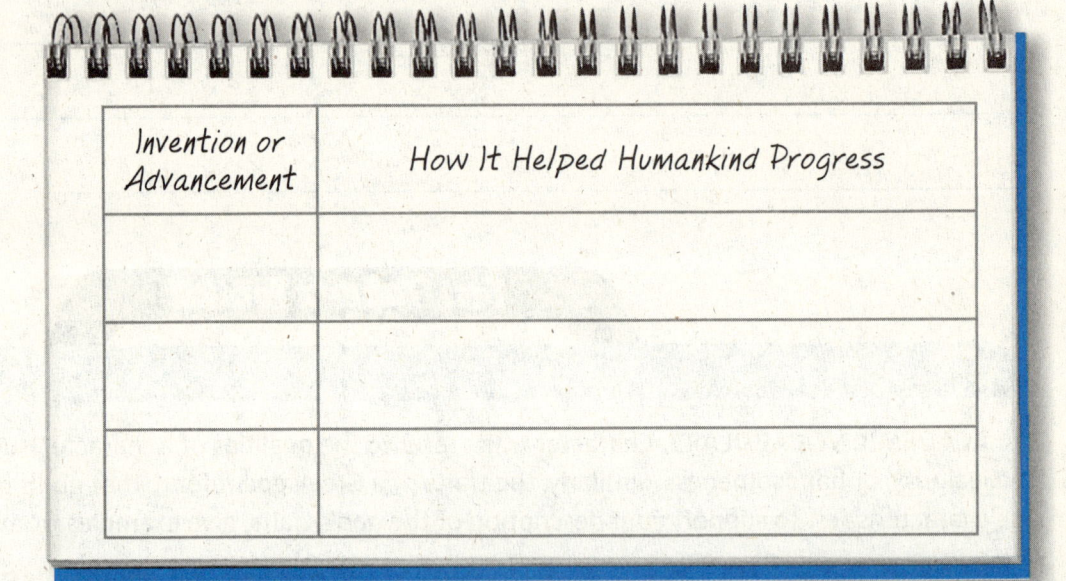

Invention or Advancement	How It Helped Humankind Progress

LEARN THE SKILL: RECOGNIZE CAUSE-AND-EFFECT RELATIONSHIPS

Nonfiction writers often explain ideas or events in terms of **cause-and-effect relationships**. Two events are related by cause and effect when one event brings about, or causes, the other. The following tips can help you recognize cause-and-effect relationships:

- Writers often use clue words and phrases such as *since*, *consequently*, *led to*, *therefore*, and *by allowing* to signal cause-and-effect relationships.

- Writers may also imply a cause-and-effect relationship by the order in which information is presented. (The cause is usually stated first.) To recognize the implied relationship, you will have to make inferences.

- Some causes can have multiple effects, and some effects can have multiple causes. Also, effects can cause other effects, forming a **cause-and-effect chain**.

For more on cause and effect, see *Nonfiction Handbook*, page R6.

156 UNIT 6: MYTHS, LEGENDS, AND TALES

An American Prometheus
by Ruby Williams

CLOSE READ

SET A PURPOSE
My purpose for reading is
_____
_____
_____

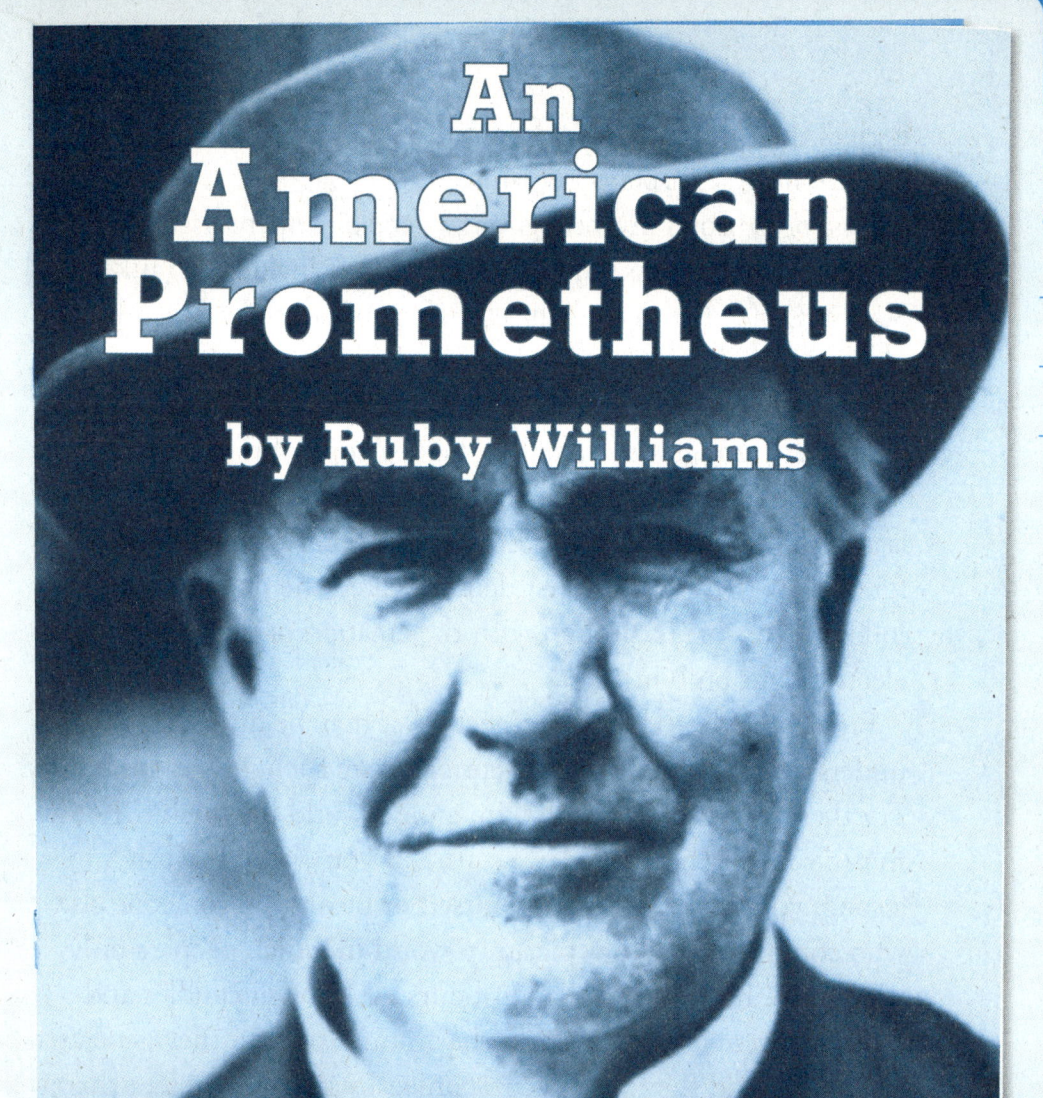

Have you ever heard a creative or inventive person called a "Prometheus"? The name fits because a creative person brings new ideas into the world. Prometheus, the Titan of Greek mythology, gave the gift of fire to humans, and he has come to symbolize the bold and pioneering spirit that infuses some scientists. For the past several centuries, those who believe that new technology, made readily available, will change the world for the better are often compared to Prometheus.

One such "Prometheus" was Thomas Edison. During his lifetime, Edison received 1,093 U.S. patents, a record that remains unequaled by any other inventor. A *patent* is legal recognition from the government of who created an invention;

RELATED NONFICTION 157

it gives the inventor the sole right to make, use, and sell that invention for a set period of time.

One of Edison's inventions was a type of cement used in building roads, dams, and other structures, including Yankee Stadium. He also created an "electric pen"—a sort of primitive photocopier. As a person wrote with the pen, a motor moved a needle that created a stencil of the written words. Ink could then be forced through the stencil to make a copy of the document.

The influence of those particular inventions was not long lasting. However, two other Edison creations changed the world forever. In 1877, Edison first demonstrated the phonograph. He followed this breakthrough with the creation of the first practical electric light bulb in 1879.

From our 21st-century perspective, it may be difficult to understand why these two inventions were such gifts to humanity. Try these two exercises: First, imagine a world in which the only music you ever heard was live music. If you wanted to listen to a song, you'd have to sing it yourself or be around someone else who could sing it. Now, picture a world in which people's only productive hours were daylight hours. (Although candles and gaslights were used after dark, the amount of light they generated was small, and they were accompanied by the ever-present threat of fire.) The phonograph and the light bulb changed all that.

Of electric light, Edison said, "In the old days man went up and down with the sun. A million years from now he won't go to bed at all. Really sleep is an absurdity, a bad habit . . . we shall throw it off." Like Prometheus's gift of fire, Edison's gift of light helped civilization expand. People could work at their jobs for longer hours, more safely. They could work in the home, study, and socialize more.

When first invented, the phonograph was viewed as even more miraculous than the light bulb. In fact, people had a difficult time believing it was real. When Edison demonstrated his creation by playing a recording of himself singing "Mary Had a Little Lamb," some accused him of using ventriloquism to make it appear that the phonograph had recorded sound. Suddenly, experiences could

---

CONNECT

What would be the most difficult part of your daily life if electric lights did not exist?

_____

_____

_____

CAUSE-AND-EFFECT RELATIONSHIPS

Reread the boxed text. Underline the sentences that state two effects the electric lightbulb had on people's lives.

Then, using your own words, fill in the lines below.

Cause: _____

_____

Effect: _____

_____

Effect: _____

_____

158   UNIT 6: MYTHS, LEGENDS, AND TALES

be relived. By allowing knowledge and experiences—speeches, lectures, concerts—to be shared, the phonograph expanded human culture.

> Did Edison's gifts to humanity have a downside, as the gift of fire did? While Prometheus's offering greatly helped humans, it also harmed them by enabling the invention of weapons, which led to conflict and war. During World War I, Edison worked for the U.S. Navy, inventing new ways to protect ships and submarines. But he always intended that his inventions would be used for defending American sailors rather than for attacking the enemy. He once stated, "I am proud of the fact that I never invented weapons to kill." ▶

Edison's work did not directly increase the violence in the world. But perhaps he paved the way for others to imagine how science could create powerful weapons. Edison's inventions inspired belief that humans could conquer nature. After all, Edison had "conquered time" with the phonograph, and overcome darkness with the light bulb. Edison himself understood the likelihood of science being used for violence, saying, "There will one day spring from the brain of science a machine or force so fearful in its potentialities, so absolutely terrifying, that even man . . . will be appalled. . . ." However, should that possibility have stopped Edison from bringing the world more light? Or perhaps the question is, could Edison have stopped himself? A Prometheus is called toward the future, even at a cost.

CAUSE-AND-EFFECT RELATIONSHIPS

Reread the boxed paragraph. Underline one possible negative effect caused by the invention of electricity.

Did Edison believe he was responsible for this possible effect?

☐ Yes
☐ No

Circle the lines that help you answer.

RELATED NONFICTION 159

Discoveries That Changed the World

1879
LIGHT BULB Made it possible to use electricity to provide safe, effective artificial light

1928
PENICILLIN Enabled the prevention and treatment of bacterial infections, a major cause of illness and death

1850

c. 1886
GASOLINE ENGINE Led to the development of the first practical automobile and other forms of transportation that increased humans' mobility

> **CAUSE-AND-EFFECT RELATIONSHIPS**
> Circle the name of each invention that appears in the timeline's captions.
>
> Do the words you circled name causes or effects?
> ☐ causes
> ☐ effects

According to Greek mythology, Prometheus is responsible for giving humankind the gift of fire. American inventor Thomas Edison is sometimes called a "modern Prometheus" because his inventions—particularly the light bulb—changed human life forever. Since Edison's first public demonstration of the light bulb in 1879, modern scientists and inventors have come a long way. "To invent," Edison once explained, "you need a good imagination and a pile of junk." Explore the timeline above to discover how far our imaginations have taken us. ◀

UNIT 6: MYTHS, LEGENDS, AND TALES

Chapter 19

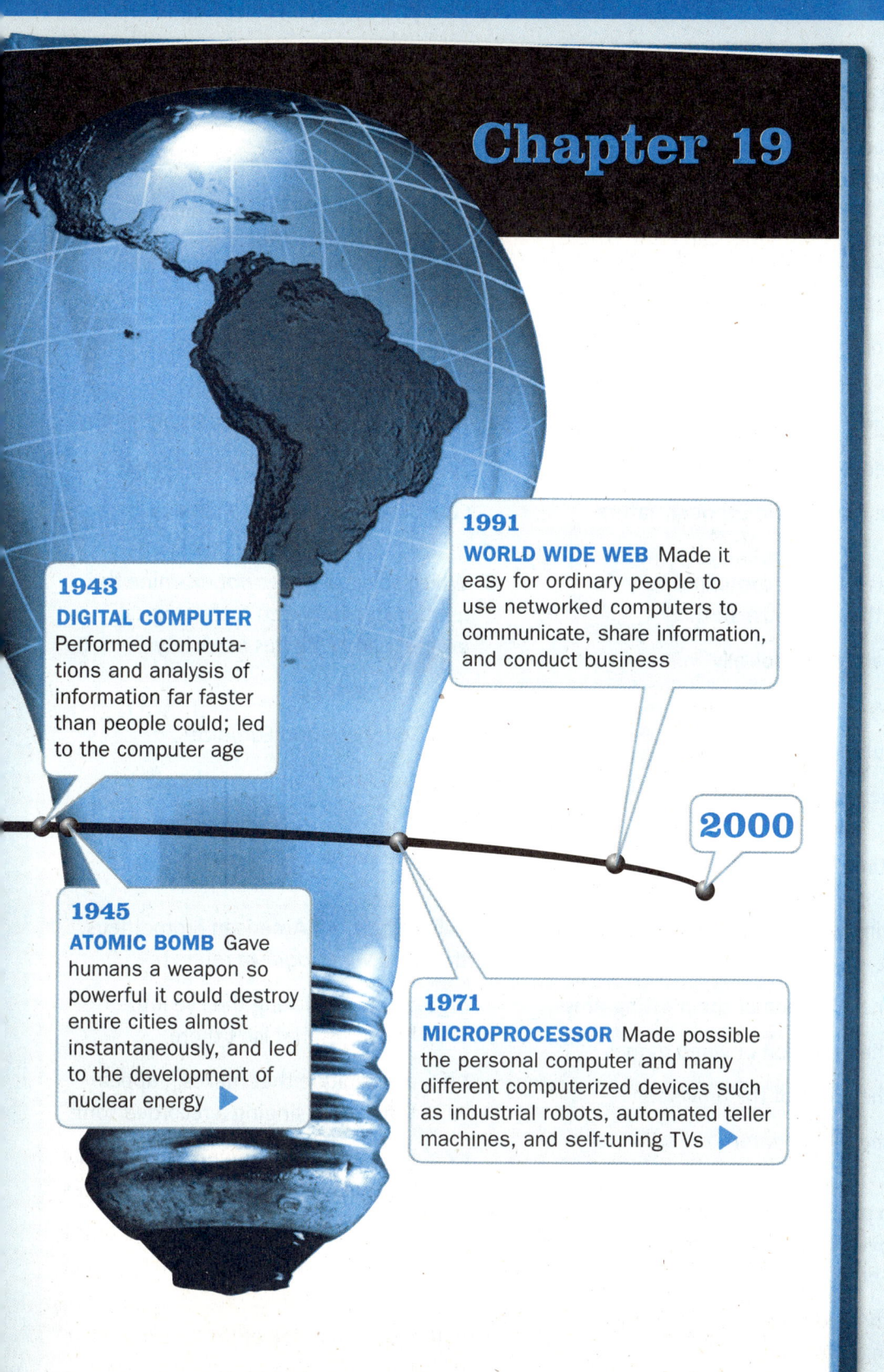

1943
DIGITAL COMPUTER Performed computations and analysis of information far faster than people could; led to the computer age

1991
WORLD WIDE WEB Made it easy for ordinary people to use networked computers to communicate, share information, and conduct business

2000

1945
ATOMIC BOMB Gave humans a weapon so powerful it could destroy entire cities almost instantaneously, and led to the development of nuclear energy ▶

1971
MICROPROCESSOR Made possible the personal computer and many different computerized devices such as industrial robots, automated teller machines, and self-tuning TVs ▶

💡 TestSmart

According to the timeline, what is one potentially positive effect of the invention of the atomic bomb?

Ⓐ created a powerful weapon

Ⓑ introduced a new source of energy

Ⓒ encouraged the enemy to surrender

Ⓓ enabled life-saving medical advancements

TIP When a question asks about a **cause-and-effect relationship,** scan that section of the text to look for signal words that make the relationship clear. In this case, review the timeline entry for the atomic bomb. Underline the signal word in that entry. What effect does it introduce?

CLASSIFY

How did each invention on this timeline improve modern life? Next to each category below, write the name of the invention that caused improvements to that aspect of life.

health _____

transportation _____

communication _____

defense/energy _____

information processing _____

_____

RELATED NONFICTION   **161**

Assessment Practice II

Reading Comprehension

DIRECTIONS *Answer these questions about the related nonfiction by filling in the correct ovals.*

1. According to "An American Prometheus," what effect did the phonograph have on human culture?
   - A) Knowledge and experience could be shared.
   - B) The entertainment industry changed.
   - C) People could work more efficiently.
   - D) Humans could conquer nature.

2. Thomas Edison is compared to Prometheus because both
   - A) behaved heroically
   - B) were great inventors
   - C) suffered consequences
   - D) helped humankind to advance

3. If the timeline on pages 160–161 started at an earlier point in history, which of the following would be the most appropriate entry?
   - A) the invention of the printing press
   - B) the invention of video games
   - C) the origin of the universe
   - D) the use of water

4. Which parts of the timeline in "Discoveries That Changed the World" name effects?
   - A) the text following the subheading in each caption
   - B) the subheading in each caption
   - C) the paragraph on page 160
   - D) the year in each caption

5. Which quotation from "Prometheus" is supported by the harnessing of atomic energy in the 1940s?
   - A) "What you call ignorance is innocence."
   - B) "Man is happy as beasts are happy."
   - C) "[Man] has the capacity for worship."
   - D) "Every gift brings a penalty."

6. Which selection does *not* examine the relationship between technological progress and changes in society?
   - A) "Prometheus"
   - B) "Orpheus and Eurydice"
   - C) "An American Prometheus"
   - D) "Discoveries That Changed the World"

7. In line 47 of "An American Prometheus," the word *ventriloquism* refers to
   - A) a way of tricking the eye into "seeing" what isn't there
   - B) a technique that makes it appear that one is singing a recorded song
   - C) the method of singing that makes one voice sound like multiple voices
   - D) the art of using one's voice so that it seems to come from another source

8. In the "1945" caption of the timeline, what does the word *instantaneously* mean?
   - A) dreadfully
   - B) completely
   - C) laboriously
   - D) immediately

162 UNIT 6: MYTHS, LEGENDS, AND TALES

Timed Writing Practice

PROMPT

Write a cause-and-effect composition about the dangers of acting without thinking ahead. Support your ideas with details from the myths you have read and what you know from your own experience.

BUDGET YOUR TIME

You have 45 minutes to complete this assignment. Decide how much time to spend on each step.

Analyze _____
Plan _____
Write _____
Review _____

Test-Taker's Toolkit

1. ANALYZE THE PROMPT

A. **Read the prompt** carefully. Draw lines between sentences to help you focus on each one.

B. **Note the key words** in each sentence. The type of writing you must complete, a cause-and-effect composition, has been noted for you. Underline the words that tell you what you should use to support your ideas.

2. PLAN YOUR RESPONSE

Make notes Before you begin, think about the type of writing you must complete. A cause-and-effect composition shows how one event causes another. Take notes on the effects different actions can have. You might want to collect examples like these shown in the notebook.

> **Example 1:** what Prometheus did and the effects his actions caused
>
> **Example 2:** what Orpheus did and the effects his actions caused
>
> **Example 3:** a story from my own experience that shows the effects of not thinking ahead

3. WRITE AND REVIEW

A. **Craft an opening** A strong opener can help your essay get a good score. You can use the ideas below to spark your creativity. Then add a third idea of your own before choosing which approach will work best for your essay.

- Ask a question, such as "How important is it to think before you act?"
- Invite readers to put themselves at the center of a conflict. You might say, "Imagine that you are at a crossroads. Your next step will decide everything."

_____

_____

_____

B. **Write out your full response** Leave time to read through it and make sure you have met all the requirements of the prompt.

RELATED NONFICTION

UNIT 7
BIOGRAPHY AND AUTOBIOGRAPHY

Names/Nombres
BY JULIA ALVAREZ

RELATED NONFICTION
Name That Child: How Culture and Tradition Influence Choices

Rodriguez
"Polo"

Aja Wuanco
"Brains"

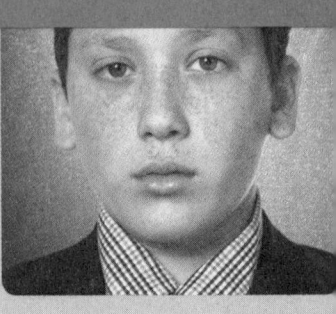

James Ngo
"Jimmy Biz"

Hannah Sobel
"Sunny"

Johnny Edelo
"Wheels"

Elena Lebowski
"Lanie"

Jared Mitchum
"Orange County"

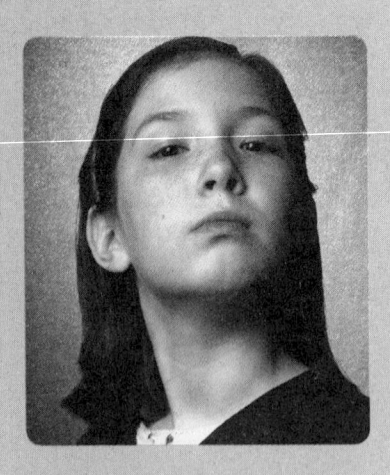

Molly VonHendrick
"Gossip"

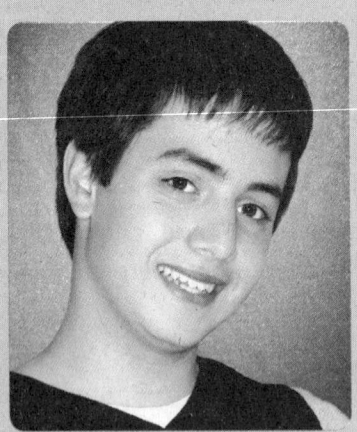

Frank Lamore
"Wizard"

Skyler Jacobsenn
"Skeeziks"

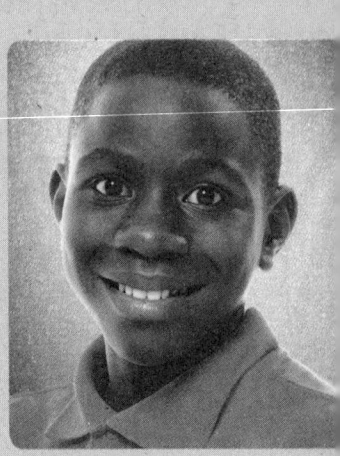

Thomas Coleman
"Indy"

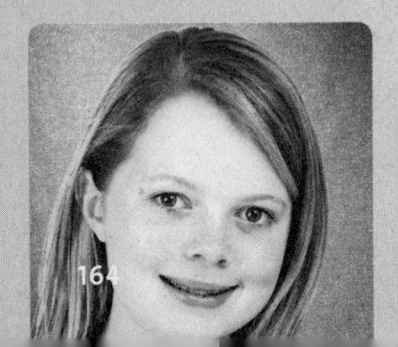

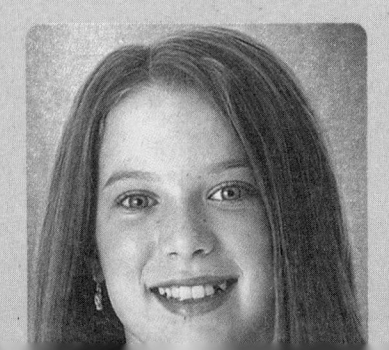

What does your name REALLY MEAN?

Parents may choose a name for their child because its original meaning is important to them. Are you named after a relative, or perhaps someone famous? Or was your name chosen simply because of the way it sounds? Whatever the answer, you've probably been called more than one name in your life.

CHART IT What names do you go by? Complete each item in the notebook. Then share your answers with a partner.

Notebook:
- THE MANY NAMES OF _____
- My full name: _____
- Why I was given this name: _____
- My nicknames: _____
- Name or nickname I would choose for myself: _____

ASSESSMENT GOALS

By the end of this lesson, you will be able to...
- understand the characteristics of autobiographical writing
- apply critical thinking skills to analyze text
- synthesize sources in nonfiction texts
- analyze a writing prompt and plan an autobiographical narrative

NAMES/NOMBRES

LEARN THE TERMS: ACADEMIC VOCABULARY

Biography and Autobiography

What was it like to be the first person on the moon? What is an athlete thinking the moment he or she crosses the finish line? How did a famous author find his or her own identity and voice? We are all curious about other people—about what they do, how they do it, and how they feel. You can satisfy this curiosity by reading biographies and autobiographies.

- A **BIOGRAPHY** is a story of a person's life told by someone else and written from the third-person point of view.

- An **AUTOBIOGRAPHY** is the story of a person's life told by that person and written from the first-person point of view.

"Names/Nombres" is a **PERSONAL ESSAY**, a form of writing that is **AUTOBIOGRAPHICAL**. In this essay, Julia Alvarez tells her own story. As a result, readers get a glimpse of the challenges she faced and how she felt about them. The chart below explains more about autobiographical writing.

AUTOBIOGRAPHY

the writer **=** the subject

He or she uses first-person pronouns such as *I, me, we, my,* and *our.*

SOURCES
- memories
- thoughts and feelings
- friends and family

FORMS
- autobiographical books
- diaries and journals
- memoirs
- personal essays

WHEN YOU READ AUTOBIOGRAPHY, YOU . . .
- get the subject's own interpretation of events
- learn the subject's private thoughts and feelings
- hear the subject's voice and get a sense of his or her personality

ADDITIONAL TERM FOR CRITICAL ANALYSIS

Like all forms of literature, biographies and autobiographies are shaped by the person who writes them. The following term will help you analyze autobiographical writing:

The **AUTHOR'S PERSPECTIVE** is the combination of ideas, values, feelings, and beliefs that influences the way an author looks at a topic. Tone, or attitude, often reveals an author's perspective.

Names/Nombres

Julia Alvarez

BACKGROUND Julia Alvarez was born in New York City. When she was still a baby, her parents took her back to their home country, the Dominican Republic. Due to political unrest in that Spanish-speaking Caribbean nation, the Alvarez family moved back to New York City in 1960. Julia was ten years old. At first, she had trouble fitting in.

When we arrived in New York City, our names changed almost immediately. At Immigration, the officer asked my father, *Mister Elbures*, if he had anything to declare.[1] My father shook his head no, and we were waved through. I was too afraid we wouldn't be let in if I corrected the man's pronunciation, but I said our name to myself, opening my mouth wide for the organ blast of the a, trilling my tongue[2] for the drumroll of the *r, All-vah-rrr-es!* How could anyone get Elbures out of that orchestra of sound? ▶

---

1. **At Immigration . . . declare:** Immigration is the place where government officials check the documents of people entering a country. People must acknowledge, or declare, certain goods or moneys that they are carrying.
2. **trilling my tongue:** rapidly vibrating the tongue against the roof of the mouth, as in pronouncing a Spanish *r*.

10   At the hotel my mother was *Missus Alburest,* and I was *little girl,* as in, "Hey, little girl, stop riding the elevator up and down. It's not a toy."

When we moved into our new apartment building, the super[3] called my father *Mister Alberase,* and the neighbors who became mother's friends pronounced her name *Jew-lee-ah* instead of *Hoo-lee-ah.* I, her namesake, was known as *Hoo-lee-tah* at home. But at school I was *Judy* or *Judith,* and once an English teacher mistook me for Juliet.

It took a while to get used to my new names. I wondered
20   if I shouldn't correct my teachers and new friends. But my mother argued that it didn't matter. <u>"You know what your friend Shakespeare said, 'A rose by any other name would smell as sweet.'"</u>[4] My family had gotten into the habit of calling any literary figure "my friend" because I had begun to write poems and stories in English class. ◀

By the time I was in high school, I was a popular kid, and it showed in my name. Friends called me *Jules* or *Hey Jude,*[5] and once a group of troublemaking friends my mother forbade me to hang out with called me *Alcatraz.*[6] I was
30   *Hoo-lee-tah* only to Mami and Papi and uncles and aunts who came over to eat *sancocho*[7] on Sunday afternoons—old world folk whom I would just as soon go back to where they came from and leave me to pursue whatever mischief I wanted to in America. JUDY ALCATRAZ: the name on the wanted poster would read. Who would ever trace her to me? ◀

---

3. **super:** superintendent, or building manager.
4. **'A rose ... smell as sweet':** In Shakespeare's *Romeo and Juliet,* the main characters' families are enemies. But when Romeo and Juliet fall in love, Juliet uses almost these words to say that Romeo is precious to her no matter what his family name is.
5. **Hey Jude:** the title of a hit song by the Beatles in 1968.
6. **Alcatraz** (ăl′kə-trăz′): the name of an island in San Francisco Bay that was once the site of a prison.
7. **sancocho** (säng-kô′chô) *Spanish*: a traditional Caribbean stew of meat and vegetables.

> **INTERPRET**
> Reread the underlined sentence and the footnote associated with it. Why do you think Alvarez's mother repeats this line from Shakespeare to Julia?

> **DRAW CONCLUSIONS**
> Based on what Alvarez says in lines 26–36 and later in the selection, what can you conclude about her **perspective** on assimilating, or adopting the habits of mainstream culture?

My older sister had the hardest time getting an American name for herself because *Mauricia* did not translate into English. **Ironically**, although she had the most foreign-
40 sounding name, she and I were the Americans in the family. We had been born in New York City when our parents had first tried immigration and then gone back "home," too homesick to stay. My mother often told the story of how she had almost changed my sister's name in the hospital.

After the delivery, Mami and some other new mothers were cooing over their new baby sons and daughters and exchanging names and weights and delivery stories. My mother was embarrassed among the Sallys and Janes and Georges and Johns to reveal the rich, noisy name
50 of *Mauricia,* so when her turn came to brag, she gave her baby's name as *Maureen.*

"Why'd ya give her an Irish name with so many pretty Spanish names to choose from?" one of the women asked her.

My mother blushed and admitted her baby's real name to the group. Her mother-in-law had recently died, she apologized, and her husband had insisted that the first daughter be named after his mother, *Mauran*. My mother thought it the ugliest name she had ever heard, and she talked my father into what she believed was an improvement, a combination of *Mauran*
60 and her own mother's name, *Felicia*.

"Her name is Mao-ree-shee-ah," my mother said to the group.

"Why, that's a beautiful name," the new mothers cried. "*Moor-ee-sha, Moor-ee-sha,*" they cooed into the pink blanket. *Moor-ee-sha* it was when we returned to the States eleven years later. Sometimes, American tongues found even that mispronunciation tough to say and called her *Maria* or *Marsha* or *Maudy* from her nickname *Maury*. I pitied her. What an awful name to have to transport across borders! ▶

My little sister, Ana, had the easiest time of all. She
70 was plain *Anne*—that is, only her name was plain, for she turned out to be the pale, blond "American beauty" in the family. The only Hispanic-seeming thing about her was the

---

ironically (ī-rŏn′ĭk-lē) *adv.* in a way that is contrary to what is expected or intended

💡 TestSmart

What does the anecdote about Mauricia suggest about why young Julia Alvarez didn't like Spanish names?

- Ⓐ She found it annoying to have a name most people couldn't pronounce.
- Ⓑ At the time, most Americans were prejudiced against Latinos.
- Ⓒ Before she went to college, she wanted an identity apart from her family.
- Ⓓ She thought Spanish names sounded ugly.

TIP When a test question asks what an anecdote, statement, or phrase suggests, you will probably have to **make an inference,** or combine clues from the text and your own knowledge to make an educated guess about the right answer. For this question, review the entire anecdote. Underline clues in the text that reveal Alvarez's feelings. Then choose the best answer.

NAMES/NOMBRES 169

MAKE INFERENCES

Reread lines 76–83 and circle the roommate's pronunciation of *Ana*.

How do you think the author felt when she heard her sister's name pronounced this way?

_____
_____
_____
_____

merge (mûrj) *v.* to blend together

CONNECT

Alvarez notes that there was a different attitude about ethnic identity in the early 1960s than there was in the late 1960s. Which attitude do you think is more similar to today's? Explain.

_____
_____
_____
_____

specify (spĕs′ə-fī′) *v.* to make known or identify

---

affectionate nicknames her boyfriends sometimes gave her. *Anita*, or as one goofy guy used to sing to her to the tune of the banana advertisement, *Anita Banana*.

Later, during her college years in the late 60's, there was a push to pronounce Third World[8] names correctly. I remember calling her long distance at her group house and a roommate answering.

80 "Can I speak to Ana?" I asked, pronouncing her name the American way.

"Ana?" The man's voice hesitated. "Oh! You must mean *Ah-nah!*"

Our first few years in the States, though, ethnicity was not yet "in." Those were the blond, blue-eyed, bobby-sock years of junior high and high school before the 60's ushered in peasant blouses, hoop earrings, *sarapes*.[9] My initial desire to be known by my correct Dominican name faded. I just wanted to be Judy and **merge** with the Sallys and Janes in my class. But, 90 inevitably, my accent and coloring gave me away. "So where are you from, Judy?"

"New York," I told my classmates. After all, I had been born blocks away at Columbia Presbyterian Hospital.

"I mean, *originally*."

"From the Caribbean," I answered vaguely, for if I **specified**, no one was quite sure what continent our island was located on.

"Really? I've been to Bermuda. We went last April for spring vacation. I got the worst sunburn! So, are you from Portoriko?"

"No," I shook my head. "From the Dominican Republic."

100 "Where's that?"

"South of Bermuda."

They were just being curious, I knew, but I burned with shame whenever they singled me out as a "foreigner," a rare, exotic friend.

---

8. **Third World:** from the developing nations of Latin America, Africa, and Asia.
9. **sarapes** (sə-rä′pāz) *Spanish:* long, blanketlike shawls.

170 UNIT 7: BIOGRAPHY AND AUTOBIOGRAPHY

"Say your name in Spanish, oh, please say it!" I had made mouths drop one day by rattling off my full name, which, according to Dominican custom, included my middle names, Mother's and Father's surnames[10] for four generations back.

"Julia Altagracia María Teresa Álvarez Tavares Perello Espaillat Julia Pérez Rochet González." I pronounced it slowly, a name as **chaotic** with sounds as a Middle Eastern bazaar or market day in a South American village.

I suffered most whenever my extended family attended school occasions. For my graduation, they all came, the whole noisy, foreign-looking lot of fat aunts in their dark mourning dresses and hair nets, uncles with full, droopy mustaches and baby-blue or salmon-colored suits and white pointy shoes and fedora hats, the many little cousins who snuck in without tickets. They sat in the first row in order to better understand the Americans' fast-spoken English. But how could they listen when they were constantly speaking among themselves in florid-sounding phrases, rococo consonants, rich, rhyming vowels? Their loud voices carried. ▶

Introducing them to my friends was a further trial to me. These relatives had such complicated names and there were so many of them, and their relationships to myself were so **convoluted**. There was my Tía Josefina, who was not really an aunt but a much older cousin. And her daughter, Aída Margarita, who was adopted, *una hija de crianza*.[11] My uncle of affection, Tío José, brought my madrina Tía Amelia and her *comadre* Tía Pilar.[12] My friends rarely had more than their nuclear family[13] to introduce, youthful, glamorous-looking couples ("Mom and Dad") who skied and played tennis and took their kids for spring vacations to Bermuda.

After the commencement ceremony, my family waited outside in the parking lot while my friends and I signed

---

10. **surnames:** last names.
11. ***una hija de crianza*** (ōō'nä ē'hä dĕ krē-än'sä) *Spanish*: a child raised as if one's own.
12. **My uncle of affection . . . Tía Pilar:** My favorite uncle, Uncle José, brought my godmother Aunt Amelia and her close friend Aunt Pilar.
13. **nuclear family:** a family unit consisting of a mother, a father, and their children.

ANALYZE

Underline the Spanish words the author uses in lines 141–145.

How does this choice of words reflect the **author's perspective** about the mixing of two cultures?

_____
_____
_____
_____

Big Question

Reread the question on page 165. How do you think the author would answer this question?

_____
_____
_____
_____

yearbooks with nicknames which recalled our high school good times: "Beans" and "Pepperoni" and "Alcatraz." We hugged and cried and promised to keep in touch.

140 Sometimes if our goodbyes went on too long, I heard my father's voice calling out across the parking lot. "*Hoo-lee-tah! Vámonos!*"[14]

Back home, my *tíos* and *tías* and *primas*, Mami and Papi, and *mis hermanas* had a party for me with *sancocho* and a store-bought *pudín*, inscribed with *Happy Graduation, Julie.*[15] There were many gifts—that was a plus to a large family! I got several wallets and a suitcase with my initials and a graduation charm from my godmother and money from my uncles. The biggest gift was a portable typewriter from my
150 parents for writing my stories and poems. ◀

Someday, the family predicted, my name would be well-known throughout the United States. I laughed to myself, wondering which one I would go by. ◀

---

14. **Vámonos** (bä'mô-nôs) *Spanish:* Let's go.
15. **Back home . . . Julie:** Back home, my uncles and aunts and cousins, Mami and Papi, and my sisters had a party for me with a stew and a store-bought pudding, inscribed with *Happy Graduation, Julie.*

Reading Comprehension

DIRECTIONS *Answer these questions by filling in the correct ovals.*

1. The author doesn't correct the immigration official's pronunciation of her family's name because
   - (A) she is too embarrassed
   - (B) her mother tells her not to
   - (C) her father corrects him first
   - (D) she fears that they will not be allowed to enter

2. Why did Mrs. Alvarez first say that her oldest daughter's name was Maureen?
   - (A) There was another child named Mauricia at the hospital.
   - (B) She was embarrassed to be different.
   - (C) Maureen was her aunt's name.
   - (D) Mrs. Alvarez loved Irish names.

3. Which statement is a clue that this is an autobiography and not a biography?
   - (A) The author includes dialogue.
   - (B) The author includes specific details.
   - (C) The author uses the pronouns *I* and *me* when referring to herself.
   - (D) The author uses the pronoun *she* when referring to her mother.

4. Based on the details given in lines 105–112, Alvarez's peers probably found her name
   - (A) easy to remember
   - (B) unusual and amazing
   - (C) not appropriate for her
   - (D) similar to their own names

5. The details Alvarez shares indicate that if she had returned to the U.S. in the late 1960s instead of the early 1960s
   - (A) she might have met more Dominicans in New York
   - (B) her classmates may not have accepted her as readily
   - (C) people might have tried harder to pronounce her name correctly
   - (D) there may have been more classes for young writers

6. Which statement best describes the author's perspective on cultural identity?
   - (A) She accepts that she should embody Latina culture.
   - (B) She believes immigrants' culture deserves more respect.
   - (C) She thinks her cultural identity doesn't matter.
   - (D) She realizes cultural identity can and should be flexible.

7. Which word below contains the base word *ethnic* and is similar in meaning?
   - (A) either
   - (B) ethical
   - (C) ethnicity
   - (D) ethernet

8. Which word below contains the base word *pronounce*?
   - (A) mispronunciation
   - (B) disproportionate
   - (C) dispassionate
   - (D) pronoun

Assessment Practice I

*For help, use the **Test-Taker's Toolkit** below.*

Responding in Writing

9. Short Response Choose one anecdote from this autobiographical personal essay. Write a paragraph explaining how it relates to the author's message about names and identity.

___

___

___

___

___

___

Test-Taker's Toolkit

ACADEMIC VOCABULARY Personal essays like "Names/Nombres" often communicate a writer's **message**, or main point. One way a writer can share this message is through **anecdotes**, which are brief stories or accounts of events.

GRAPHIC ORGANIZER Use the chart below to help you plan your response. First, jot down Alvarez's message about names and identity. Then review the essay, looking for an anecdote that you think helps communicate this message.

TITLE:	AUTHOR:
MESSAGE:	
ANECDOTE:	

174 UNIT 7: BIOGRAPHY AND AUTOBIOGRAPHY

What's the Connection?

Julia Alvarez is not the only person whose name reflects different parts of her. Most of us have names that say something about our individual identity as well as our family and cultural background. The online article "Name That Child" examines the naming traditions of different groups around the world.

CHART IT Work in a group to complete the first two columns of the chart below. In the first column, write what you know about naming traditions. In the second column, write what you would like to find out about this topic. After you have read the online article, complete the third column by telling what you have learned.

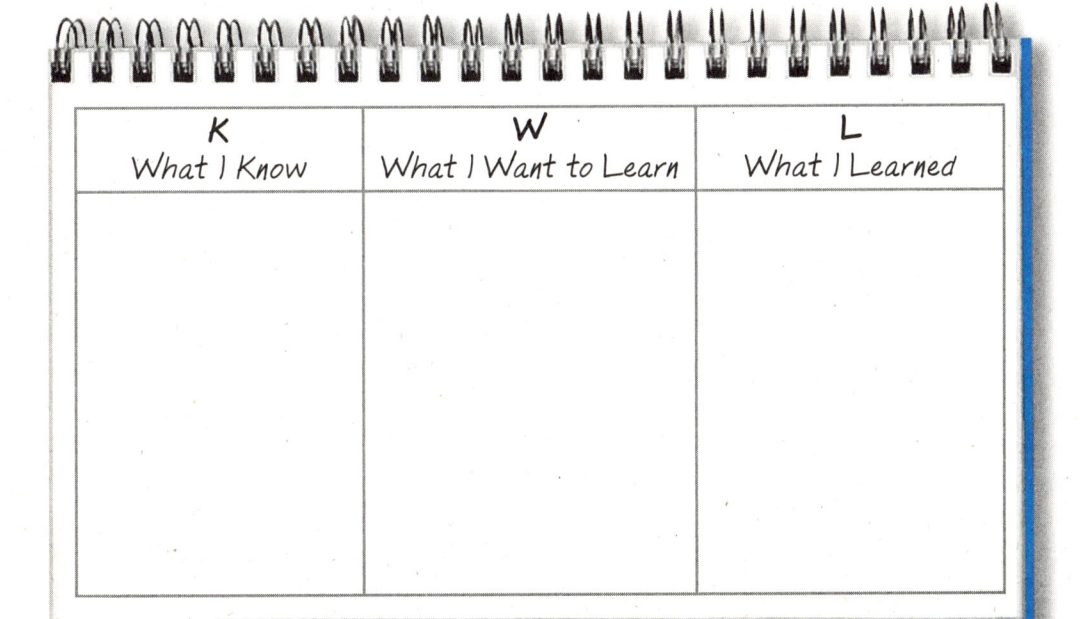

K What I Know	W What I Want to Learn	L What I Learned

Related Nonfiction

Name That Child: How Culture and Tradition Influence Choices
ONLINE ARTICLE

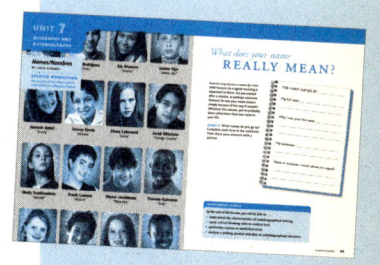

Use with "Names/Nombres," p. 164

LEARN THE SKILL: SYNTHESIZE SOURCES

When you **synthesize**, you gather information from a variety of sources, and then you combine that information to gain a better understanding of the topic. Synthesizing sources can help you form your own well-informed ideas and opinions. Here are some ways to synthesize nonfiction sources:

- **Connect** information you read in one source to what you've learned from other sources that deal with the topic.
- **Compare and contrast** the information in your sources. Think about what you can learn from each one.
- **Draw conclusions** about the topic based on the information in the sources and on your own experiences.

For more on synthesizing sources, see *Nonfiction Handbook* page R21.

CLOSE READ

SET A PURPOSE

My purpose for reading is

_____

_____

_____

SYNTHESIZE SOURCES

Why can a name immediately identify a child as belonging to a certain group? Underline the answer in the first paragraph.

What does this information help you to understand about why Julia Alvarez might have felt differently about her full name at various points in her life?

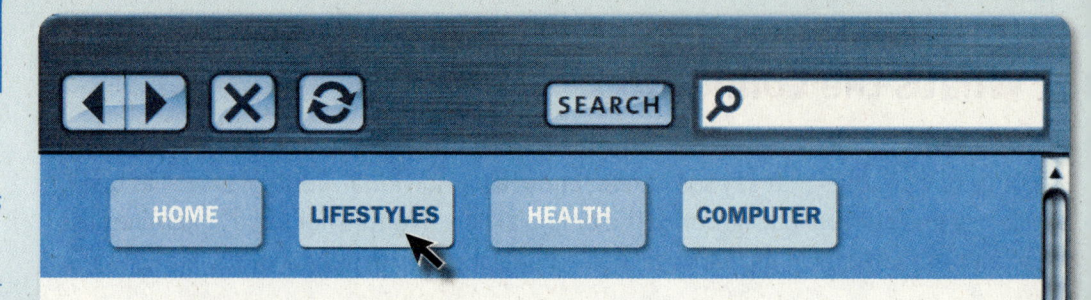

_____

_____

_____

HOME | LIFESTYLES | HEALTH | COMPUTER

1 | 2 | 3 | 4 | 5 | 6

Name That Child: How Culture and Tradition Influence Choices

No matter what their background or what their heritage, everybody in the world has a name. Names are the most distinctive things that children carry from their families and their cultures. Each person's name is, at base, nothing more than a
10 collection of sounds. But those sounds are both unique to the person that carries them and part of the language of the person's family. When a child is given a name, it marks him or her as different from anyone else. The name identifies the child by language, gender, and family. It may link a child to his or her religion, class, caste, clan, or family totem. A name demonstrates that a person is part of a group.

THE TRADITION OF NAMING CEREMONIES

Giving a name to a new child is such an important task that many cultures wait for several days after a baby is born to formally do so. Names not only identify children as part of a family, but they also make
20 them part of traditions, and even part of a spiritual world.

American children may not be allowed out of the hospital without a valid name for their birth certificate. But in Hindu tradition the baby isn't named until twelve days after it is born. On that day the new name is commemorated with a *Namkaran,* or naming ceremony. The baby's father whispers the new name in the baby's ear, and then announces it to the world.

176 UNIT 7: BIOGRAPHY AND AUTOBIOGRAPHY

In the Native American Hopi nation, an ear of corn is placed close to the newborn. This corn represents Mother Earth. It is kept with the baby for twenty days after birth. On the twentieth day the baby is held up to face the rising sun, the ear of corn is rubbed over its body, and the name is bestowed when the first ray of light hits the baby's forehead.

MANY NAMES AND MANY MEANINGS

Jewish families also hold naming ceremonies, and like some other cultures, their naming traditions reflect family histories. The Ashkenazi Jews[1] have a tradition of giving a baby the name of a relative. But that relative cannot be anyone who is still alive. If the child and another person have the same name, the Angel of Death might be confused and choose the child when they were looking for the older person.

Many cultures bestow several names on a single person over the course of their lives. Nigerian children are first given an *oruku* name, which tells the circumstances of their birth. For example, a girl born during the rainy season might be called Bejide to signify "born in a rainy time." Later, that same child would be given an *oriki,* or praise name, which would state the parents' hopes for the child's future. These are names like Dunsimi, which means "don't die before me."

Members of the Native American Sioux nation didn't traditionally have surnames, but they had an entire naming system that included birth order, honor, special deed, nicknames, and secret or spirit names. A child could be called by several names over a lifetime, most of which reflected aspects of the child's character or history.

The famous Sioux warrior Sitting Bull was called "Jumping Badger" as a boy and then nicknamed "Slow" as he grew up because he always took extra time in getting things done. Today, it is not uncommon for Native Americans to have a name that they use with family or only within their reservation, as well as a more Americanized name that they use away from home. ▶

---

1. **Ashkenazi** (äsh′kə-nä′zĭ): relating to Jewish people of eastern European descent.

COMPARE

What similarities are there between Nigerian naming traditions and Native American naming traditions?

_____
_____
_____
_____

◀ 1 | 2 | **3** | 4 | 5 | 6 ▶

    Some cultures create names with meanings that represent the child's position in the family. Japanese boys may be given names to describe
60 their birth order. Ichiro means "first son," Jiro means "second son," and Saburo means "third son." A Japanese girl might be given a name ending in "ko"; this is a feminine ending that means "child." This ending can be used to create names like Nayako, Yoshiko, or Kiyiko, which mean "obedient child," "good child," and "clean child."

THE HISTORY OF AFRICAN-AMERICAN NAMES

Slave traders and slaveholders renamed Africans who were enslaved and brought to America. The new names were usually chosen randomly and were meant to be easy for English speakers to say. Losing their given names often meant that enslaved people lost a part of their
70 African identity.

    Once African Americans gained their freedom, they began to create original names to help get that identity back. After the Civil War, freed slaves created original names with unique suffixes and prefixes. They often added the suffix -inda to popular European names. Thus Clara became Clarinda, Flora became Florinda, and Lucretia became Lucinda.

    After the birth of the Civil Rights Movement, African Americans began to adopt names from African and Islamic culture. Names like Ahana, Kwame, and Jabari from Africa and Malik, Jamal, and Aaliyah from Islam are now common. And after the 1960s, African-American parents began
80 to again use prefixes and suffixes to create truly original names.

    Suffixes like –on, -won, -quon, -el, and –ell have been used to create boys names like Davon from David and Marquon from Mark. For girls, names are often made with both prefixes and suffixes. *Chan-, Shan-, Ka-* and *La-* are combined with suffixes like –isha, -el, -onda, -ika, and –ae to create names like Monisha, LaShonda, and Danel.

    The attempt to create truly unusual names has been successful. Even in big states such as Texas, each year the average African-American girl is given a name that no one else has. Names like Azane, Kyaire, and Zaterria set girls apart, but there are many unique boys'
90 names as well, such as Ladarius, Deonte, and Quantavious. ◀

SUMMARIZE

Reread the text under the subheading "The History of African-American Names." What are three inspirations of African-American names?

1. _____

_____

2. _____

_____

3. _____

_____

HISPANIC NAMES REFLECT TRADITION AND TRENDS

Hispanic names often come from Roman Catholic saints or other religious figures. Names like Jesus, Salvador, and Angel link boys to religious traditions. For girls, names often relate to the Virgin Mary. Maria is popular, but there are other names related to Mary, including Mercedes, Consuelo, and Aracelli.

Lots of names from non-religious Spanish traditions live on in the Hispanic community. These include Isabel, Gabriella, Adriana, Beatriz, Daniela, and Carolina for girls, and Carlos, Enrique, Javier, Juan, Miguel, Francisco, Jaime, and Marcos for boys.

Hispanic parents may also follow the tradition of including the last names of both parents in the name of a child. For example, in a name like Maria Isabel Hernandez Soto, Maria is the first name, Isabel is the middle name, Hernandez is the father's last name, and Soto is the mother's.

Popular culture has introduced many unique and nontraditional names into the Hispanic community. Telenovelas have popularized the names of their stars in the community. Parents in second and third generations of Hispanic-American immigrants often look for unique names. One popular trend is using the prefix y- to make names like Yanelis and Yaritza.

Nontraditional names are popular in the global Hispanic culture, as well, but the trend is controversial in Venezuela. There, the government has recently proposed a bill to limit parents to only 100 possible names for children. Some Venezuelan lawmakers want to cut back on the very original names that are populating the country. These names can be family-related, as is the case for the child who was named Mariangela, from the combination of grandmothers named Maria and Angela. But it's also becoming common to give children long, one-of-a-kind names or to name children after historical figures such as Hitler and Dwight Eisenhower, which some people don't approve of.

SYNTHESIZE SOURCES

Recall the names of the three Alvarez sisters, and write them below.

_____

_____

_____

Draw on your own knowledge and the information in lines 92–111 of this article to explain whether Julia Alvarez's parents gave their daughters traditional Hispanic names.

_____

_____

_____

_____

SPECIALIZED Vocabulary

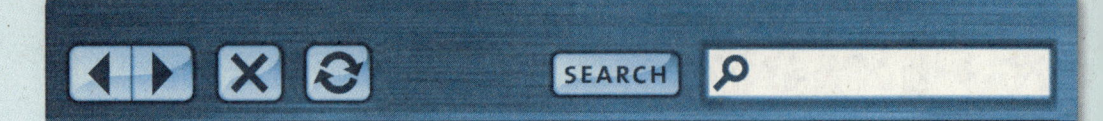

The word **assimilated** in line 131 is a cultural term that refers to how integrated the members of a culture have become within a society after they move to a new country. *Assimilate* is related to the word *similar*. Both share the Latin root *sim*, meaning "alike." WORD ANALYSIS

CLASSIFY

Reread lines 128–140. Underline the author's description of the naming customs of second-, third-, and fourth-generation immigrants.

Based on this information, put a check next to the generation that is *least* likely to give their children names that reflect their ancestry.

☐ second
☐ third
☐ fourth

◀ 1 | 2 | 3 | 4 | **5** | 6 ▶

IMMIGRANTS ON THE FRONT LINES OF CHANGE

In New York in 2004, there were more Fatoumas born than Lisas. Meanwhile, the most popular name for Hispanic-American boys was Justin, a name without strong ties to Hispanic culture. Statistics like that can suggest a lot about how immigration affects baby-naming traditions.

Immigrants from the first generation to come to the United States often try to pick names that help their children fit in to their new culture. 130 They hope that a typically American name will help their child become **assimilated** more quickly. However, because newly arrived parents probably aren't yet fully familiar with the general American society, some children might end up with names that are already out of fashion in the mainstream culture. ◀

By the second generation, the children of immigrants often choose familiar American names for their own children—just think of all those Hispanic-American Justins. In 2004, Emily was the most popular name for Asian Americans. By the third and fourth generations, the grandchildren and great-grandchildren of immigrants often choose names that reflect the 140 traditions and heritage of their family's country of origin. ◀

That explains why in New York there are many children named Aaliyah, Moshe, and Ahmed. Mohammed, with lots of different spellings, came in as a top 50 name in New York. That name is common among groups with roots in places like the Middle East, South Asia, and Southeast Asia. In 2004, Mohammed was a more popular name than both Richard and Charles in New York.

GLOBAL NAMING TRENDS

Names that are given to children go through trends in every part of the world. This is especially true if that place has seen immigration or other 150 cultural change. But in many communities, parents continue to choose names that retain and reflect national and ethnic heritage. Names help parents and children connect to ancestors and histories. Names remind children of where they come from and what they'll take with them into the future. The following chart details names that have been popular in various countries.

180 UNIT 7: BIOGRAPHY AND AUTOBIOGRAPHY

◀ 1 | 2 | 3 | 4 | 5 | **6**

Country	Girl Names	Boy Names
United Kingdom	Emily, Ellie, Jessica, Amy, Sophie, Chloe, Lucy, Katie, Olivia, Charlotte	Jack, Joshua, Thomas, James, Daniel, Samuel, Oliver, William Benjamin, Joseph
Ireland	Emma, Aoife, Sarah, Ciara, Amy, Katie, Sophie, Rachel, Chloe, Leah	Sean, Jack, Adam, Conor, James, Daniel, Cian, Michael, Eoin, David ▶
Israel	Adi, Chen, Feigel, Hallel, Maayan, Maya, Neta, Noa, Noam, Shira	Bar, Fishel, Gai, Ido, Nachman, Natan, Oren, Tom, Yisrael, Zalman
Philippines	Maricel, Michelle, Jennifer, Janice, Mary Grace, Jocelyn, Catherine, Mary Anne, Rowena, Grace	Michael, Ronald, Ryan, Joseph, Joel, Jeffrey, Marlon, Richard, Noel, Jonathan
Jordan	Rawan, Suzan, Lana, Diana, Tala, Leena, Tamara, Reem, Randa, Amal	Sami, Rani, Samer, Kamal, Bisher, Imad, Raed, Hazem, Nader, Amjad
Russia	Anna, Antonia, Elena, Galina, Irina, Mariya, Olga, Svetlana, Tatyana, Valentina	Aleksey, Alexander, Ivan, Konstantin, Mikhail, Nokolai, Pavel, Sergey, Vladimir, Yuri
Spain	Lucia, Maria, Paula, Laura, Marta, Alba, Andrea, Claudia, Sara, Nerea	Alejandro, David, Daniel, Pablo, Adrian, Alvaro, Javier, Sergio, Carlos, Marcos
Botswana	Ambreen, Hada, Abba, Ujana, Dikeledi, Goitsemedi, Kagiso, Kefilwe ▶	Akuji, Alake, Agu, Jabilo, Ja, Baruti, Fenyang, Mosegi, Kefentse, Tebogo, Kopano

SYNTHESIZE SOURCES

Read the Irish names in the chart, circling the names of any people you know. Then underline the sentences on page 180 that explain why these names might be popular today.

Why might parents choose to name their children to reflect the culture of a country they no longer live in?

_____
_____
_____

TestSmart

Which girls' names are popular throughout the British Isles, which includes, both the United Kingdom and Ireland?

Ⓐ Amy, Emma, Aoife, Katie

Ⓑ Emma, Sophie, Charlotte, Olivia

Ⓒ Rachel, Chloe, Sophie, Leah

Ⓓ Amy, Katie, Sophie, Chloe

TIP When a reading selection on a test includes a **graphic aid**, you are likely to be asked a question about it. To answer this question about names, first find the rows of the chart that refer to any of the British Isles. Next, circle or list the girls' names that appear in *both* of these rows. Then compare each answer choice with the names you circled or listed.

RELATED NONFICTION **181**

Assessment Practice II

Reading Comprehension

DIRECTIONS *Answer these questions by filling in the correct ovals.*

1. According to "Name That Child," which naming tradition is common in Hindu tradition?
   - A naming a child after its parents
   - B giving a child its name at puberty
   - C naming a child a month after birth
   - D whispering a newborn's name to the baby

2. According to "Name That Child," three Japanese children named Ichiro, Jiro, and Saburo are
   - A sons and daughters born in spring
   - B children born in the same village
   - C sons born in the same generation
   - D daughters born in the same generation

3. Based on the information in lines 86–90 of "Name That Child," what generalization is true of names given to most African-American girls today?
   - A They are unique; no other girl in the state is likely to have the same one.
   - B They are Muslim names from the Arabic language, such as *Aaliyah*.
   - C They contain the prefix *Sha-, La-, Ka-,* or *Ty-*.
   - D They reflect the names of earlier generations.

4. In which country are the names Laura and Carlos both popular?
   - A Ireland
   - B France
   - C Jordan
   - D Spain

5. Which statement is supported by information in both "Name That Child" and "Names/Nombres"?
   - A Hispanic-American children are unlikely to have traditional names.
   - B Many immigrants try to choose names that are easy for Americans to pronounce.
   - C Some immigrants choose names based on the generation in which a child is born.
   - D Ethnic names have become more popular in the United States since the late 1960s.

6. When you syntheize the anecdote about Mauricia in "Names/Nombres" and the information in "Name That Child," you can conclude that
   - A girls are often named after saints
   - B names can be used to break with a troubled past
   - C invented names can also reflect family and heritage
   - D families choose girls' and boys' names for different reasons

7. In line 43 of "Name That Child," the word *signify* means
   - A to create
   - B to spell
   - C to mean
   - D to sing

8. In line 48 of "Name That Child," the word *surnames* refers to
   - A last names
   - B common names
   - C first names
   - D African names

182 UNIT 7: BIOGRAPHY AND AUTOBIOGRAPHY

Timed Writing Practice

PROMPT

Who we are depends in part on the events we have experienced. Write an (autobiographical narrative) about a key event in your life. Choose an event that helped you realize something important or that says something about the kind of person you are. Remember to use the first-person point of view.

BUDGET YOUR TIME

You have 45 minutes to complete this assignment. Decide how much time to spend on each step.

Analyze _____
Plan _____
Write _____
Review _____

Test-Taker's Toolkit

1. ANALYZE THE PROMPT

A. **Read the prompt** carefully. Note key words that tell you what you must do. The writing form has been circled. Underline the topic. Double-underline the point of view the prompt requires.

B. **Restate the prompt** in your own words. List all key ideas. Be sure you understand that the required point of view means that you should use pronouns such as *I, me, we,* and *our.*

2. PLAN YOUR RESPONSE

A. **Make notes** Use the key elements you identified in the prompt to take notes. Organize your notes into a list like the one shown.

B. **Organize your information** A narrative is the telling of a story, and these events are usually told in sequence. In the first part of your response, retell the story in sequence. In the second part, explain why the event was important to you, or what you learned from it.

Essay Topic: An Important Event in My Life
When the event happened:
What happened:
Why I remember the event:
What I learned about myself:

3. WRITE AND REVIEW

A. **Write your response** Use your notes to guide you as you write. If you have trouble getting started, try writing a draft of your conclusion first. The conclusion should show readers why the experience was meaningful, and drafting it might help you clarify what to focus on in the rest of your narrative.

B. **Review your work** Be sure to leave enough time to reread your narrative carefully. Correct any errors, and make sure you have met all the requirements of the prompt.

UNIT 8

INFORMATION, ARGUMENT, AND PERSUASION

LESSON 8A

What Do You Know About Sharks?
BY SHARON GUYNUP

RELATED NONFICTION
A Real Can of Worms: Animal Figures of Speech

Can appearances DECEIVE?

Cute doesn't always mean cuddly, and frightening doesn't always mean vicious. Humans are often quick to make snap judgments about animals based on how they look, but appearances can deceive.

DISCUSS IT Sharks attract a lot of interest from people, but how much do you really know about them? Form a small group and discuss whether each statement in the notebook is true or false. Once you've come to an agreement with your group, put a T next to each true statement and an F next to each false one. Then read the article to discover whether or not you were correct.

TRUE OR FALSE?

1. The great white is the largest shark. _____

2. There are more than 300 species of sharks. _____

3. Most shark species are dangerous to humans. _____

4. Sharks lived at the time of dinosaurs. _____

ASSESSMENT GOALS

By the end of this lesson, you will be able to...
- identify and use text features to locate and understand information
- apply critical thinking skills to analyze text
- examine an author's treatment of ideas
- analyze a writing prompt and write an expository essay

LEARN THE TERMS: ACADEMIC VOCABULARY

Text Features

Flipping through a magazine or surfing the Web can be an overwhelming experience. Information overload can keep you from knowing where to find the facts you need. To help readers find and understand key ideas, many writers use text features.

TEXT FEATURES are special design elements that that help organize and call attention to important information. They include headings, subheadings, graphic aids, and captions. Notice how much you can tell about the article below by scanning its text features.

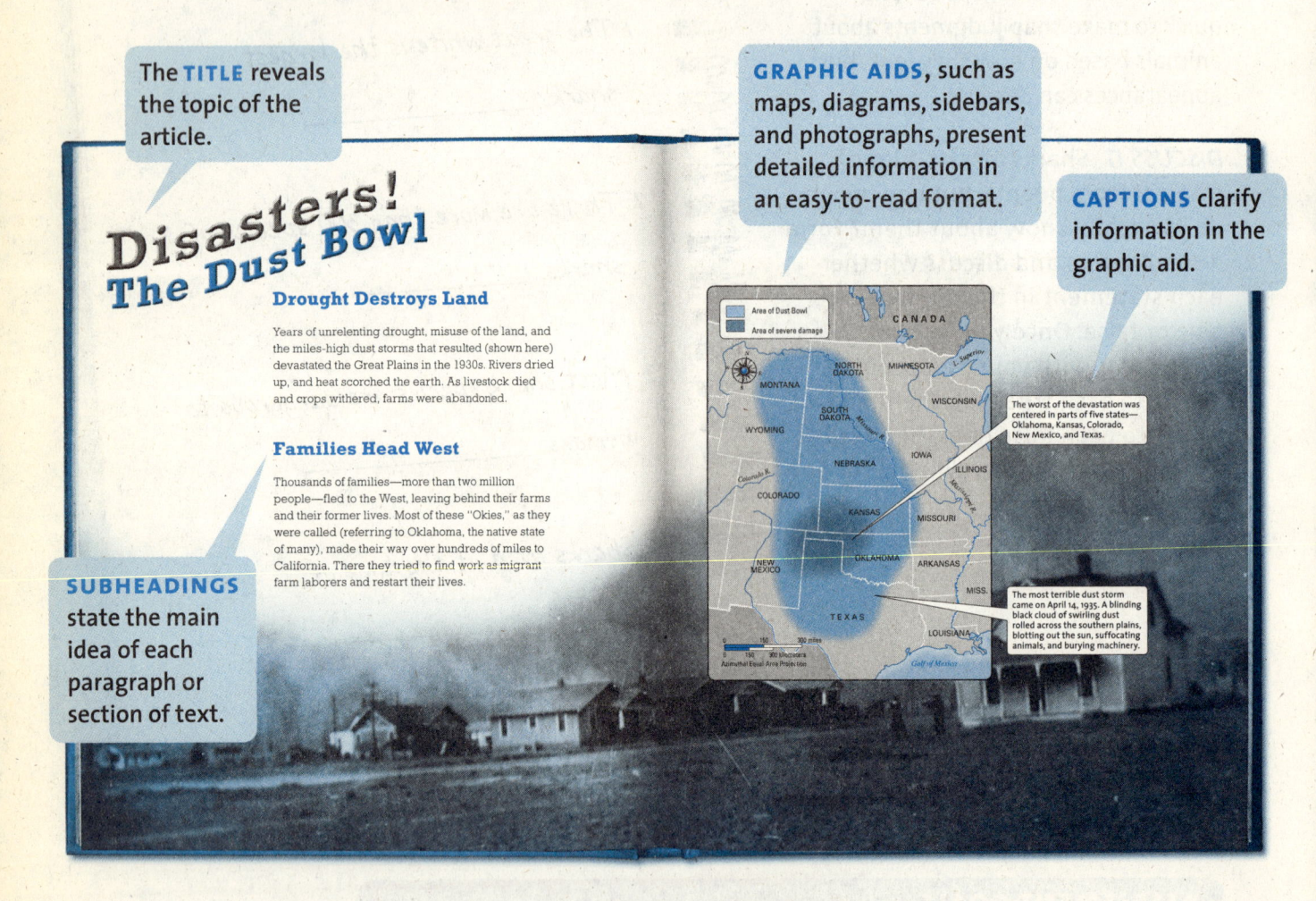

The **TITLE** reveals the topic of the article.

GRAPHIC AIDS, such as maps, diagrams, sidebars, and photographs, present detailed information in an easy-to-read format.

CAPTIONS clarify information in the graphic aid.

Disasters! The Dust Bowl

Drought Destroys Land

Years of unrelenting drought, misuse of the land, and the miles-high dust storms that resulted (shown here) devastated the Great Plains in the 1930s. Rivers dried up, and heat scorched the earth. As livestock died and crops withered, farms were abandoned.

Families Head West

Thousands of families—more than two million people—fled to the West, leaving behind their farms and their former lives. Most of these "Okies," as they were called (referring to Oklahoma, the native state of many), made their way over hundreds of miles to California. There they tried to find work as migrant farm laborers and restart their lives.

The worst of the devastation was centered in parts of five states—Oklahoma, Kansas, Colorado, New Mexico, and Texas.

The most terrible dust storm came on April 14, 1935. A blinding black cloud of swirling dust rolled across the southern plains, blotting out the sun, suffocating animals, and burying machinery.

SUBHEADINGS state the main idea of each paragraph or section of text.

ADDITIONAL TERM FOR CRITICAL ANALYSIS

The following term will help you analyze how the author has organized the information in the upcoming selection:

STRUCTURE is the way in which parts of a piece of writing are put together. A text's structure can highlight or emphasize certain aspects of is content.

186   UNIT 8A: INFORMATION, ARGUMENT, AND PERSUASION

WHAT DO YOU KNOW ABOUT SHARKS?

SHARON GUYNUP

They're ferocious predators. They haunt us in nightmares. But the scariest thing about sharks may be that they're vanishing from the world's oceans. . . .

Why do sharks need protection? Sharks are top predators in the aquatic food chain—a web that interconnects all organisms, in which smaller creatures become food for larger predators. Without sharks, the ocean's delicate ecosystem would be disrupted. Species that sharks devour, like seals, for example, would overpopulate and in turn decimate other species, like salmon. Read the following questions and answers to learn more about the world's most fear-inspiring fish.

WHAT ARE SHARKS?

Sharks are fish with skeletons made of rubbery cartilage (tough, flexible tissue) instead of bone. They're cold-blooded (unable to generate their own body heat), breathe through gills (respiratory organs), and have a two-chambered heart. Though most live in warm seas, the Greenland shark thrives in frigid Arctic seas.

WHAT'S THE LARGEST SHARK? THE SMALLEST?

Weighing in at 15 tons and stretching up to 14 meters (46 feet) long, the whale shark is the world's largest fish—bigger than a school bus! Nine hundred meters (2,953 feet) below the ocean surface lives the smallest shark: the dwarf shark. An adult measures only 25 centimeters (10 inches) long!

SECOND READ: CRITICAL ANALYSIS

MARK & ANALYZE

Read this selection once on your own, marking the text in any way that is helpful to you.

Then read the story a second time, using the questions in the margins to help you analyze the literature. When you see this pencil, you'll be asked to mark up the text.

aquatic (ə-kwăt'ĭk) *adj.* growing or living in the water

ecosystem (ē'kō-sĭs'təm) *n.* a physical environment, such as an ocean, and the community of things that live in it

decimate (dĕs'ə-māt') *v.* to kill or destroy a large part of

ANALYZE

On the lines below, answer the question asked in each **subheading** on this page.

1. _____
_____

2. _____
_____

3. _____
_____

Then, consider the **structure** of this article. What is the function of the subheadings? What does each introduce?

_____
_____
_____
_____
_____

ARE ALL SHARKS DANGEROUS TO PEOPLE? ◀

Most sharks are harmless. "Out of 375 shark species, only two dozen are in any way really dangerous to us," says Robert Hueter, director of the Center for Shark Research at Mote Marine Laboratory. Still, scientists don't know for sure why sharks sometimes attack humans. One theory: sharks may mistake the sound of swimming humans for that of injured fish—which are easy prey.

WHICH SHARK IS THE MOST DANGEROUS TO HUMANS?

"In terms of fatal attacks, it's a tossup between the great white, the tiger, and the bull shark," Hueter says. People fear the massive great white the most because of its size—up to 6.4 meters (21 feet) long—and its large razor-like teeth, not to mention the terror stirred up by *Jaws* flicks. But great whites usually inhabit deep seas—not shallow waters where people swim. Worldwide, fewer than 100 human attacks by all shark species are reported each year.

WHERE DO MOST SHARK ATTACKS HAPPEN?

Florida leads the world in shark bites, with 22 to 25 reported incidents each year. But, claims Hueter, they're not repeated shark attacks—usually a single bite. . . . "Most really bad attacks occur off the coasts of California, Hawaii, Australia, and South Africa," Hueter says.

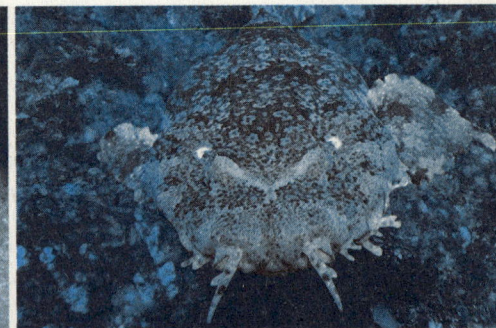

Nurse Shark
Nurse sharks are sluggish bottom dwellers found in the Atlantic Ocean. They're usually not dangerous and are one of the few sharks that breathe by pumping water through their gills while lying motionless. They sometimes suck in prey as well.

Wobbegong Shark
Wobbegongs are found resting on the sea floor in shallow waters of the Indo-Pacific and the Red Sea. The barbels, or fringe of flesh around their mouths, are feelers that act as camouflage.

JUST HOW POWERFUL IS A SHARK'S BITE?

Scientists built a "shark-bite meter" that measures the jaw strength of one species, the dusky shark. It exerts 18 tons of pressure per square inch on a victim. That's like being crushed beneath the weight of ten cars!

WHAT DO SHARKS EAT?

Sharks chow down on what they can when they can—usually smaller animals from shrimp and fish to turtles and seabirds. Some, like the bull shark, consume large mammals like sea lions or dolphins; others, like the whale shark, eat only plankton, tiny drifting animals. And tiger sharks devour just about anything—mammal **carcasses**, tin cans, plastic bags, coal, and even license plates have been found inside their stomachs!

HOW DO SHARKS FIND PREY?

Sharks can hear a wide range of sounds but are attracted by bursts of sound—like those made by an injured fish—or occasionally humans romping in water. At close range, sharks also sense vibration with their lateral line, a sensory system that runs from head to tail on each side of a shark's body. Inside the lateral line, which helps a shark maintain balance as well as detect sound, are canals filled with fluid and tiny "hair cells." Sound causes the liquid to vibrate, alerting the shark to the presence of another creature. This sense allows sharks to hunt even in total darkness.

carcass (kär′kəs) *n.* the dead body of an animal

Goblin Shark
Goblin sharks feature needle-like teeth. They're rarely spotted—only 36 specimens have been counted—most found in waters deeper than 1,150 feet. Scientists think they inhabit seas from Europe to Australia.

Hammerhead Shark
Hammerheads inhabit shorelines and deep seas worldwide. The head, or cephalofoil, provides greater maneuverability—and enlarged nostrils and eyes at the ends of their "hammer" receive more information giving them a hunting advantage.

DRAW CONCLUSIONS

Examine the **photographs** and accompanying **captions**. Based on the information presented here, what general statement can you make about sharks?

_____
_____
_____
_____
_____
_____
_____

TestSmart

VOCABULARY

The word *swarm* in line 65 most likely means

- Ⓐ a mate
- Ⓑ a pair
- Ⓒ a family
- Ⓓ a large group

TIP When a test question asks you to choose a definition for a word you don't know, review the sentence in which it appears. Look for **context clues**. For example, if the unfamiliar word is contrasted with a familiar word, that is a clue to the unfamiliar word's meaning. In this case, the word *but* signals a contrast between the word *solo* and the word *swarm*. If a shark usually swims solo, or alone, what might a swarm of sharks be?

---

diffuse (dĭ-fyo̅o̅z′) *v.* to spread out or through

EVALUATE

Sidebars are special **graphic aids** that are set off from the main text. Review the sidebar along the bottom of pages 188–190. Why might the author have chosen these sharks to highlight?

_____
_____
_____

WHAT'S A "FEEDING FRENZY"?

Sharks usually travel solo, but if one finds easy prey, an excited, competitive swarm of sharks may join in the feast, biting anything that lies in its path. ◀

HOW DO SHARKS BREATHE?

A shark usually swims with its mouth open to force oxygen-rich water to pass over a set of gills housed in a cavity behind its head—a
70　process known as ramjet ventilation. Gill flaps called lamellae absorb and help **diffuse** oxygen into the shark's bloodstream. Lamellae also help sharks expel carbon dioxide, a gaseous waste product of breathing, from the bloodstream.

ARE SHARKS SMART?

Experiments show that sharks recognize and remember shapes and patterns. Using shark snacks as rewards, scientists have taught lemon sharks to swim through mazes, ring bells, and press targets. "Although we learn new things about sharks every day, there's still a lot we don't know about them," says Hueter.

Whale Shark
The largest fish in the sea—whale sharks—are very docile. They feed on plankton, tiny drifting animals. They swim with their enormous mouths open, filtering food from the water with 15,000 tiny teeth.

Leopard Shark
Leopard sharks are commonly found near shore, often in large schools along the Pacific coast from Oregon to Mexico. They feed on small fish and crustaceans and are generally harmless.

Brushing and Flossing ▶

Sharks continually lose their teeth, but some species grow new teeth as often as every week to replace worn or lost ones. During their lifetime, some species shed 30,000 teeth. Shark teeth vary according to what's on the menu:

left: mako shark teeth, which grind up squid and big fish like tuna and mackerel

right: tiger shark teeth, which crunch everything from fish and birds to tin cans and other garbage

SUMMARIZE

On the lines below, summarize the main idea presented in the **graphic aid** "Brushing and Flossing."

Now examine each photograph and accompanying caption. Explain why the shape of each shark's teeth makes sense.

80 **WHAT ARE SHARKS' NATURAL ENEMIES?**

Large sharks sometimes eat smaller sharks, and killer whales also dine on sharks. But the shark's greatest enemy is people. Humans kill sharks for food, use their skins for leather, make medicine from their liver oil, and use shark teeth for jewelry. Many sharks are killed senselessly for sport or get trapped and die in fishing nets. And it takes a long time for shark populations to rebound. Most shark species take ten years to reach reproductive age and produce small litters of less than a dozen pups. ▶

COMPARE

In what way is this paragraph similar to the introductory paragraph? Explain.

Bite-Size Facts

- The first sharks appeared in the ancient oceans about 400 million years ago—200 million years before the dinosaurs!
- Sharks are carnivores (meat-eaters). Most gobble their prey whole or rip it into large, shark-size bites.
- Most sharks are found in the ocean but some, like the bull shark, also swim in lakes and rivers. Most shark attacks occur in warm waters—20° to 30°C (68° to 86°F).
- Sharks lack the inflatable swim bladder that allows bony fish to control **buoyancy**. Most sharks must swim endlessly. If they stop, they sink to the bottom and may drown from a lack of water flowing over the gills.

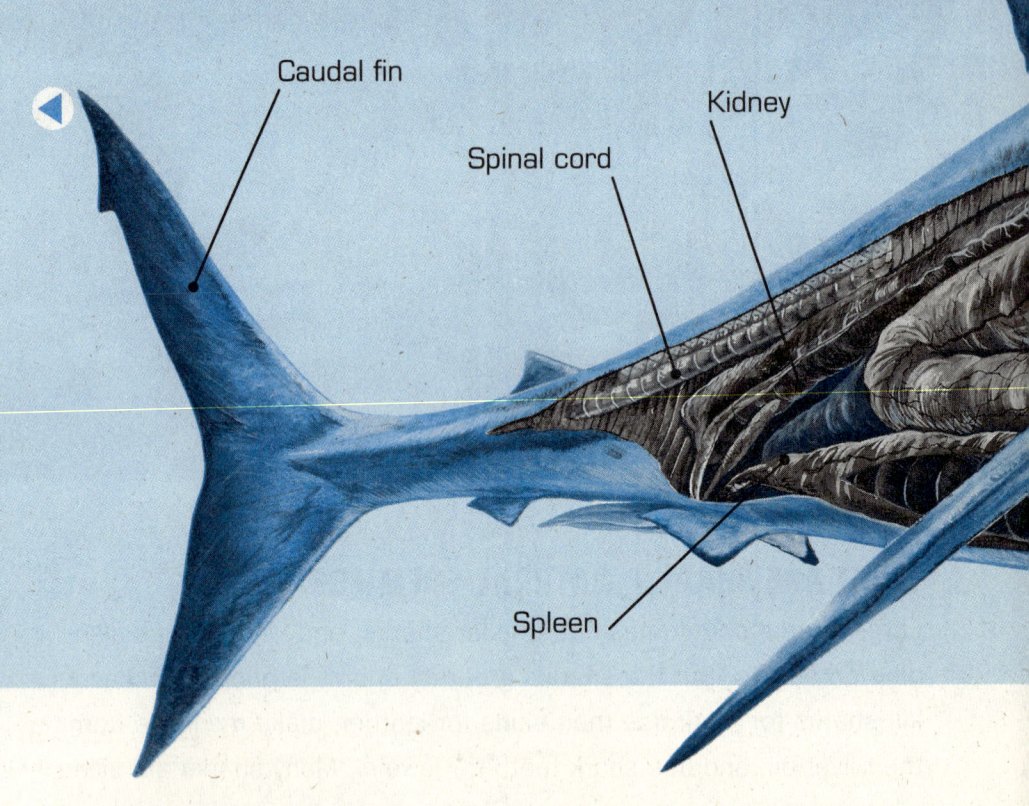

buoyancy (boi'ən-sē) *n.* the ability to remain afloat in liquid

DRAW CONCLUSIONS

A **cutaway diagram** is a drawing that shows what the inside of something looks like. Locate each of the shark's fins on the diagram and read the **caption** about the tail. What can you conclude about the function of each fin listed below?

Caudal fin _____

_____

_____

Pectoral fin _____

_____

_____

Caudal fin

Spinal cord

Kidney

Spleen

Top-Powerful Tail

Since its upper lobe is larger than the lower one, the great white's thrashing tail movements drive the shark forward and push its head down. This nosedive is countered by the fish's wedge-shaped head and its pectoral fins, which lift the front end.

192 UNIT 8A: INFORMATION, ARGUMENT, AND PERSUASION

Great White Shark ▶

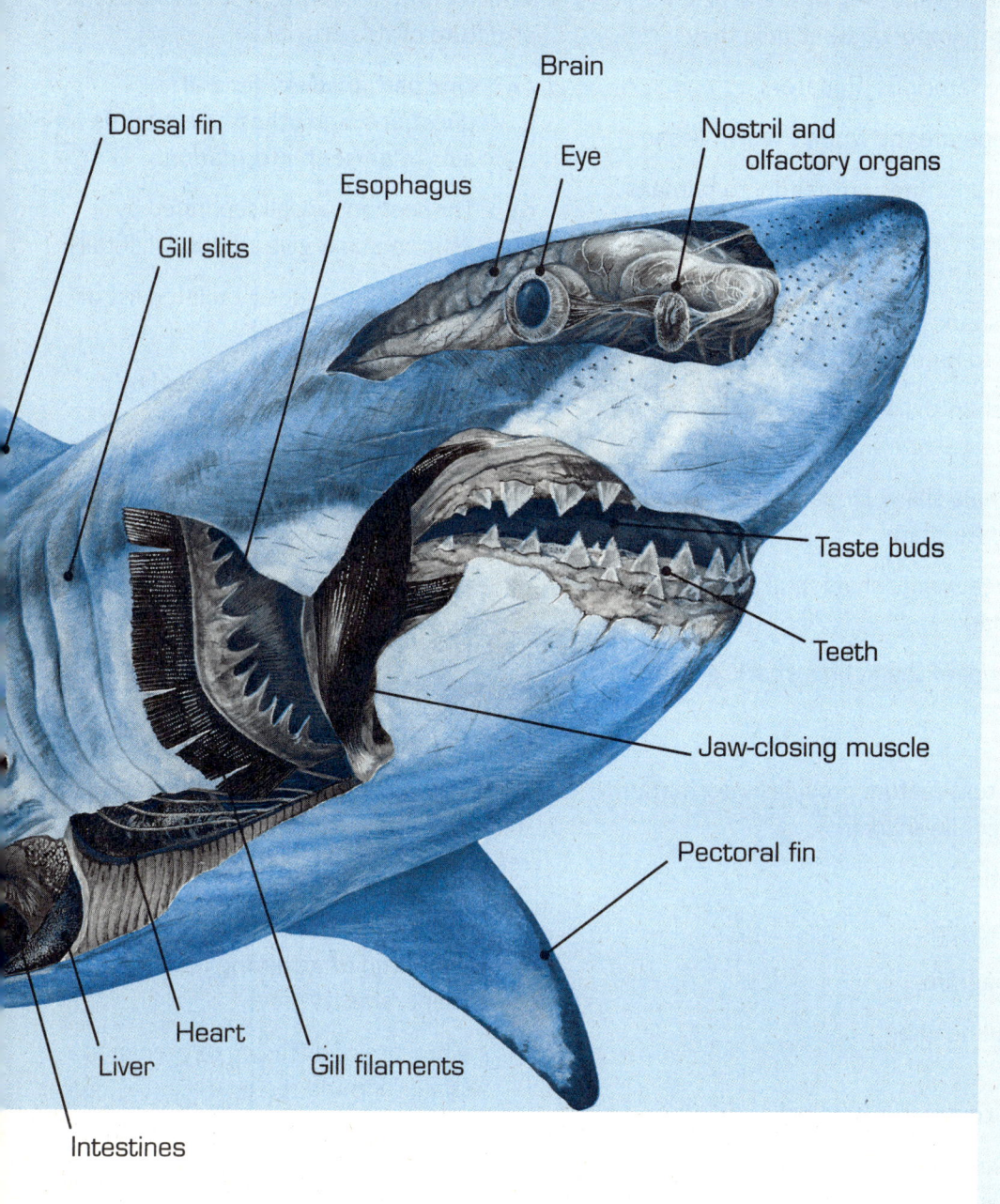

Labels on diagram:
- Dorsal fin
- Gill slits
- Esophagus
- Brain
- Eye
- Nostril and olfactory organs
- Taste buds
- Teeth
- Jaw-closing muscle
- Pectoral fin
- Gill filaments
- Heart
- Liver
- Intestines

Sandpaper Skin
Rough and tough, shark skin is made of hard, platelike scales, like tiny teeth pointing backward.

Gills
Water flows in the mouth and over blood-rich gill filaments. Some dissolved oxygen passes into the bloodstream before the water flows out through gill slits. ▶

TestSmart

From the diagram and captions, you can tell that a shark's gill slits are

- A like teeth within the shark's body
- B on the outside of a shark and help it to breathe
- C next to the heart within a shark's chest
- D the external organs that allow a shark to sense prey

TIP When asked a question about **graphic aids,** make sure you review the visuals and any related text. For this question, locate the gill slits on the diagram, and reread the text under the caption "Gills." Which answer choice most closely matches both the visual and written information presented in this graphic aid?

Big Question ?

Based on what you have learned, is a shark's scary appearance deceptive? Use examples from the article to support your answer. MAKE JUDGMENTS

WHAT DO YOU KNOW ABOUT SHARKS?

Assessment Practice I

Reading Comprehension

DIRECTIONS *Answer these questions by filling in the correct ovals.*

1. According to lines 1–9 of the article, sharks are important because they
   - A are ferocious predators
   - B populate the world's warm oceans
   - C kill creatures unfriendly to humans
   - D keep the ocean's ecosystem in balance

2. Which shark species pose the greatest danger to humans?
   - A goblin shark, hammerhead shark, great white shark
   - B whale shark, leopard shark, great white shark
   - C great white shark, bull shark, tiger shark
   - D leopard shark, tiger shark, goblin shark

3. Which text feature provides information about goblin sharks?
   - A title
   - B caption
   - C diagram
   - D subheading

4. Which commonly held belief is true?
   - A The larger the shark, the more dangerous it is.
   - B Most sharks must keep moving to stay alive.
   - C Sharks will not eat other sharks.
   - D Most sharks will attack people.

5. Which of the following *best* describes the structure of this article?
   - A One part answers general questions, and others use graphic aids to present information.
   - B The sections are all separated by diagrams that give additional details.
   - C Each part includes a bulleted list of facts and statistics.
   - D Each section is accompanied by a sidebar.

6. From the diagram and labels on pages 192–193, you can tell that a shark's caudal fin
   - A is used as defense against predators
   - B allows a shark to hunt
   - C is part of the tail
   - D covers the gills

7. In line 70 of the article, *ramjet ventilation* refers to
   - A a way of getting rid of carbon dioxide
   - B a method of attacking in which a shark rams its prey
   - C a process of diffusing oxygen in a shark's bloodstream
   - D a process that forces oxygen-rich water over a shark's gills

8. In the text under the caption "Top-Powerful Tail" on page 192, *countered* means
   - A balanced out
   - B counted on
   - C measured out
   - D driven forward

194 UNIT 8A: INFORMATION, ARGUMENT, AND PERSUASION

Responding in Writing

9. Short Response Do humans have more to fear from sharks, or do sharks have more to fear from humans? Write two or three sentences that explain your answer.

_____
_____
_____
_____
_____
_____
_____

For help, use the *Test-Taker's Toolkit* below.

Test-Taker's Toolkit

GRAPHIC ORGANIZER Use the chart below to collect facts that will help you answer the question.

DANGERS SHARKS POSE TO HUMANS	DANGERS HUMANS POSE TO SHARKS

WHAT DO YOU KNOW ABOUT SHARKS?

Related Nonfiction

A Real Can of Worms: Animal Figures of Speech
MAGAZINE ARTICLE

Use with "What Do You Know About Sharks?," p. 184

What's the Connection?

Have you ever read a story about a character who borrowed money from a "loan shark"? *Loan shark* is an expression based on our perception of sharks as dangerous and hungry. The magazine article "A Real Can of Worms: Animal Figures of Speech" explores other expressions based (rightly or wrongly) on our perceptions of animals.

CHART IT Working with a partner, read each expression in the first column of the chart below. In the second column, write what you think the expression means. Then write the animal characteristic you think the expression is based on.

EXPRESSION	ITS MEANING	ANIMAL CHARACTERISTIC
monkey-see, monkey-do	This expression describes someone who copies another person's behavior.	Monkeys sometimes mimic other creatures' movements.
rat race		
chicken out		
bull-headed		

LEARN THE SKILL: EXAMINE TREATMENT

The way a writer handles a topic is called its **treatment.** To examine how writers treat their subject matter, pay attention to

- the **author's purpose** for writing about the topic. For example, does the author want to persuade, inform, correct, or entertain?
- the **form** and **structure** the author has chosen to use. For example, what exactly is the author writing? Is it a personal essay, a feature article, or something else? Notice whether the author uses subheadings, questions, or some other structural device to present the information.
- the author's **tone,** or attitude toward the subject. For example, is the author writing a humorous, light-hearted piece? Or does he or she treat the topic in a serious or business-like manner?

For more on examining treatment, see *Nonfiction Handbook,* page R25.

A Real Can of Worms

ANIMAL FIGURES OF SPEECH

By Sydney Groll

Human beings share many characteristics with other living creatures. Since animals constitute an important part of our world, we often see ourselves reflected in their behavior. It's not surprising, therefore, that our everyday speech includes numerous animal expressions.

Many of these figures of speech are clichés, overused statements that have lost their freshness and meaning. Some are accurate and are based on facts; others are inaccurate and stem from misinformation or misinterpretation. As you examine these familiar expressions, be aware that you just might be opening a can of worms that will make you see the English language as a horse of a whole different color. ▶

INACCURATE

Laughing like a hyena

Though this expression describes someone who is overcome with amusement, hyenas don't actually laugh at all. When under attack or excited by the prospect of food, spotted hyenas
20 make a snickering noise that may sound like a person laughing, but that indicates a much more serious state of mind. When a hyena makes this noise, it is disturbed or has a kill to share—not laughing matters.

Eating like a bird

We say that someone who consumes hardly any food eats like a bird. The eating habits of birds, though, are precisely the opposite. Birds have a rapid metabolism, and most eat from a quarter to half their body weight daily. Tiny hummingbirds often consume eight times that much—up to twice their weight. A 150-pound
30 man who ate like that bird would have to consume about 1,200 quarter-pound hamburgers a day.

Wise as an owl

Although this expression highly praises someone's intelligence, it is actually another example of misinterpretation of animal behavior. Owls appear intelligent to us because of their calmness and their uncanny ability to rotate their heads almost completely around. The fact is that they are no smarter than other predators
40 that have the skills needed to survive as a species. ◀

Dumb as a dodo

If you're trying to insult someone's intelligence, calling him or her a "dodo" isn't the way to go. This now-extinct bird once inhabited the Isle of Mauritius, an island in the Indian Ocean. Mauritius was completely isolated from human contact until

---

EXAMINE TREATMENT

Examine the way the author has structured the ideas in this article. Then describe the function of each type of text feature listed below.

The main subheading in line 14:
_____
_____
_____

The boldface subheadings, such as the one in line 15:
_____
_____
_____

The text beneath the subheadings:
_____
_____
_____

Portuguese sailors landed on its shores in 1598. The sailors were greeted by flightless birds that had no fear of humans. The men mistook the birds' lack of fear for stupidity. Thus, the sailors christened the birds dodos, a name that comes from the Portuguese word for "simpleton." Though they were not unintelligent, the dodos' fearlessness did lead to their extinction. By 1681, the whole species was wiped out.

Quiet as a mouse

If you want to describe someone who doesn't make much noise, this isn't the factual expression to use. Actually, baby mice require a great deal of food and attention and squeak almost nonstop to get those needs met. Adult mice are not necessarily quiet, either. The tiny grasshopper mouse, which lives in the deserts of the Southwest, gives off extended high-pitched squeals to mark its territory.

Filthy as a pig ▶

For much of history, pigs have gotten a bad reputation. You have probably heard a number of unflattering idioms involving pigs: "filthy as a pig," "living in a pigsty," and "acting like a hog" are all common sayings. But these unsavory comparisons are based on a misconception. Pigs are not actually filthy. Pigs—among the most intelligent of all domestic animals—are actually as clean or cleaner than other creatures. Misconceptions about pigs' cleanliness stems in part from the animals' love of wallowing in the mud. Pigs have thick skins covered with stiff, bristly hair. Their sweat glands are ineffective and don't lower their body temperature sufficiently, so pigs wallow in mud or shallow water holes simply to beat the heat. ▶

CONNECT
Underline the animal expressions on pages 198–199 that you have heard before.

What other animal expressions do you know?

EXAMINE TREATMENT
Underline the words that rhyme in line 79.

What effect does the rhyme have on the **tone** of this article?

80 **ACCURATE**

Crying crocodile tears

When we say someone is crying crocodile tears, we mean that the person is trying to appear sad, but doesn't really feel that way. This expression is based on the fact that, although crocodiles appear to be crying when they're lying out in the sun, their eyes are actually only producing tears to stay moist and comfortable.

90 ### Lazy as a sloth

The word *sloth* has two main meanings: it can refer to a slow-moving, tree-dwelling animal, or it can mean laziness. Is it fair that the animal called the sloth has such a reputation for laziness? Though zoologists might take issue with that exact term, these creatures are anything but energetic. Sloth, who hang upside down from tree branches for most of their lives, move only when necessary. They eat, sleep, and even give birth to their young hanging from tree limbs. When sloth are forced to move, they do so extremely slowly. Even 100 when chased by a predator, the animal's top speed is about 15 feet per minute. ◂

Hungry as a bear

Someone who we call hungry as a bear truly could eat a horse. Bears consume an enormous amount of food, particularly in preparation for winter. To store up a surplus of nutrition, Alaskan grizzlies can eat up to 90 pounds of fish, and polar bears, over 110 100 pounds of whale meat and blubber in one day.

MAKE JUDGMENTS

Do you think sloths are really lazy, or are they just acting according to their nature?

Sly like a fox

This figure of speech has been around for millennia. It is recorded in some of the earliest literature—including the Bible. Foxes live in a huge variety of habitats, from the frigid Artic tundra to the most arid deserts. They adapt to their environment extremely well, and they are clever **scavengers**. Because they are able to get used to living in areas populated by humans, we have been able to witness the cunning hunting and scavenging that
120 earned these animals their sly reputation. ▶

Busy as a bee

Like the workaholic we characterize with this expression, bees are busily active most of the time. Each bee has its specific task, which it performs diligently. The queen's full-time occupation is laying eggs. The workers have a variety of duties, including gathering nectar and building
130 wax honeycombs, feeding the queen and the larvae, cooling down the hive, and protecting it from intruders. ▶

SPECIALIZED Vocabulary

To scavenge is to search through discarded material to find something useful. Once you know this, you can figure out other forms of the word. A scavenger is an animal that includes a wide variety of living and nonliving things, including the remains of other animals, in its diet. Underline another word in this section that is contains a form of the word *scavenge*. **WORD ANALYSIS**

TestSmart

How are all the expressions on pages 200–201 alike?

A They are based on the behavior of mammals.

B They are based on the way animals really behave.

C They have to do with how animals mimic people.

D They describe negative characteristics.

TIP When a test question asks how a group of things are alike, you must find the answer that states their similarities. Sometimes, the **structure** of a selection can make it easier for you. In this case, the **subheading** in line 80 tells how all the expressions on these pages relate to each other. You can use this clue to choose the right answer.

RELATED NONFICTION   **201**

Assessment Practice II

Reading Comprehension

DIRECTIONS *Answer these questions about the two selections in this lesson by filling in the correct ovals.*

1. Which of the following expressions is based on an accurate understanding of the animal?
   - A The silly girls laughed like hyenas.
   - B The workers are as busy as bees.
   - C Your room looks like a pigsty!
   - D Paul was as quiet as a mouse.

2. If a man truly ate like a bird, he might eat
   - A more than 1,000 hamburgers a day
   - B eight times his body weight
   - C twigs and leaves
   - D very little food

3. Pigs have a reputation of being filthy because they
   - A really are filthy
   - B avoid clean water
   - C wallow in mud to stay cool
   - D are less clean than other animals

4. Which statement *best* describes how "A Real Can of Worms" treats its topic?
   - A an article that entertainingly describes true and false beliefs about animals
   - B an essay that explains how certain animal expressions developed
   - C a list that matter-of-factly presents facts and fictions about animals
   - D a chart showing the humor in certain animal expressions

5. Based on the information in "What Do You Know About Sharks?" which expression below is accurate?
   - A soft as a shark's skin
   - B nasty as a nurse shark
   - C tame as a tiger shark
   - D ferocious as a feeding shark

6. How is the structure of "What Do You Know About Sharks?" similar to the structure of "A Real Can of Worms"?
   - A In both, the ideas are sorted into categories.
   - B Both selections are organized by a sequence of steps.
   - C Both selections are organized by question and answer.
   - D In both, each paragraph has a heading and explains one idea.

7. What is the meaning of the word *cliché* in line 7 of "A Real Can of Worms"?
   - A a stale, overused expression
   - B an accurate figure of speech
   - C a statement of misinformation
   - D a statement that makes no sense

8. What is the meaning of the word *diligently* in line 126 of "A Real Can of Worms"?
   - A with dedication and effort
   - B occasionally
   - C with pleasure
   - D reluctantly

Timed Writing Practice

PROMPT

Write an (expository essay) about why people should or should not be afraid of sharks. Organize your essay by first stating your claim and then supporting it with at least three supporting details from "What Do You Know About Sharks?"

BUDGET YOUR TIME

You have 45 minutes to complete this assignment. Decide how much time to spend on each step.

Analyze _____
Plan _____
Write _____
Review _____

Test-Taker's Toolkit

1. ANALYZE THE PROMPT

A. **Read the prompt** carefully to get a clear idea of what this prompt requires.

B. **Note key words** that tell you exactly what you must do. The writing form has been circled for you. Underline the topic. Double-underline the elements your essay must include.

2. PLAN YOUR RESPONSE

Create an outline of what you must include in your essay. You may want to organize your ideas this way: in the first paragraph, state your claim and briefly summarize your three reasons. Then write one paragraph for each supporting detail. In your concluding paragraph, sum up your essay.

Claim:

Supporting Detail:

Supporting Detail:

Supporting Detail:

Conclusion:

3. WRITE AND REVIEW

A. **Craft an essay body** that contains all necessary details. Each paragraph in the body should state the main idea in a topic sentence. The other sentences should support the main idea. Try writing the topic sentence for your first paragraph here:

_____
_____
_____

B. **Add an introduction and conclusion** to the body of your essay. Then rewrite your full response on a second sheet of paper. Be sure to leave time to check your spelling and grammar.

RELATED NONFICTION 203

UNIT 8

INFORMATION, ARGUMENT, AND PERSUASION

LESSON 8B

Remarks at the Dedication of the Aerospace Medical Health Center

BY JOHN F. KENNEDY

RELATED NONFICTION
Inventions Inspired by Apollo

What INSPIRES people?

It's sometimes hard to do the right thing, especially if you feel as if you're doing it all alone. Every once in a while, a leader emerges who can inspire people to join together to help make our society the best it can be. You're about to read a speech by one such leader—President John F. Kennedy. He helped the country realize that we should reach as far as outer space to achieve greatness.

CHART IT Think of three things people can do to make the world a better place. Jot down your ideas in the first column of the chart. In the second column, write ideas for how you would inspire people to do these things.

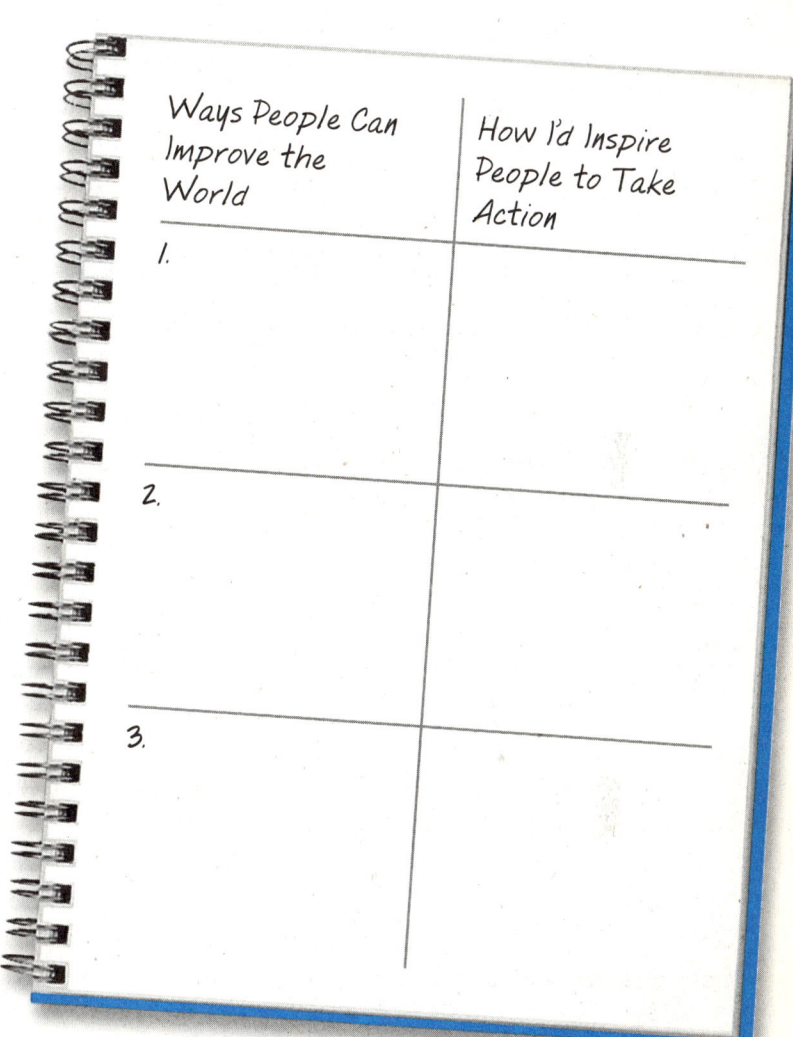

Ways People Can Improve the World	How I'd Inspire People to Take Action
1.	
2.	
3.	

ASSESSMENT GOALS

By the end of this lesson, you will be able to...
- analyze argument and persuasion in a speech
- apply critical thinking skills to analyze text
- analyze patterns of organization
- analyze a writing prompt and plan a persuasive essay

LEARN THE TERMS: ACADEMIC VOCABULARY

Argument and Persuasion

When you hear the word *argument*, you might think of a fight between two people, complete with angry shouting and hurt feelings. In formal speaking and writing, however, an **ARGUMENT** is a claim supported by reasons and evidence.

A **CLAIM** is a writer's position on a problem or an issue. The strength of an argument depends not on the claim but on the **SUPPORT**, or the reasons and evidence that are used to prove the claim. Evidence can include facts, statistics, and examples. Speakers and writers also use **PERSUASIVE TECHNIQUES** to get people to agree with their claim. This chart lists several persuasive techniques.

APPEALS BY ASSOCIATION
Link an idea or a product to something or someone positive or influential

▼

BANDWAGON APPEAL
Taps into people's desire to belong

> See the movie and discover the surprise ending that everybody's talking about.

TESTIMONIAL
Uses celebrities or satisfied customers to persuade

> As an Olympic athlete, I need all the energy I can get. That's why I drink Quench-Ade.

TRANSFER
Connects a product, a candidate, or a cause with a positive image or idea

> A vote for Proposition 43 is a vote for freedom.

EMOTIONAL APPEALS
Use strong feelings, rather than facts, to persuade

▼

APPEAL TO PITY
Taps into people's compassion for others

> Won't you give this abandoned puppy a home?

APPEAL TO FEAR
Preys upon people's fear for their safety

> Is your home safe? ProAlarm Systems—because you shouldn't take any chances.

APPEAL TO VANITY
Uses flattery to win people over

> Bring your creativity and intelligence to our team. Join the yearbook staff!

ADDITIONAL TERMS FOR CRITICAL ANALYSIS

RHETORICAL DEVICES are persuasive techniques writers and speakers use to enhance their arguments. Rhetorical devices include the following:

- **REPETITION:** when a sound, word, phrase, or idea is repeated for emphasis
- **PARALLELISM:** the use of similar wording or grammatical constructions to express related ideas
- **ANALOGY:** a comparison between two things that are alike in some way

Remarks at the Dedication of the Aerospace Medical Health Center

President John F. Kennedy

BACKGROUND In 1957, the country then known as the Soviet Union launched *Sputnik I*, the first satellite to orbit the earth. After becoming president in 1961, Kennedy was determined that America must beat the Soviets in the "space race." He made the following speech on November 21, 1963—the day before he was assassinated.

Mr. Secretary, Governor, Mr. Vice President, Senator, Members of the Congress, members of the military, ladies and gentlemen:

For more than 3 years I have spoken about the New Frontier. This is not a **partisan** term, and it is not the exclusive property of Republicans or Democrats. It refers, instead, to this Nation's place in history, to the fact that we do stand on the edge of a great new era, filled with both crisis and opportunity, an era to be characterized by achievement and by challenge. It is an era which calls for action and for the best efforts of all those who would test the unknown and the uncertain in every phase of human **endeavor**. It is a time for pathfinders and pioneers.

I have come to Texas today to salute an outstanding group of pioneers, the men who man the Brooks Air Force Base School of Aerospace Medicine and the Aerospace Medical Center. It is fitting that San Antonio should be the site of this center and this school as we gather to dedicate this complex of buildings. For this city has long been the home of the pioneers in the air. It was here that Sidney Brooks, whose memory we honor today, was born and raised. It was here that Charles Lindbergh and Claire Chennault,[1] and a host of others, who, in World War I and World War II and Korea, and even today have helped demonstrate American mastery of the skies, trained at Kelly Field and Randolph Field,[2] which form a major part of aviation history. And in the new frontier of outer space, while headlines may be made by others in other places, history is being made every day by the men and women of the Aerospace Medical Center, without whom there could be no history.

Many Americans make the mistake of assuming that space research has no values here on earth. Nothing could be further from the truth. Just as the wartime development of **radar** gave us the transistor, and all that it made possible, so research in space medicine holds the promise of substantial benefit for those of us who are earthbound. For our effort in space is not, as some have suggested, a competitor for the natural resources that we need to develop the earth. It is a working partner and a coproducer of these resources. And nothing makes this clearer than the fact that medicine in space is going to make our lives healthier and happier here on earth.

---

1. **Sidney Brooks...Charles Lindbergh...Claire Chennault** (shən-ôlt'): Sidney Brooks was a young flyer killed in a training accident. Charles Lindbergh was the first transatlantic solo pilot, and Claire Chennault was an important figure in the development of air-war theories.
2. **Kelly Field and Randolph Field:** airfields in the San Antonio area where many military pilots were trained.

I give you three examples: first, medical space research may open up new understanding of man's relation to his environment. Examinations of the astronaut's physical, and mental, and emotional reactions can teach us more about the differences between normal and abnormal, about the causes and effects of <u>disorientation</u>, about changes in <u>metabolism</u> which could result in extending the life span. When you study the effects on our astronauts of exhaust gases which can contaminate their environment, and you seek ways to alter these gases so as to reduce their toxicity, you are working on problems similar to those we face in our great urban centers which themselves are being corrupted by gases and which must be clear. ▶

And second, medical space research may revolutionize the technology and the techniques of modern medicine. Whatever new devices are created, for example, to monitor our astronauts, to measure their heart activity, their breathing, their brain waves, their eye motion, at great distances and under difficult conditions, will also represent a major advance in general medical instrumentation. Heart patients may even be able to wear a light monitor which will sound a warning if their activity exceeds certain limits. An instrument recently developed to record automatically the impact of acceleration upon an astronaut's eyes will also be of help to small children who are suffering miserably from eye defects, but are unable to describe their <u>impairment</u>. And also by the use of instruments similar to those used in Project Mercury, this Nation's private as well as public nursing services are being improved, enabling one nurse now to give more critically ill patients greater attention than they ever could in the past.

---

disorientation (dĭs-ôr′ē-ĕn-tā′shən) *n.* mental confusion or impaired awareness

metabolism (mĭ-tăb′ə-lĭz′əm) *n.* all the processes a living thing uses to continue to grow and live

💡 TestSmart

According to President Kennedy, which of the following is *not* a benefit of medical space research?

- **A** It can find new uses for radar.
- **B** It can help explain disorientation.
- **C** It can teach us about changes in metabolism.
- **D** It can lead to cleaner exhaust gases.

TIP Answer choices may contain vocabulary that is not familiar to you. However, it's not always necessary to have a perfect understanding of the words in order to pick the correct answer. For example, to answer this question, **scan the text** and look for **key words** such as *radar, disorientation, metabolism,* and *exhaust.* When you locate them, reread the sentences in which the words are used. The important thing to figure out is whether or not the benefits come from space research.

impairment (ĭm-pâr′mənt) *n.* the condition of being damaged, injured, or harmed

REMARKS AT THE DEDICATION OF THE AEROSPACE MEDICAL HEALTH CENTER

ANALYZE

Reread the sentence in lines 43–45. Then underline two sentences in lines 56–79 that have a **parallel structure** to it.

What ideas does the **parallelism** in these sentences emphasize?

_____
_____
_____
_____

impetus (ĭm′pĭ-təs) *n.* a driving force; a motivation

tedious (tē′dē-əs) *adj.* tiresome; boring

And third, medical space research may lead to new safeguards against hazards common to many environments. Specifically, our astronauts will need fundamentally new devices to protect them from the ill effects of radiation which can have a profound influence upon medicine and man's relations to our present environment. ◀

80 Here at this center we have the laboratories, the talent, the resources to give new **impetus** to vital research in the life centers. I am not suggesting that the entire space program is justified alone by what is done in medicine. The space program stands on its own as a contribution to national strength. And last Saturday at Cape Canaveral I saw our new Saturn C-1 rocket booster,[3] which, with its payload,[4] when it rises in December of this year, will be, for the first time, the largest booster in the world, carrying into space the largest payload that any country in the world has ever sent into space.

90 I think the United States should be a leader. A country as rich and powerful as this which bears so many burdens and responsibilities, which has so many opportunities, should be second to none. And in December, while I do not regard our mastery of space as anywhere near complete, while I recognize that there are still areas where we are behind—at least in one area, the size of the booster—this year I hope the United States will be ahead. And I am for it. We have a long way to go. Many weeks and months and years of long, **tedious** work lie ahead. There will be setbacks and frustrations and 100 disappointments. There will be, as there always are, pressures in this country to do less in this area as in so many others, and temptations to do something else that is perhaps easier. But this research here must go on. This space effort must go on. The conquest of space must and will go ahead. That

---

3. **booster:** a rocket used to launch a spacecraft.
4. **payload:** the load carried by a rocket or other vehicle.

210 UNIT 8B: INFORMATION, ARGUMENT, AND PERSUASION

much we know. That much we can say with confidence and conviction. ▶

Frank O'Connor, the Irish writer, tells in one of his books how, as a boy, he and his friends would make their way across the countryside, and when they came to an orchard wall that seemed too high and too doubtful to try and too difficult to permit their voyage to continue, they took off their hats and tossed them over the wall—and then they had no choice but to follow them.

This Nation has tossed its cap over the wall of space, and we have no choice but to follow it. Whatever the difficulties, they will be overcome. Whatever the hazards, they must be guarded against. With the vital help of this Aerospace Medical Center, with the help of all those who labor in the space endeavor, with the help and support of all Americans, we will climb this wall with safety and with speed—and we shall then explore the wonders on the other side.

Thank you. ▶

TestSmart

VOCABULARY
What does the word *conviction* mean in line 106?

- A a punishment
- B a guilty verdict
- C a strong nation
- D a strong belief

TIP Vocabulary tests often ask questions about **multiple-meaning words.** Since you won't always know which words have more than one definition, make sure to reread the sentence in which the tested word appears. For example, to answer this question, reread the sentence in which *conviction* appears. If you are familiar with a definition of *conviction*, does that definition make sense in this context? If not, try the other definitions offered.

ANALYZE
What **persuasive technique** does Kennedy use in the last paragraph of the speech?

_____

_____

Big Question
Do you think President Kennedy's speech was inspiring? Why or why not? **MAKE JUDGMENTS**

_____

_____

_____

Assessment Practice 1

Reading Comprehension

DIRECTIONS *Answer these questions about "Remarks at the Dedication of the Aerospace Medical Health Center" by filling in the correct ovals.*

1. By describing space researchers as "pathfinders and pioneers," what persuasive technique is President Kennedy using?
   - A testimonial
   - B transfer
   - C appeal to pity
   - D appeal to fear

2. In lines 31–36, President Kennedy uses the wartime development of radar to support the idea that
   - A competitors can work together
   - B natural resources can be developed
   - C one development can lead to another
   - D space medicine can help the earthbound

3. According to President Kennedy, which of the following might result from medical space research on environmental hazards?
   - A a cure for eye disease
   - B protection from radiation
   - C improved nursing services
   - D better medical instruments

4. President Kennedy uses Frank O'Connor's story (lines 107–121) as what type of rhetorical device?
   - A analogy
   - B repetition
   - C alliteration
   - D parallelism

5. What sentences in the last paragraph of President Kennedy's speech are parallel?
   - A sentences 1 and 2
   - B sentences 2 and 3
   - C sentences 3 and 4
   - D sentences 1 and 4

6. The main claim President Kennedy argues in his speech is that
   - A medical research is a new frontier
   - B medical space research will improve technology
   - C the Aerospace Medical Center belongs in San Antonio
   - D the United States should lead the world in space exploration

7. What does the word *exclusive* mean in line 6?
   - A sole
   - B shared
   - C expensive
   - D honorary

8. What does the word *endeavor* mean in line 119?
   - A effort
   - B difficulty
   - C hazard
   - D support

Responding in Writing

*For help, use the **Test-Taker's Toolkit** below.*

9. Short Response Which persuasive technique does President Kennedy use most effectively? In a few sentences, identify this technique and give two examples of its use in this speech.

___

Test-Taker's Toolkit

ACADEMIC VOCABULARY When you are asked to identify a speaker's **persuasive techniques,** look for instances in which he or she is trying to sway people's feelings or actions. Then decide which appeal by association or emotional appeal is most effective.

GRAPHIC ORGANIZER Use a chart like the one below to help you plan your response.

PERSUASIVE TECHNIQUE:	
Example 1	Example 2

Related Nonfiction

Inventions Inspired by Apollo
ONLINE ARTICLE

Use with "Remarks at the Dedication of the Aerospace Medical Health Center," p. 204

What's the Connection?

In his speech, President Kennedy spoke of how space research could someday benefit people on Earth. The online article "Inventions Inspired by Apollo" shows that Kennedy was right—many things invented for the Apollo space crew have developed into products we use today.

INVENT IT Invent a product that would make your everyday life easier. Describe the invention below and the problem it would help you solve. Then take an informal poll of your classmates to see if they would find your invention useful. Tally their responses in the chart shown.

My invention: _____

What problem would this help me solve? _____

Classmates who would use my invention	Classmates who wouldn't use my invention

LEARN THE SKILL: ANALYZE PATTERNS OF ORGANIZATION

When you analyze a text's **pattern of organization,** you look at how the ideas and information are arranged. This will help you to understand what you read and to determine a text's most important ideas and details.

Problem-solution organization is one common pattern of organization. In a text that uses problem-solution organization, ideas are arranged in the following way:

- A **problem** is stated and analyzed.
- One or more **solutions** to the problem are described.

Sometimes the pattern of presenting problems and solutions will repeat itself within a single nonfiction text.

For more on analyzing patterns of organization, see *Nonfiction Handbook* pages R15 and R17.

CLOSE READ

SET A PURPOSE
My purpose for reading is
_____
_____
_____

Inventions Inspired by Apollo

by Gloria Chang

When US president John F. Kennedy boldly stated on May 25, 1961 that his country would send a man to the Moon by the end of the decade, it seemed an impossible feat. At the time, only one American had flown in space—less than a month earlier—and the country had not yet sent a man into orbit. But, motivated by a competition with the Soviet Union during the Cold War, Kennedy set the wheels of invention in motion. The effort to send a man to the Moon was labeled the Apollo program, and it triggered a massive burst of technological creativity. Some of the materials and technologies that were developed to take a three-man crew to the Moon have spun off into products we use everyday. The Apollo program has not only enriched our understanding of the world, it has also enhanced life in it. Here's a look at some of the inventions inspired by the Apollo missions.

AN INSIDE LOOK AT THE HUMAN BODY

When NASA was preparing for the first lunar landing, engineers weren't just thinking about how to get a man to the surface of the Moon. They were also thinking about how they could get the best pictures once they got there. Scientists at the Jet Propulsion Laboratory in Pasadena, California developed a technology called digital image processing. This technology allowed them to

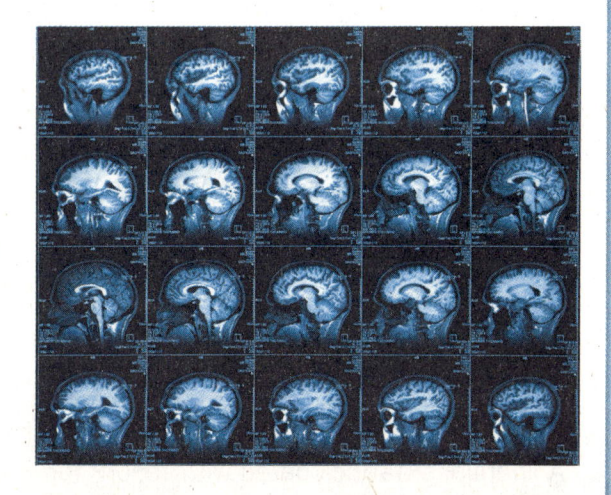

RELATED NONFICTION 215

PATTERNS OF ORGANIZATION

The section "An Inside Look at the Human Body" describes a problem that NASA was trying to solve, a solution to the problem, and how that solution was applied to life on Earth. Underline each element and label them *P*, *S*, and *A*.

MAKE INFERENCES

Reread the section "Cordless Tools and Appliances." What was a key technological advance that made the battery-powered drill possible? Circle the answer in the text.

Why is this an important feature for space travel?

_____

_____

_____

---

enhance pictures of the Moon with computers, giving us detailed images of the Moon. Today, this technology is used by doctors around the world to take photos of the human body. Two of the most well known and commonly used are computer-aided tomography (CATScan), and Magnetic Resonance Imaging (MRI). While CATScans are good for seeing bone, MRIs are used to image soft tissue. Both help doctors diagnose a wide range of illnesses. ◀

CORDLESS TOOLS AND APPLIANCES

Photos took care of surface studies of the Moon, but scientists wanted a core sample to bring back to Earth to analyze. This required drilling into the Moon as deep as ten feet. The drill also had to be lightweight and compact. Most importantly, it had to have its own source of power so that the astronauts could take samples from a variety of locations, including some far away from the spaceship. NASA chose Black and Decker for the job, a manufacturing company in Towson, Maryland that met the challenge with a battery-operated drill. A key technological advance was a computer program used to design the drill's motor so that it used as little power as possible. That program, along with the general knowledge and experience gained from developing the lunar drill, provided the technology for the company to become a household name as a maker of battery-powered tools and appliances. ◀

MOONSUIT ROOFS

What should the astronauts wear? It wasn't a question about fashion, but of durability and flexibility. To work in space, Apollo astronauts needed a suit that was lightweight and flexible so that they could move easily, but strong enough to withstand the extreme conditions of space. A fiberglass[1] fabric coated with Teflon[2] for added strength met NASA

---

1. **fiberglass:** a material made of very fine glass fibers, used to make structural objects or parts.
2. **Teflon:** the trade name for a material with a durable nonstick surface.

specifications. Soon after, the technology found its way onto the roofs of sports stadiums and shopping malls as well. Pound for pound, the moonsuit fabric is stronger than steel, but weighs 1/30th as much as a conventional roof of the same size. It's also cheaper. It lets in light but reflects heat, which reduces lighting and cooling costs.

THE SKIN OF THE MOON

Take a close look at the surface of the moon through a telescope, and you'll see craters, boulders, furrows, hills and valleys. If you look at your own skin through a microscope, you'll see that you have the same features. In the early days of the Apollo program, NASA used unmanned satellites[3] orbiting the Moon to photograph possible landing sites for its astronauts. But getting a detailed look was tough. Unlike Earth, the Moon doesn't have an atmosphere to filter the light. That makes

---

3. **satellite:** a manufactured object or vehicle intended to orbit the earth, the Moon, or something else in space.

THE APOLLO MISSIONS

On May 25, 1961, President John F. Kennedy announced that the United States had a new goal: to send astronauts to the moon within a decade. According to the National Aeronautics and Space Administration (NASA), Kennedy's "bold challenge set the nation on a journey unlike any before in human history."

The Apollo missions were made up of 17 different flights into space. Apollo 1, the first of the missions, was delayed when a fire erupted inside the still-grounded spacecraft, killing all three astronauts inside. The next several missions were unmanned, but Apollo 7 and its three-man crew orbited the earth successfully.

The next three Apollo missions carried out lunar research, and then, on July 20, 1969, a nation's dream was realized. Apollo 11 commander Neil A. Armstrong became the first man to walk on the moon. "That's one small step for man," Armstrong famously intoned from the moon's surface, "one giant leap for mankind."

Five more missions—Apollos 12, 14, 15, 16, and 17—went on to make successful lunar landings. All in all, 12 American astronauts walked on the moon during the course of the Apollo missions.

PATTERNS OF ORGANIZATION

Identify the problem, solution, and application on Earth that are presented in lines 52–68.

Problem:
_____
_____

Solution:
_____
_____

Application:
_____
_____

TestSmart

Humans first walked on the moon during Apollo Mission

(A) 1 (C) 7
(B) 11 (D) 17

TIP It can be difficult to remember all the facts mentioned in a passage. If you are asked about a specific fact, **refer back to the text** to make sure you select the correct answer. In this case, scan the sidebar "The Apollo Missions" and look for the key words *walk on the moon*. This will help you identify the correct mission.

the Moon's shadows look different from the shadows on Earth. By enhancing the photos with image processing software, scientists were able to "decode" the lunar shadow patterns. Cosmetic firms now use the same software to test their skin products. "Before" and "after" pictures of skin treated with a skin care product will show if they are effective or not.

EMERGENCY RESCUE

You've seen them being used to get injured people out of serious car accidents. Sometimes called the "Jaws of Life," the tool cuts the doors and roofs of cars to get victims out—fast. But tools like these are usually powered by hydraulic[4] pumps. Hydraulic pumps are powered by gasoline engines, which can take a long time to set up. So how do you speed up the process? Think of the space shuttle. Minutes after lift off, two solid rocket boosters separate from the rest of the vehicle. Bolts that hold the boosters in place are designed to explode, releasing the boosters in the process. Hi-Shear Technology Corporation of Torrance, California, the company who developed the exploding bolts, made a miniature version to power the metal-cutting tools. Using small explosive charges, the rescue cutters take only 30 seconds to set up, shaving off precious time that can make the difference between life and death. ▶

---

4. **hydraulic:** operated by the pressure that results when liquid is forced through a small opening or tube.

DRAW CONCLUSIONS

Why is it important for the directors of a space mission to view the moon's surface accurately?

_____
_____
_____

SPACE TECHNOLOGY SPINOFFS

Since the Apollo program, space technology continues to have spinoff benefits in our everyday world. Freeze dried food was the answer to creating meals that could stay fresh for long periods of time in space.

120 Smoke detectors were first used in the Earth-orbiting space station called Skylab to help detect toxic vapours. Kidney dialysis[5] machines were developed as a result of a chemical process that could remove toxic waste from used dialysis fluid. A new molding process used to make space helmets is what led to the shock-absorbing materials on athletic shoes, forever changing the shoes' design. The list goes on. What started as a seemingly impossible challenge spawned countless innovations we now take for granted. US president John F. Kennedy launched the Apollo program, saying: "No single space project in this period will be more impressive to mankind, or more important in

130 the long-range exploration of space; and none will be so difficult or expensive to accomplish." And so it was. ▶

---

5. **dialysis** (dī-ăl′ĭ-sis): a method of removing toxic substances from the blood when the kidneys are unable to do so.

MAKE JUDGMENTS

Does this article change your opinion about the importance of space research? Explain why or why not.

Assessment Practice II

Reading Comprehension

DIRECTIONS *Answer these questions about the two selections in this lesson by filling in the correct ovals.*

1. Battery-powered tools and appliances developed as a result of astronauts' need to
   - A drill down into the moon's core
   - B examine the moon's surface
   - C separate rocket boosters from a spaceship
   - D withstand the extreme conditions of space

2. Teflon is a valuable invention on Earth because of its ability to
   - A polarize harmful light
   - B replace steel in buildings
   - C accurately process images
   - D provide a lightweight protective surface

3. What is the problem identified in the section "The Skin of the Moon"?
   - A The shape of the Moon is changing.
   - B There are no safe landing sites on the Moon.
   - C The Moon's surface has many boulders and craters.
   - D Scientists couldn't accurately interpret photos of the Moon.

4. Which item allowed the "Jaws of Life" to become a more effective rescue tool?
   - A hydraulic pumps
   - B gasoline engines
   - C small explosive charges
   - D two solid rocket boosters

5. What pattern of organization is repeated in most sections of the article?
   - A problem/solution/application
   - B first problem/resulting problem/solution
   - C problem/attempted solution/final solution
   - D problem in space/problem on Earth/joint application

6. Which invention supports Kennedy's claim that medical space research will help people lead healthier lives?
   - A Teflon
   - B moonsuits
   - C freeze-dried foods
   - D kidney dialysis machines

7. What does the word *enhance* mean in line 28?
   - A improve
   - B distort
   - C notice
   - D enrich

8. The word *tomography* in line 31 is related to the root
   - A *morph*, meaning "change"
   - B *graph*, meaning "write"
   - C *gram*, meaning "letter"
   - D *geo*, meaning "earth"

UNIT 8B: INFORMATION, ARGUMENT, AND PERSUASION

Timed Writing Practice

PROMPT

What inspires people to work for positive change in the world? Write a persuasive essay in which you try to inspire people to work for a cause you think is important. Include facts and examples as evidence to support your ideas.

BUDGET YOUR TIME

You have 45 minutes to complete this assignment. Decide how much time to spend on each step.

Analyze _____
Plan _____
Write _____
Review _____

Test-Taker's Toolkit

1. ANALYZE THE PROMPT

A. **Read the prompt** carefully to make sure you understand it.
B. **Underline** the type of writing you are being asked to do.
C. **Circle key words** that tell you what you need to include to get a good score.

2. PLAN YOUR RESPONSE

A. **Choose a topic** List several problems that need attention, such as pollution, violence, or poverty. Select a topic you feel strongly about.

B. **Make notes** Think of reasons and evidence you can use to support your topic. For example, if your topic is recycling, note three reasons why recycling can make a positive change in the world. For each reason, think of facts or examples that can help you convince your readers to recycle.

C. **Organize your information** Use a planning chart like the one shown here to help you organize your ideas. You could write an introduction that states your cause and why it's important. Then you could write a paragraph for each reason, including related evidence. End with a conclusion that makes a call to action.

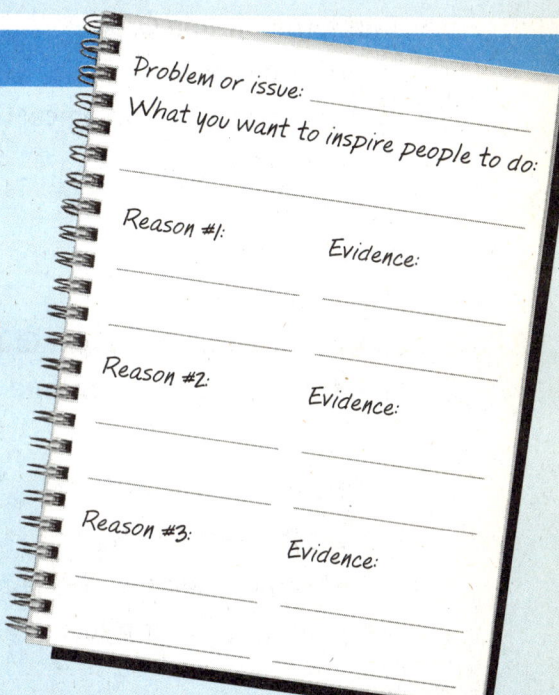

Problem or issue: _____
What you want to inspire people to do: _____

Reason #1: _____   Evidence: _____
Reason #2: _____   Evidence: _____
Reason #3: _____   Evidence: _____

3. WRITE AND REVIEW

A. **Write a powerful opening sentence** that will appeal to your readers' emotions. Reread the descriptions of emotional appeals on page 206 for ideas.

B. **Compose your full response** on a separate sheet of paper. Leave enough time to read through it and make sure you have met all the requirements of the prompt.

RELATED NONFICTION

Student Handbooks

Nonfiction Skills Handbook

Author's Credibility or Bias	R3
Author's Perspective	R4
Author's Purpose	R5
Cause-and-Effect Order	R6
Charts and Other Graphic Aids	R7
Classification Order	R8
Compare-and-Contrast Order	R9
Electronic Texts	R10
Evaluate Support	R11
Evaluate Usefulness	R12
Forms of Nonfiction Texts	R13
Main Ideas and Supporting Details	R14
Patterns of Organization	R15
Problem-Solution Order	R17
Rhetorical Devices	R18
Sequence and Chronological Order	R19
Spatial Order	R20
Synthesize	R21
Text Features	R22
Textbooks	R23
Transitions and Other Text Clues	R24
Treatment, Organization, and Scope of Ideas	R25

Test-Taking Handbook

Successful Test Taking	R26
Functional Reading Tests	R30
Revising-and-Editing Tests	R34

Nonfiction Skills Handbook

Author's Credibility or Bias

ACADEMIC VOCABULARY

author: the person who wrote a book or an article or who created a Web page; some texts do not name an individual but only an organization

bias: an inclination for or against a particular person, group, topic, or issue

credibility: the knowledge and trustworthiness of an author

loaded words: words that show bias because of their intensely positive or negative associations

STEP 1 **Look for the name of the author or authors.** Get in the habit of asking who wrote a piece. If there is no name—individual or organization, credited for the work, then no one is responsible, or accountable for factual, truthful content. It may not be credible. Look in the following places for a name:

- **Book:** on the cover or title page
- **Article** or **periodical:** at the beginning or end of the text
- **Web site:** on the home page or "contact" page

STEP 2 **Examine the author's credibility.** To examine **credibility** means to determine if the author has enough **knowledge** to write factually and accurately, and whether the author has **balance** or **bias,** is truthful and fair, or leans toward one belief or interest.

- **Background:** First, look for information about the author (for example, "Director, Excelsior University Museum of Art"). If you don't see any information given with the author's name, try a reference book, such as *Current Biography*, or try a search engine.
- **Knowledge:** As you read about an author, ask yourself: Does the author have direct experience with the topic? What are the author's credentials—recognition and achievement such as, education, training, experiences, job title, and publishing record?
- **Bias:** As you read an author's work, ask yourself: Does the author make direct statements or give hints about opinions, beliefs and interests? Is the author well-regarded? Does the author work for a group that advocates a certain position? Does the author use loaded words?

  EXAMPLE
  "The electoral college has served us well."

STEP 3 **Evaluate the usefulness and importance of the work.** In light of the author's credibility, ask yourself whether you should discount the piece, rely on it as a source, or get the viewpoint of another author.

Author's Perspective

ACADEMIC VOCABULARY

background: facts about an author's experience and knowledge

bias: an author's preference or slant on a particular topic

perspective: the way an author looks at a topic

selective details: information an author includes—and decides not to include—in a text

word choice: the words an author uses to create a specific effect on readers

STEP 1 **Identify the author.** Look for the author's name and any additional information about the person. This usually can be found at the beginning or end of a text, sometimes set off as a separate feature. Ask the following questions for clues about the author's experiences, values, and beliefs:

- What does the author's name suggest about the person's sex and possibly nationality?
- What is the author's education? Did he or she earn degrees from a respected institution?
- What do the author's activities, responsibilities, and publications say about his or her reliability?

STEP 2 **Examine the text for clues to the author's point of view.** Carefully read the text, looking for indications of the author's point of view. Focus on:

- **word choice**—words with strong positive or negative emotional associations, or connotations
- **selective details**—facts and opinions that support a specific point of view
- **biased language**—statements that reveal a one-sided belief
- **direct statements**—clear admissions of point of view, often beginning with the words "I believe" or "In my opinion"

Then record specific instances of these elements in a chart like the one below:

TYPE OF EVIDENCE	SPECIFIC INSTANCE
word choice selective details biased language direct statements	

STEP 3 **Identify the author's perspective.** Review the evidence you entered in your chart and ask yourself, "What does this information tell me about the author's point of view on the topic?" Then write a sentence describing that point of view. Finally, read through the text again, keeping the author's perspective in mind. Write down questions, comments, or counterevidence that occurs to you as you read. Take this information into account as you evaluate the reliability or usefulness of the text.

Author's Purpose

> **ACADEMIC VOCABULARY**
> **author's purpose:** the reason(s) an author has for writing a particular work

STEP 1 **Learn common purposes.** Keep the four common author purposes in mind as you read: to explain or inform, to persuade, to entertain, and to express emotion and ideas.

STEP 2 **Identify clues to author's purpose.** As you read a text, look for clues in the work's title, subject, and tone; the choice of details and words; the context, or intended audience; the effects on you as a reader; and the pattern of organization or structure. There are some common match-ups between text structure and purpose, but beware that there are no firm rules.

> **EXAMPLE**
> **Sequence, cause-effect,** or **main idea and details** are often used to explain or to inform.
>
> **Problem-solution, proposition-support,** or **compare-contrast** order may signal that the author's purpose is to persuade.
>
> **Chronological order** is often used in dramatic histories or storytelling and may signal that the purpose is to entertain.
>
> **Order of degree** or **spatial order** may be used to express emotion.

STEP 3 **Infer the author's main purpose.** Review the clues and recall the common purposes. Decide what is *most likely* the main purpose the author has for the writing. Check your answer by ruling out the other purposes.

STEP 4 **Use purpose to evaluate the work.** Evaluate the piece in light of the author's purpose: How well did the passage achieve the goal? How well were you entertained, informed, persuaded, or instructed?

Cause-and-Effect Order

> **ACADEMIC VOCABULARY**
> **cause-and-effect order:** a method of organizing ideas and information in an essay that shows causal relationships
> **cause:** why something happens
> **effect:** a result; what happened as an outcome of the cause

STEP 1 Look for effects. Ask: "What was the outcome?" Check for multiple effects.

> **EXAMPLE**
> Because Harry left the cage open, the canary escaped and flew around the room.

STEP 2 Look for causes. Ask: "Why did it happen?" Check for multiple causes.

> **EXAMPLE**
> Because Harry left the cage open and never noticed, the canary escaped.

STEP 3 Check for cause-effect chains. A cause can lead to an effect that then causes another effect, and so on. A series of such linked events is a cause-effect chain.

> **EXAMPLE**
> Harry left the cage open, allowing the canary to escape. As a result, Harry chased the bird around the room for an hour.

STEP 4 Find signal words. Signal words and phrases for cause and effect include: *because, since, as a result, therefore,* and *due to.*

> **EXAMPLE**
> I forgot to study, and as a result, I didn't do very well on the quiz.

STEP 5 Use a Graphic Organizer. Arrange ideas in a cause-and-effect diagram or chain.

> **EXAMPLE**
>
> | Cause: Angel oversleeps. | → | Effect: Angel misses bus. |

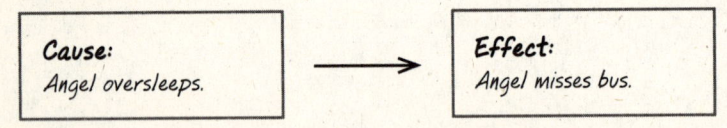

STEP 6 Check your logic. The cause must spark, or set in motion the result. They do not have to be presented in sequence. In many sentences, the effect appears first.

> **EXAMPLE**
> Angel missed the bus due to oversleeping.

Charts and Other Graphic Aids

> **ACADEMIC VOCABULARY**
>
> **bar graph:** a coordinate grid with shaded bars, used to compare amounts or levels in various categories
>
> **chart:** a table, displaying information in rows and columns or in boxes
>
> **diagram:** a sketch or plan designed to explain how something works or to show the relationship of parts to the whole
>
> **illustration:** usually a drawing designed to explain a concept or to show relationships of parts to the whole
>
> **map:** a drawing of a region of the earth, showing the location of places
>
> **pie chart/circle graph:** a circle divided into sliced sections, measured to represent percentages of a whole

STEP 1 **Read the title.** Ask yourself: What information does the graphic aid display? Does the title include time periods, locations, ages, or other details about the subject?

STEP 2 **Study the data.** Read all the headings, labels, and captions. Make sure you understand any symbols or abbreviations. Look at the lines, bars, slices, row and column heads, and other labels. Try comparing just two bars, points, rows, or slices to be sure you understand the information in a chart or graph. Ask yourself: what question might be answered from this display?

STEP 3 **Draw conclusions.** Decide why the information in the graphic aid is useful and how it could be used. Ask yourself:
- What can I conclude from the information in the graphic aid?
- Which data allow me to make that conclusion?
- What further information would be helpful?
- What new questions arise from learning this data?

Classification Order

> **ACADEMIC VOCABULARY**
> **classification order:** a pattern of organization in which objects, ideas, and/or information are presented in groups, or classes, based on common characteristics

STEP 1 **Look for words and phrases that signal groups.** Words and phrases writers use to indicate a subject's class include *group, category, kind, set, type, class, classification, division, divided into,* and *common characteristics*. Notice how many groups there are.

STEP 2 **Look for how classes or groups are defined.** What do each of these objects, ideas, or facts have in common? What qualities or attributes unite the items in each group?

STEP 3 **Look for subgroups.** Under each of your major groups or classes, are there other items that share common attributes with each other?

STEP 4 **Write categories and subcategories in a graphic organizer.** A classification organizer like the one shown can help you keep track of the major groups and subgroups mentioned in the text. Recognizing classification order can help you understand the relationships between ideas and details and help you remember important information.

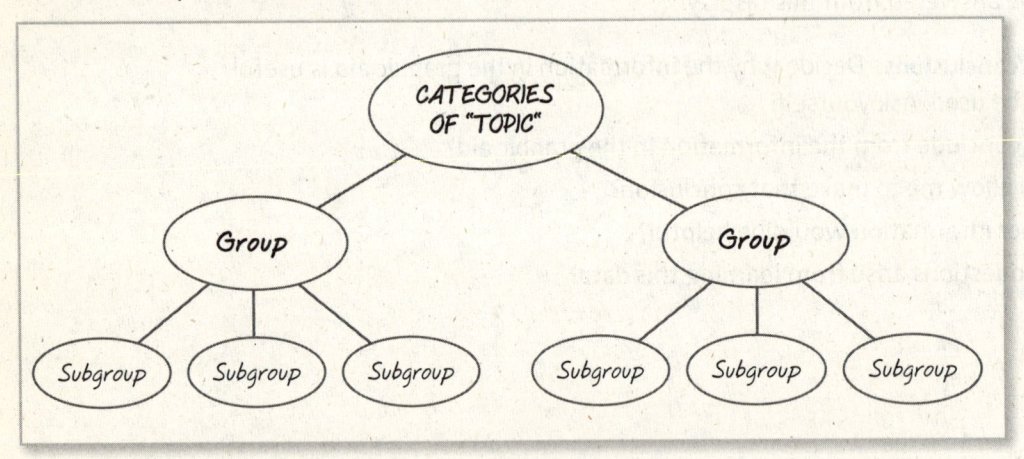

```
                CATEGORIES
                OF "TOPIC"
               /          \
           Group          Group
          / | \          / | \
    Subgroup Subgroup Subgroup   Subgroup Subgroup Subgroup
```

R8 INTERACTIVE READER & WRITER

Compare-and-Contrast Order

> **ACADEMIC VOCABULARY**
>
> **compare-and-contrast order:** organization of writing to show the similarities and differences between two or more subjects.
>
> **feature-by-feature:** a text pattern in which a writer compares and contrasts two subjects one feature or characteristic at a time.
>
> **subject-by-subject:** a text pattern in which a writer presents the features of one subject first, then moves on to features of a second subject, showing how they are alike and different.

STEP 1 **Look for signal words and phrases:**

- **Similarities:** To **compare** subjects, writers use words and phrases such as *like, likewise, both, similarly, are similar* and *neither*.
- **Differences:** To **contrast** subjects, writers use words and phrases such as *unlike, in contrast, different from,* and *on the other hand*.

STEP 2 **Identify the subjects being compared or contrasted.** Usually the subjects have similar characteristics. They may be works in one genre or items in one category.

STEP 3 **Identify the pattern.** Does the text use feature-by-feature or subject-by-subject order?

Subject-by-subject	Feature-by-feature
Subject A 　Feature 1 　Feature 2	Feature 1 　Subject A 　Subject B
Subject B 　Feature 1 　Feature 2	Feature 2 　Subject A 　Subject B

STEP 4 **Organize similarities and differences in a graphic.** Use a Venn diagram or other graphic to take notes on the similarities and differences described in the text.

Electronic Texts

> **ACADEMIC VOCABULARY**
>
> **credits and sponsor:** information about the creator of an electronic text
>
> **home page:** opening or main page of an electronic text that gives introductory information and links to other features included in the text
>
> **icons:** pictures that you can click on to perform a function or access information in the text
>
> **menus and hyperlinks:** drop-down lists or highlighted or underlined words in an electronic text that you can click on to move to another page of related information
>
> **URL:** Universal Resource Locator, address of an electronic text on the World Wide Web

STEP 1 **Analyze the features of the Website.** Before gathering information from an electronic text, or Website, familiarize yourself with its features. Identify and ask yourself questions about the following elements:

- **URL**—Look at the address of the Website in the locator box on your search engine. What clues does the address give you about the sponsor and purpose of the site? Websites whose addresses end in *.gov* or *.edu* usually publish reliable information.
- **Credits and sponsor**—At the top of the home page, find the name and any supporting details about the individual or organization that is responsible for the text. What does this information suggest about the point of view of the site?
- **Menus**—Click on any menu tabs along the top or sides of the home page. What options do these features offer?
- **Hyperlinks**—Locate words in the text that are highlighted or underlined and click on two or three. Do these links take you to other pages within the same Website, to other Websites, or to both?

STEP 2 **Analyze the purpose of the Website.** What do you learn from the features you have identified as well as from the title, headings, and subheadings of the text?

- Is the purpose of the site primarily to convey information, to persuade, or to entertain?
- What point of view does the text support?

STEP 3 **Evaluate the purpose and usefulness of the site.** Based on your answers to the questions in Step 2, identify the purpose of the Website. Compare this purpose with your need for information. For example, if you want to learn many points of view about a topic and the Website focuses only on one side of a topic or issue, you should look for other sites that present different approaches to the topic.

Evaluate Support

ACADEMIC VOCABULARY

evaluate evidence: determine the strength and quality of the facts, statistics, reasons, examples, and sources that support a position or claim

evidence: a reason, fact, statistic, example, or expert opinion that supports a proposition or claim

objective: not influenced by emotions or personal prejudices; factual

proposition or claim: the writer's position on an issue or problem

subjective: personal to a given person; existing only in the mind

STEP 1 **Look for opinions to be sure they are supported.** No one can check whether an opinion is true or false. So a writer must support any claims, positions, or personal opinions with examples, facts, and reasons. For any expert opinions, be sure that sources are clearly identified. Don't accept vague language, such as "experts agree."

STEP 2 **Look for facts-statistics, examples, and expert opinions.** Part of a writer's job is to present enough facts to support each claim. Facts include quotations from experts, anecdotes and examples, and definitions, as well as **statistics** (mathematical data). Decide whether there is enough evidence. Decide if the evidence is up to date. If there are no data to back up the ideas, don't accept the claim.

STEP 3 **Look for ways in which sources are documented.** Writers should name the source of their facts. Look for sources that are **objective** and **credible**, like an encyclopedia, rather than **subjective** and **biased** like a personal blog. Good documentation includes the *who, where,* and *when* of each source, so readers can check it.

STEP 4 **Weigh the evidence.** After evaluating the support, the hard data, and the documentation, a reader can decide whether to accept or agree with the writer's position or not. You can also weigh how reasonable, valuable, or useful the writer's ideas are to you.

Evaluate Usefulness

> **ACADEMIC VOCABULARY**
>
> **accuracy:** correctness of statements and facts
>
> **author credibility:** author's education and background
>
> **evaluation:** rating the strength of a source
>
> **incomplete information:** missing facts or explanations
>
> **realistic suggestions:** plans of action that make sense and are possible to carry out
>
> **solid information:** facts that are complete, well-supported, and reliable

STEP 1 **Make a checklist.** To help you decide whether or not you should use the information in a source, create a checklist of questions to ask about it. Copy the form below or use it as an example to create your own:

Yes	No	
☐	☐	Is the author an expert in the field?
☐	☐	Is he/she affiliated with a respected institution?
☐	☐	Does the information seem solid and accurate?
☐	☐	Are statements supported by facts that can be verified?
☐	☐	Do you need more information after reading?
☐	☐	Are the author's suggestions realistic?

STEP 2 **Evaluate the text.** Read through the text with the questions on your checklist in mind. Pay special attention to the following text features:

- the author's byline and biographical information
- boldfaced statements
- charts and graphs

STEP 3 **Determine the usefulness of the source.** Tally the "yes" and "no" marks on your checklist.

- If you answered "no" to any question about the author or the reliability of the information, DO NOT use the source.
- If you answered "yes" to the question about needing more information after reading, you may be able to use the source and look for the missing information in other sources.

Forms of Nonfiction Texts

ACADEMIC VOCABULARY

accuracy: correctness of statements and facts

bias: a person's particular ideas about and approach to a topic

feature articles: in-depth coverage of human-interest or lifestyle topics found in newspapers or magazines

instructions: information on how to do something, often including diagrams and numbered steps, found in manuals and product inserts

interviews: conversations between two people in which one person asks questions and the other person responds, often presented with text features such as subheads that help readers follow the conversation

thoroughness: complete coverage of all aspects of a topic from several perspectives

STEP 1 **Identify the author's purpose.** Look at the title, subheads, and graphics and skim the article for clues to the subject, tone, and intended audience. Does the author intend to

- describe?
- inform?
- persuade?
- entertain?

STEP 2 **Identify the form.** Look for the features that characterize three main forms of nonfiction texts:

- **feature articles**—front-page or main articles including subheadings, graphics, illustrations, and often multiple pages
- **instructions**—numbered steps, illustrations or diagrams, and short paragraphs
- **interviews**—alternating statements by the interviewer and person being interviewed sometimes introduced by the name or initials and a colon

STEP 3 **Evaluate for effectiveness.** Ask yourself these questions about the text:

- **How thorough is it?** Look for complete explanations of all steps in a process or complete background information on a topic.
- **How accurate is it?** Find facts from reliable sources that support statements.
- **What is the author's bias?** Identify how the author's beliefs about the topic affect the ideas presented.

Main Ideas and Supporting Details

ACADEMIC VOCABULARY

main idea: the most important idea about a topic. It can be the central idea of an entire work or of just a paragraph.

supporting details: words, phrases, or sentences that tell more about the main idea or topic sentence. Types of supporting details include:

examples: specific instances that explain or support a point

sensory details: details that appeal to one or more of the five senses

reasons: details that tell why an opinion is valid or why something occurs

facts: statements that can be proved

statistics: facts expressed in numbers

topic: what a piece of nonfiction writing is about; its subject matter

topic sentence: a sentence that states the main idea of a paragraph

STEP 1 Identify the topic. Ask yourself: What is this passage or paragraph about?

STEP 2 Think about the main idea. Ask yourself: What idea does the writer express?

STEP 3 Look for a topic sentence. The topic sentence is usually either the first or last sentence in a paragraph, although it can occur anywhere. In some paragraphs, the main idea is not stated directly, but is implied by the supporting details.

STEP 4 Identify the supporting details. Writers use different types of details to support different purposes and main ideas. Sensory details describe, examples illustrate, reasons persuade, and facts and statistics explain.

STEP 5 Use a graphic organizer. A chart can help you take notes on the main idea and supporting details in a paragraph. List a main idea, then note all the details that support it.

Patterns of Organization

> **ACADEMIC VOCABULARY**
> **cause-and-effect order:** shows the relationship between events and their results
> **chronological order:** shows the sequence of events in time
> **classification:** assigns people, places, things, or events to groups based on specific characteristics
> **comparison-contrast order:** presents the similarities and differences between people, places, things, or events
> **problem-solution:** explains a problem and offers a solution
> **spatial order:** presents things or events according to their arrangement in space

STEP 1 **Get a general sense of the organization.** To form an initial impression of how a text is organized, skim it quickly, asking yourself, "Am I learning about:
- time sequence?"
- relation in space?"
- relative ranking?"
- membership in a category?"
- causes and effects?"
- similarities and differences?"
- the solution to a problem?"

STEP 2 **Look for clues to the organization.** Each organizational pattern uses a variety of signal words and structural patterns.

Cause-and-Effect Order
- Look for signal words like *because, therefore, since, as a result, the effect of, consequently*.
- Look for answers to the question, "What happens next?"
- Study the text for clues to implied causes and effects.

Chronological Order
- Look for signal words like *first, next, then, afterward, before*.
- Study the text for times, dates, or numbers that show order.

Classification
- Look for words or phrases that signal groups: *group, category, kind, set, type, class, classification, division, divided into, common characteristics*.
- Look for definitions of the groups used in the text. What do each of these objects, ideas, or facts have in common?
- Look for subgroups under the major groups.

Comparison-Contrast Order
- Signal words for this pattern are *similarly, also, both, like, neither, unlike, instead, in contrast*.
- Identify the subjects being compared or contrasted. The subjects usually have similar characteristics.
- Look for the pattern. Does the text compare each subject in turn, or does it compare each subject feature by feature?

Problem-Solution Order
- Look for words like *problem, solution, pros, cons,* and *recommendation*.
- Examine the text for a clear statement of the problem, an analysis of the problem, and a proposed solution.
- Look for a discussion of the causes and effects of the problem.

Spatial Order
- Look for signal words such as *in front of, behind, under, above, left, right, top, bottom*.
- Identify the specific way in which the spatial details are organized. A writer usually arranges spatial details in a certain order such as front to back, near to far, low to high, and so on.

STEP 3 Determine the most important ideas and supporting details. Once you have determined how the text is organized, focus on the main ideas the author is presenting and the support that he/she provides. Making an informal outline like the one below can help you understand how he organizational pattern helps convey author's message.

Organizational pattern _____

I. Main idea
  A. Supporting detail
  B. Supporting detail
II. Main idea related to first idea by _____
  A. Supporting detail
  B. Supporting detail
III. Main idea related to first and second ideas by _____
  A. Supporting detail
  B. Supporting detail

Problem-Solution Order

ACADEMIC VOCABULARY
problem-solution order: presents a problem, explores various solutions, and identifies a solution, or outcome

STEP 1 **Identify the problems or problems.** To signal a **problem,** writers may use words and phrases like *problem, difficulty, issue, conflict,* and *need for change.*

STEP 2 **Look for solutions.** Signal words and phrases can help you.
- **solutions**—words like *solution, answer, approach, method, way, option, remedy, alternative*
- **outcomes**—words and phrases like *but, however, can lead to, would result in, most likely, might also, on the other hand*
- **preferred solution**—words and phrases like *best, most effective, useful, helpful, valuable*

STEP 3 **Use a graphic organizer** to keep track of the problem, solutions, and possible outcomes.

State Problem

Solution 1	Pros
	•
	•
	•
	Cons
	•
	•
	•
Solution 2	Pros
	•
	•
	•
	Cons
	•
	•
	•

Decision

Rhetorical Devices

> **ACADEMIC VOCABULARY**
>
> **analogies:** comparison of one idea or object with another
>
> **parallelism:** use of similar grammatical structures to stress the similarity of ideas
>
> **repetition:** duplication of sounds, words, or phrases for emphasis
>
> **rhetoric:** effective use of language

STEP 1 Scan the text for rhetorical devices. Read quickly through the text looking for clues to the following rhetorical devices:

- **analogies**—the phrases *is like* and *is to the* _____ *as* _____ *is to the* _____
- **parallelism**—repeated grammatical structures, such as similar parts of speech, phrases, or sentence types
- **repetition**—words or phrases that appear several times

STEP 2 Determine how each rhetorical device contributes to the text. Ask the following questions about each rhetorical device you identified:

Analogies
- What two things are being compared?
- How are they similar?
- How are they different?
- What idea is the author trying to convey?

Parallelism
- What do the ideas being expressed have in common?
- Why might the author want to stress these ideas?

Repetition
- Why is this word or phrase especially important?
- What is the effect of repeating it?

STEP 3 Determine the key ideas in the text. Review your answers to the questions in Step 2. Then examine the entire text closely. As you read, keep the ideas conveyed by the rhetorical devices in mind. Integrate them with additional ideas that you learn.

Sequence and Chronological Order

ACADEMIC VOCABULARY

chronological order: organization in order of occurrence, forward in time, usually used to tell stories, to report events, or to record histories.

sequence order: the order in which events should, may, or usually occur; sequence order is used to give directions or to show steps or events in a process.

STEP 1 **Look for times, dates, or numbers that show order.** Clue words such as *first, second,* and so on indicate sequence of information. Numerals (*1, 2, 3, . . .*) or dates and times may give order of events.

STEP 2 **Organize information in a graphic.** Based on any time-order clue words, place the events in a graphic organizer. The organizer can be a numbered list. Or you can create a left-to-right series of boxes and arrows to track information.

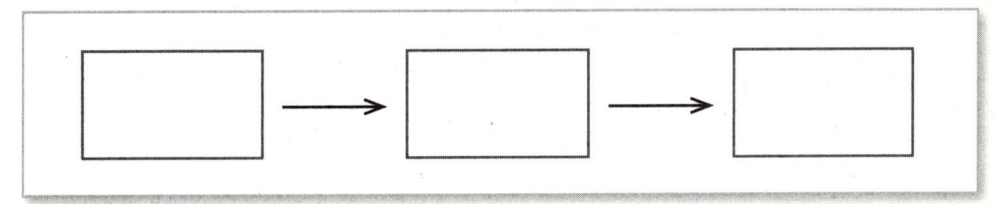

STEP 3 **Look for words and phrases that show duration or sequence.** Certain signal words and phrases help structure both chronological and sequential texts: *then, next, before, after, during, finally,* and so on.

STEP 4 **Infer the author's purpose.** The author may want to explain how to carry out a task or report a story about how events unfolded in time. Ask yourself: Why does the author arrange details in this way? What is he or she trying to achieve?

Spatial Order

> **ACADEMIC VOCABULARY**
>
> **spatial order:** the arrangement of details according to their physical position or relationship
>
> **specific spatial order:** details can be arranged in specific ways, such as *top to bottom, back to front, outside to inside, left to right, near to far,* or the reverse of any of these.

STEP 1 **Look for signal words or phrases** that show physical position or location—words such as *top, bottom above, below,* phrases, such as *away from, close to, in front of.*

EXAMPLE

What words signal a spatial position or location in the following sentences? The kitten curled up *beneath* the rocking chair *beside* the stove. The tea kettle simmered slowly, its steam blowing *past* the open door. *Just to the right,* the clock ticked toward noon, hanging *above* the sink, whose dripping faucet drummed.

STEP 2 **Identify the specific way in which the spatial details are organized.** Usually a writer arranges spatial details in a certain order, such as near to far, front to back, low to high, and so on.

EXAMPLE

In the passage that follows, how has the writer organized the information?

At the bottom of the totem pole, there was a fish. In the middle, a man's hard face stared out. A sun with rays crowned the top of the totem pole, as though the sun were shining down on the face.

STEP 3 **Take notes.** Once you have identified how the details are organized, you can take notes, by listing details, such as people, objects, or actions, in order. You can also create a drawing or map that helps you see clearly see whatever is being described. If the text is a guide or instruction, your graphic may help you use the information.

STEP 4 **Infer author's purpose.** An author may use spatial order to create effects such as a tense or tranquil mood, a confused or orderly character, a or other effects in a literary work. Other writers organize factual information or directions spatially to make them clear and easy to follow.

EXAMPLE

What is the writer's purpose in the following sentence? "Turn *left* after the library, and *in front of* you there will be a small yellow building. Your class is *inside* the yellow building."

Synthesize

> **ACADEMIC VOCABULARY**
>
> **synthesize:** to combine individual ideas, influences, or materials to create a new product or idea
>
> **synthesizing information:** drawing from a variety of research materials, combining new ideas with prior knowledge, and applying the information to some new work or creation

STEP 1 **Determine the message in each source.** Decide what is most memorable or important about each work you are using. Then look for details the writers use to support these main ideas.

STEP 2 **Paraphrase the main ideas.** You will find the main ideas easier to work with after you have rephrased them in your own words. You should also paraphrase difficult concepts and wording in each selection to improve your understanding.

STEP 3 **Compare sources in light of author's purpose and audience.** Determine whether each selection was written to explain, inform, express an opinion, persuade, tell a story, or express emotion. You may interpret information in different ways depending on its purpose and audience.

STEP 4 **Ask questions about your sources.** The right questions will help you view your subject from different perspectives. Ask questions starting with *who, what, where, when, why, how,* and even *what if*. For example:

- How do the sources differ?
- What approach has the author of each work taken?
- Whose perspective is, or is *not*, represented?
- Who is the intended audience?
- Why is the message important to the author? To me?
- When and where is the writing set? When and where was it created?

STEP 5 **Connect to other sources, or your own experiences.** Look for ways that key ideas relate to other works on the same subject, or to your prior knowledge of the subject. Use your imagination to find connections that may not seem obvious at first. Ask yourself:

- How does the information confirm or refute other material?
- How does the information relate to my life or to world affairs?

STEP 6 **Synthesize.** After reviewing your sources as a group, piece the information together to create something new—an essay, story, poem, research paper, map, poster or other work. Be sure to offer your own original insights about the topic.

Text Features

> **ACADEMIC VOCABULARY**
>
> **text features:** design elements that highlight the organization and especially important information in a text
>
> **boldface type:** thicker, darker type, often used for key terms
>
> **bulleted list:** each listed item is signaled with a dot or "bullet"
>
> **caption:** written information about an illustration, photograph, or graphic
>
> **graphic aid:** visual tool (a photograph, table, graph, or other illustration)
>
> **head or heading:** title that identifies the topic of the content that follows it
>
> **key word:** important term, may be italicized, boldfaced, or highlighted
>
> **sidebar:** additional information set in a box or apart from the main text
>
> **subhead or subheading:** signals the beginning of a new topic or section under a more general heading
>
> **title:** name given to a book, chapter, play, film, or poem

STEP 1 **Before you read, identify the text features.** Knowing the kinds of features that a text contains can help you find information.

STEP 2 **Preview the text features.** As you preview, follow these steps:
- Read the heads and subheads to get an overview of the material and to determine which details go with which main ideas.
- Scan for boldfaced terms, other key words, and lists to get a sense of the important details you will encounter in this text.
- Glance at the graphic aids (and corresponding captions) to see what kind of data the text offers besides words.
- Familiarize yourself with the kind of material that is covered in the sidebars, but don't read them yet.

STEP 3 **Now read the text and organize information.** As you read, paragraph by paragraph, work in the graphic aids and sidebars as convenient. Use the text features to help your note taking, outlining, summarizing, and questioning.

Textbooks

> **ACADEMIC VOCABULARY**
>
> **bulleted or numbered lists:** each of these brief items of information or explanation is preceded by a dot or "bullet" or by a number
>
> **captions:** information about photographs, illustrations, or other graphics
>
> **footnotes:** numbered notes placed at the bottom of a page that provide additional or source information
>
> **graphic aids:** information presented visually, such as graphs, charts, maps, photographs, and diagrams, to help clarify ideas in the text
>
> **headings/subheadings:** boldfaced text titles that indicate the start of a new section of text and identify its main idea
>
> **review questions:** a way for readers to focus or assess their understanding
>
> **side bars:** focused information set apart from the main text that relates to or contrasts with the topic
>
> **specialized vocabulary:** boldfaced words with definitions in the text or in a separate list that help readers understand the topic
>
> **timeline:** graphic showing dates or periods of time along with captions

STEP 1 **Scan text features to help identify the overall topic and purpose of the text.** To get a good idea of what an instructional text is about, follow these steps:

- **Read the title, headings and subheadings.** What do they tell you about the topic?
- **Read any opening questions or boldfaced text.** Often a textbook chapter will open with signals about the key ideas.

STEP 2 **Analyze the text features.** Focus carefully on the text features you've identified.

- **Note the main ideas** you have identified from the heads and subheads.
- **Examine the photographs**, illustrations, maps, charts, and graphs in detail. These graphic aids help explain the concepts discussed in the text.
- **Read the review questions** to identify the concepts you are expected to learn.

STEP 3 **Identify key ideas.** Finally, read the full text. Make a list of important details. Then examine all your notes, looking for main ideas that they support. It is these ideas that the author wants you to remember.

Transitions and Other Text Clues

> **ACADEMIC VOCABULARY**
>
> **demonstrative pronouns:** words like *this, these,* and *those* that refer to people, places, and things and clarify relationships between ideas
>
> **synonyms:** words with similar meanings that help define and elaborate on ideas
>
> **transitions:** signal words that indicate how ideas relate to each other, such as *but* and *however* for contrast; *like* and *similarly* for comparison; and *first, then,* and *next* for sequence

STEP 1 **Scan the text for an overall impression.** As you skim the title, subheads, graphics, and first few paragraphs, ask yourself:

- What is this text about?
- What is the author's purpose?
- Who is the intended audience?
- What is the author's tone?

STEP 2 **Preview the text clues.** Look for words that signal relationships between the ideas and list them in a three-column chart like this one.

Demonstrative Pronouns	Synonyms	Transitions

Then add the following information for each entry:

- **demonstrative pronouns**—the word each refers to
- **synonyms**—the meaning (using a dictionary if necessary)
- **transitions**—the type of relationship each transition word signals—comparison, contrast, sequence, or some other connection

STEP 3 **Analyze the flow of ideas.** Then read the text carefully, using your chart to help you understand the main ideas and how they relate to each other. Make an informal outline as you read or summarize the information afterward to make sure you understand the author's point.

Treatment, Organization, and Scope of Ideas

> **ACADEMIC VOCABULARY**
> **organization:** a particular arrangement, or pattern, of ideas in text
> **scope:** the focus of a text, the depth and breadth of detail included
> **tone:** the writer's attitude toward his or her subject
> **treatment:** the way a topic is handled; includes the form a writer uses, the writer's purpose, and tone

STEP 1 Identify and compare treatment. Look for differences and similarities in form, purpose, and tone between two works. Ask yourself:

- **What is the form, or genre, or each text?** Examples of forms include news reports, summaries, editorials, interviews, and reviews.
- **What is the writer's purpose?** Is it to inform, persuade, instruct, advise, warn, critique, promote, amuse, or inspire readers?
- **What is the tone of the writing?** Is it serious? Comical? Angry? Fearful?

STEP 2 Identify and compare organization. Some common patterns of organization include:

- **Chronological order** arranges events from earliest to latest in time. Reverse chronological order starts with recent events.
- **Deductive order** begins with a general statement, followed by facts and evidence, building toward a specific conclusion.
- **Main idea and supporting details** begins with the main idea, followed by reasons, facts, and examples that strengthen the reader's understanding of it.
- **Cause-effect organization** shows that a certain event, idea, or trend causes a change. The writing may begin with the cause or begin with the effects.

STEP 3 Identify and compare scope. Two texts about one subject may each have a different focus, such as an overview versus a close-up look. Ask:

- **What is the topic?** This may appear in the title or first sentence.
- **What aspects of the topic are covered?** Scan headings or topic sentences throughout the work to see what the focus is.
- **How much and what sort of details are used?** In articles with wide scope, facts and statistics are given and background is provided. A narrow piece covers personal anecdotes and minor incidents.

Test-Taking Handbook

Successful Test Taking

You can prepare for tests in several ways. First, study and understand the content that will be on the test. Second, learn as many test-taking techniques as you can. These techniques will help you better understand the questions and how to answer them. Following are some general suggestions for preparing for and taking tests. Starting on page R30, you'll find more detailed suggestions and test-taking practice.

Study Content Throughout the Year

1. **Master the content of your language arts class.** The best way to study for tests is to read, understand, and review the content of your language arts class. Read your daily assignments carefully. Study the notes that you have taken in class. Participate in class discussions. Work with classmates in small groups to help one another learn. You might trade writing assignments and comment on your classmates' work.

2. **Use your textbook for practice.** Your textbook includes many different types of questions. Some may ask you to talk about a story you just read. Others may ask you to figure out what's wrong with a sentence or how to make a paragraph sound better. Try answering these questions out loud and in writing. This type of practice can make taking a test much easier.

3. **Learn how to understand the information in charts, maps, and graphic organizers.** One type of test question may ask you to look at a graphic organizer, such as a spider map, and explain something about the information you see there. Another type of question may ask you to look at a map to find a particular place, such as the Indian setting of the story "Rikki-tikki-tavi." You'll find charts, maps, and graphic organizers to study in your literature textbooks. You'll also find charts, maps and graphs in your science, mathematics, and social studies textbook. When you look at these, ask yourself, What information is being presented and why is it important?

4. **Practice taking tests.** Use copies of tests you have taken in the past or in other classes for practice. Every test has a time limit, so set a timer for 15 or 20 minutes and then begin your practice. Try to finish the test in the time you've given yourself.

5. **Talk about test-taking experiences.** After you've taken a classroom test or quiz, talk about it with your teacher and classmates. Which types of questions were the hardest to understand? What made them difficult? Which questions seemed easiest, and why? When you share test-taking techniques with your classmates, everyone can become a successful test taker.

Use Strategies During the Test

1. **Read the directions carefully.** You can't be a successful test taker unless you know exactly what you are expected to do. Look for key words and phrases, such as *circle the best answer, write a paragraph,* or *choose the word that best completes each sentence.*

2. **Learn how to read test questions.** Test questions can sometimes be difficult to figure out. They may include unfamiliar language or be written in an unfamiliar way. Try rephrasing the question in a simpler way using words you understand. Always ask yourself, What type of information does this question want me to provide?

3. **Pay special attention when using a separate answer sheet.** If you accidentally skip a line on an answer sheet, all the rest of your answers may be wrong! Try one or more of the following techniques:

   - Use a ruler on the answer sheet to make sure you are placing your answers on the correct line.
   - After every five answers, check to make sure you're on the right line.
   - Each time you turn a page of the test booklet, check to make sure the number of the question is the same as the number of the answer line on the answer sheet.
   - If the answer sheet has circles, fill them in neatly. A stray pencil mark might cause the scoring machine to count the answer as incorrect.

4. **If you're not sure of the answer, make your best guess.** Unless you've been told that there is a penalty for guessing, choose the answer that you think is likeliest to be correct.

5. **Keep track of the time.** Answering all the questions on a test usually results in a better score. That's why finishing the test is important. Keep track of the time you have left. At the beginning of the test, figure out how many questions you will have to answer by the halfway point in order to finish in the time given.

Understand Types of Test Questions

Most tests include two types of questions: multiple choice and open-ended. Specific strategies will help you understand and correctly answer each type of question.

A multiple-choice question has two parts. The first part is the question itself, called the stem. The second part is a series of possible answers. Usually four possible answers are provided, and only one of them is correct. Your task is to choose the correct answer. Here are some strategies to help you do just that.

1. Read and think about each question carefully before looking at the possible answers.

2. Pay close attention to key words in the question. For example, look for the word *not*, as in "Which of the following is *not* a cause of the conflict in this story?"

3. Read and think about all of the possible answers before making your choice.

4. Reduce the number of choices by eliminating any answers you know are incorrect. Then, think about why some of the remaining choices might also be incorrect.

    - If two of the choices are pretty much the same, both are probably wrong.
    - Answers that contain any of the following words are usually incorrect: *always, never, none, all,* and *only*.

5. If you're still unsure about an answer, see if any of the following applies:

    - When one choice is longer and more detailed than the others, it is often the correct answer.
    - When a choice repeats a word that is in the question, it may be the correct answer.
    - When two choices are direct opposites, one of them is likely the correct answer.
    - When one choice includes one or more of the other choices, it is often the correct answer.
    - When a choice includes the word *some* or *often*, it may be the correct answer.
    - If one of the choices is *All of the above*, make sure that at least two of the other choices seem correct.
    - If one of the choices is *None of the above*, make sure that none of the other choices seems correct.

An **open-ended test item** can take many forms. It might ask you to write a word or phrase to complete a sentence. You might be asked to create a chart, draw a map, or fill in a graphic organizer. Sometimes, you will be asked to write one or more paragraphs in response to a writing prompt. Use the following strategies when reading and answering open-ended items:

1. If the item includes directions, read them carefully. Take note of any steps required.

2. Look for key words and phrases in the item as you plan how you will respond. Does the item ask you to identify a cause-and-effect relationship or to compare and contrast two or more things? Are you supposed to provide a sequence of events or make a generalization? Does the item ask you to write an essay in which you state your point of view and then try to persuade others that your view is correct?

3. If you're going to be writing a paragraph or more, plan your answer. Jot down notes and a brief outline of what you want to say before you begin writing.

4. Focus your answer. Don't include everything you can think of, but be sure to include everything the item asks for.

5. If you're creating a chart or drawing a map, make sure your work is as clear as possible.

MODEL

Functional Reading Test

DIRECTIONS *Study the following directions for recording an answering machine announcement. Then answer the questions that follow.*

READING STRATEGIES FOR ASSESSMENT

Examine organization. Skim this set of directions to see how the information is organized before reading it carefully. Circle the two major headings under Answering System Operation.

Note sequence of steps. Circle or highlight the numbered steps that explain the actual process of recording the announcement.

Study diagrams. Look closely at the first diagram. Refer to it as you read through each step. Do the same with the second diagram.

Answering System Operation

Recording Your Announcement

Before using your new answering system, you should record an announcement message. This is the message callers will hear when you set the system to answer calls automatically.

1. Prepare your announcement. Your announcement message may be up to 2 minutes long.

EXAMPLE: "Hello. I can't come to the phone right now. Please leave your name, telephone number, and a short message after you hear the beep. I will return your call as soon as I can. Thank you."

2. Check to make sure the MESSAGES light is on. If it is not, press ON/OFF (Figure 1) to turn the answering system on.

3. Press and hold ANNC (Figure 1).

4. When the system beeps, speak toward the microphone in a normal tone of voice. Release ANNC when finished.

5. To play back your announcement, wait for the tape to reset, then press and release ANNC.

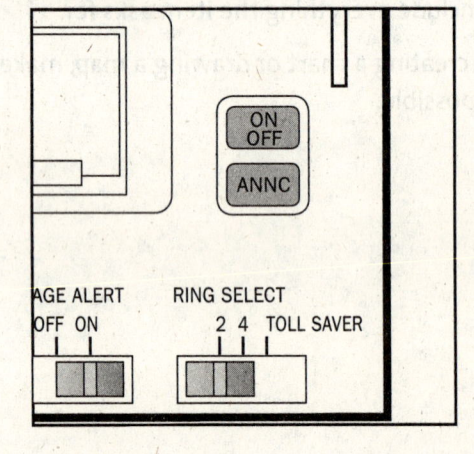

To adjust volume, see "Message Volume Control" on page 11.

9

R30 INTERACTIVE READER & WRITER

Answering System Operation, continued

Changing Your Announcement

To change your announcement, repeat Steps 3, 4, and 5 under "Recording Your Announcement."

When you change your announcement, there must be no messages waiting—*MESSAGES* light (Figure 2) is on steady.

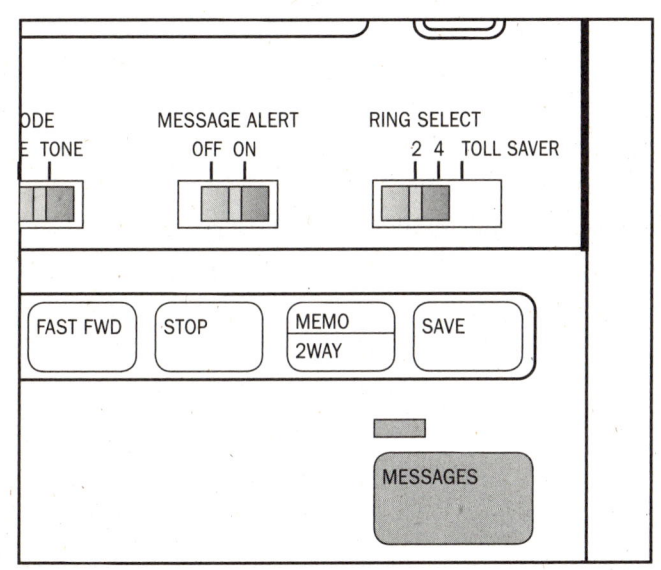

Figure 2

If there are messages:

1. Press MESSAGES (Figure 2).
2. Wait for all messages to be played—or press FAST FWD (Figure 2).
3. Wait 10 seconds after the 5 beeps, allowing the unit to reset and clear the messages.

Identify important instructions. What must be done before the announcement can be changed?

_____

_____

_____

_____

Test-Taking Handbook

TEST-TAKING HANDBOOK **R31**

ANSWER STRATEGIES

> Note the sequence of steps. Composing the announcement is Step 1. What is Step 2?

1. What is the first step you should take after you have prepared your announcement?
   - (A) Hold the button labeled *ANNC*.
   - (B) Speak toward the microphone.
   - (C) Make sure the *MESSAGES* light is on.
   - (D) Press "Release."

> Reread the steps that explain how to record the announcement. Which answer contains the same instructions?

2. What must you do while recording your announcement?
   - (E) Press *ON/OFF* to be sure the *MESSAGES* light is on.
   - (F) Press and hold the *ANNC* button and speak toward the microphone after the beep.
   - (G) Press and release the *ANNC* button.
   - (H) Position yourself several inches away from the microphone.

> Recall that the directions are organized in two parts. Review the section entitled "Changing Your Announcement" to identify the correct answer.

3. What must you do if you want to change your announcement and the *MESSAGES* light is blinking?
   - (A) Press and hold *ANNC* while speaking toward the microphone.
   - (B) Play all messages and wait 10 seconds after the 5 beeps for the machine to reset.
   - (C) Press the *ON/OFF* button and hold for 5 beeps; then record your message.
   - (D) Do B, then A.

Answers: 1.C, 2.F, 3.D

PRACTICE

Functional Reading Test

DIRECTIONS *Study the following nutrition label from a package of provolone cheese. Notice the information it provides and how the information is organized. Then answer the multiple-choice questions that follow.*

Nutrition Facts
Serv. Size 1 slice (19 g)
Servings Per Container 12

Amount Per Serving

Calories 70   Calories from Fat 45

Amount/Serving	% Daily Value*
Total Fat 5g	8%
Sat. Fat 3.5g	17%
Cholesterol 15 mg	5%
Sodium 125 mg	5%
Total Carbohydrate 0g	0%
Dietary Fiber 0g	0%
Sugars 0g	
Protein 5g	

Vitamin A 4%   •   Vitamin C 0%
Calcium 15%   •   Iron 0%

*Percent Daily Values are based on a 2,000 calorie diet. Your daily values may be higher or lower depending on your calorie needs.

1. How many calories does one slice of this cheese contain?
   - (A) 12
   - (B) 19
   - (C) 45
   - (D) 70

2. What major nutrients and vitamins are *not* supplied by this cheese?
   - (E) sodium, protein, fat
   - (F) calcium, protein, vitamin A
   - (G) dietary fiber, iron, vitamin C
   - (H) sugars, saturated fat, vitamin A

3. If you are on a 2,000 calorie diet, what percentage of your daily supply of saturated fat is provided by one slice of this cheese?
   - (A) 3.5
   - (B) 5
   - (C) 8
   - (D) 17

4. If you need calcium but don't need saturated fat, is this cheese a good food choice for you?
   - (E) No. Although the % Daily Value of calcium per serving is high, the % Daily Value of saturated fat is higher.
   - (F) Yes. The % Daily Value of calcium is 15%.
   - (G) There is not enough information given to make a decision.
   - (H) Yes. There is no saturated fat in this product.

TEST-TAKING HANDBOOK   **R33**

MODEL

Revising-and-Editing Test

DIRECTIONS *Read the following paragraph carefully. Then answer the multiple-choice questions that follow. After answering the questions, read the material in the side columns to check your answer strategies.*

¹ Our principle, Mr. Dollinger, thinks that we don't need to have dances at our school. ² He says, you students already have too many activities." ³ It is true that some students are involved in sports others participate in the newspaper and the yearbook. ⁴ However, only 40 percent of the students take part in these activities. ⁵ Having dances on Valentine's Day, the first day of spring, and other special occasions would help to build school spirit. ⁶ Dances is one school activity that everyone can enjoy.

READING STRATEGIES FOR ASSESSMENT

Watch for common errors. Highlight or underline errors such as incorrect punctuation, spelling, or capitalization; incomplete or run-on sentences; and missing or misplaced information.

ANSWER STRATEGIES

Commonly Confused Words *Principle* means "code of conduct" or "basic truth." A *principal* is the head of a school.

Quotations Remember that a direct quotation is enclosed in quotation marks, and the first word is capitalized.

Run-on Sentences Three choices use incorrect punctuation to join the two thoughts and do not show the relationship between them. The correct answer shows that the two thoughts elaborate on the same idea by combining them with a conjunction.

1. What is the correct spelling of *principle* as it is used in sentence 1?
   - **A** principul
   - **B** principel
   - **C** principle
   - **D** principal

2. What change, if any, should be made in sentence 2?
   - **E** change *He says, you students* to *He says, "you students*
   - **F** change *He says, you students* to *He says "You students*
   - **G** change *He says, you students* to *He says, you, students*
   - **H** change *He says, you students* to *He says, "You students*

3. What is the best way to rewrite sentence 3 in this paragraph?
   - **A** It is true that some students are involved in sports, others participate in the newspaper and the yearbook.
   - **B** It is true that some students are involved in sports, however others participate in the newspaper and the yearbook.
   - **C** It is true that some students are involved in sports and others participate in the newspaper and the yearbook.
   - **D** It is true that some students are involved in sports—others participate in the newspaper and the yearbook.

R34 INTERACTIVE READER & WRITER

4. Where should the sentence *I don't agree* be added to the paragraph?
   - (E) between sentences 1 and 2
   - (F) between sentences 2 and 3
   - (G) between sentences 3 and 4
   - (H) between sentences 5 and 6

5. Which of the following is the best way to rewrite sentence 6?
   - (A) Dances is one school activity enjoyed by everyone.
   - (B) One school activity enjoyed by everyone are dances.
   - (C) Everyone can be enjoying the school activity of dances.
   - (D) Dances are one school activity that everyone can enjoy.

6. Which of the following details would best support the student's argument?
   - (E) In a recent poll, 80 percent of the students said that they would attend school dances.
   - (F) School dances were very popular 20 years ago.
   - (G) On Valentine's Day, students only exchange cards and have a bake sale.
   - (H) A dance could be held for the entire student body in the new gymnasium.

Transitions The sentence *I don't agree* indicates a change in the direction of the paragraph. Where does the writer begin to present his or her argument disputing Mr. Dollinger's opinion?

Subject-Verb Agreement Identify the subject in each choice and determine whether the verb agrees with it in number. Choose the answer that is correct and most clearly phrased.

Supporting Details Reread the paragraph to identify the main idea. Decide which detail would strengthen the argument that school dances would provide enjoyment for many students.

Answers: 1.D, 2.H, 3.C, 4.F, 5.D, 6.E

PRACTICE

Revising-and-Editing Test Practice

DIRECTIONS *Read the following paragraph carefully. As you read, circle each error that you find and identify the error in the side column—for example, write* misspelled word *or* not a complete sentence. *When you have finished, fill in the letter of the correct choice for each question that follows.*

¹ A good sailor can determine their latitude by looking at the sun or stars. ² Calculating longitude depends on time, however. ³ The difference between the time on a ship and the time in its home port can be converted into longitude. ⁴ Nowadays that process seems simple years ago it was almost impossible. ⁵ Many ships became lost at sea, for instance, the *Eva Doran* sank in the Pacific Ocean when she hit land unexpectedly. ⁶ The problem in the late 18th century was not solved until John Harrison developed an accurate ship's clock. ⁷ Harrison's invention began a new era in navigation.

1. Which of the following is the correct way to rewrite sentence 1?
   - (A) A good sailor can determine they're latitude by looking at the sun or stars.
   - (B) Good sailors can determine their latitude by looking at the sun or stars.
   - (C) A good sailor, can determine his latitude, by looking at the sun or stars.
   - (D) Good sailors can determine their latitude. By looking at the sun or stars.

2. What type of sentence is sentence 2?
   - (E) exclamatory
   - (F) imperative
   - (G) interrogative
   - (H) declarative

3. Which sentence is a run-on sentence?
   - (A) sentence 2
   - (B) sentence 3
   - (C) sentence 4
   - (D) sentence 7

4. Which sentence in this paragraph is the topic sentence?
   - (E) sentence 1
   - (F) sentence 2
   - (G) sentence 4
   - (H) sentence 7

5. What change should be made to sentence 5?
    - A replace the comma after *sea* with a semicolon
    - B insert a comma after *Doran*
    - C insert a comma after *Ocean*
    - D delete the comma after *sea*

6. Which of the following is the best way to rewrite sentence 6?
    - E In the late 18th century, the problem was not solved until John Harrison developed an accurate ship's clock.
    - F Until John Harrison developed an accurate ship's clock, the problem was not solved in the late 18th century.
    - G The problem was not solved in the late 18th century until John Harrison developed an accurate ship's clock.
    - H The problem was not solved until John Harrison developed an accurate ship's clock in the late 18th century.

Acknowledgments

UNIT 1
National Geographic Society: Excerpt from "King Cobras: Feared, Revered" by Mattias Klum, from *National Geographic,* November 2001. Copyright © 2001 by National Geographic. Reprinted with permission from the National Geographic Society.

UNIT 3
Pantheon Books: "The War of the Wall," from *Deep Sightings and Rescue Missions* by Toni Cade Bambara. Copyright © 1996 by The Estate of Toni Cade Bambara. Used by permission of Pantheon Books, a division of Random House, Inc.

Rick Olivo: Excerpt from "Veteran's mural honors those who served" by Rick Olivo, from *The Daily Press,* August 15, 2005. Copyright © 2005 by Rick Olivo. Used by permission of the author.

UNIT 4
Don Congdon Associates: "Dark They Were, and Golden-Eyed" as "The Naming of Names," from *Thrilling Wonder Stories* by Ray Bradbury. Copyright © 1949 by Standard Magazines, renewed 1976 by Ray Bradbury. Reprinted by permission of Don Congdon Associates, Inc.

How Stuff Works: Excerpt from "How Terraforming Mars Will Work" by Kevin Bonsor, from HowStuffWorks.com. Copyright © by How Stuff Works. Used courtesy of HowStuffWorks.com.

UNIT 5A
Copper Canyon Press: "the earth is a living thing," from *The Book of Light* by Lucille Clifton. Copyright © 1993 by Lucille Clifton. Used with the permission of Copper Canyon Press, www.coppercanyonpress.org

Little, Brown and Company: "Sleeping in the Forest," from *Twelve Moons* by Mary Oliver. Copyright © 1972, 1973, 1974, 1976, 1977, 1978, 1979 by Mary Oliver. By permission of Little, Brown and Company, Inc.

Curtis Brown: "Gold" by Pat Mora, first appeared in *Home: A Journey Through America,* published by Silver Whistle Books. Copyright © 1998 by Pat Mora. Reprinted by permission of Curtis Brown, Ltd.

Scholastic: From "Cool School" by Emily Costello, from *Scholastic Science World,* April 17, 2006. Copyright © 2006 by Scholastic Inc. Reprinted by permission.

UNIT 5B
Faber and Faber: "Scaffolding," from *Death of a Naturalist* by Seamus Heaney. Copyright © 1966 by Seamus Heaney. Reprinted by permission of Faber and Faber, Ltd.

HarperCollins: "The World Is Not a Pleasant Place to Be," from *My House* by Nikki Giovanni. Copyright © 1972 by Nikki Giovanni. Reprinted by permission of HarperCollins Publishers.

UNIT 6
Scholastic: "Prometheus," from Heroes, *Gods and Monsters of the Greek Myths* by Bernard Evslin. Copyright © 1966, 1967 by Scholastic Inc. Reprinted by permission.

Houghton Mifflin Company: "The Great Musician," from *Greek Myths* by Olivia E. Coolidge. Copyright © 1949 by Olivia E. Coolidge. Copyright renewed © 1977 by Olivia E. Coolidge. Adapted by permission of Houghton Mifflin Company. All rights reserved.

UNIT 7
Susan Bergholz Literary Services: "Names/Nombres" by Julia Alvarez, first published in *Nuestro,* March 1985. Copyright © 1985 by Julia Alvarez. Reprinted by permission of Susan Bergholz Literary Services, New York, New York and Lamy, New Mexico. All rights reserved.

UNIT 8A
Sharon Guynup: Excerpts from "What Do You Know About Sharks?" by Sharon Guynup, from *Science World*. Copyright © 2001 by Scholastic Inc. Reprinted by permission of the author.

UNIT 8B
Gloria Chang: "Inventions Inspired by Apollo" by Gloria Chang. Copyright © 2007. Used by permission of the author.

Art Credits

FRONT PAGES
ix Untitled (1986), Jerry N. Uelsmann. © Jerry N. Uelsmann; x © Getty Images; xii *left* © Jan Erasmus/ShutterStock; *center* © Jupiterimages Corporation; *right* © Jupiterimages Corporation; xiii NASA; xix © Getty Images; xx NASA/JPL/Caltech; xxi NASA.

UNIT 1
2 Illustration by Lucy Kirchner; © Telnov Oleksii/ShutterStock; 4 © Getty Images; 5 Illustration by Lucy Kirchner; 6–21 Public Domain; 24 Illustration by Lucy Kirchner; © Telnov Oleksii/ShutterStock; 25 © Jupiterimages Corporation; 27 Map by GeoNova LLC; 29 © Jupiterimages Corporation.

UNIT 2
34, 37 © Dynamic Graphics/Jupiterimages Corporation; 38–46 © Matkovskyy Artur/ShutterStock; 49 © Dynamic Graphics/Jupiterimages Corporation; 50 © p|s/ShutterStock; 52 © Frederick M. Brown/Getty Images.

UNIT 3
58 © Agb/ShutterStock; © Jupiterimages Corporation; © Kirsty Pargeter/ShutterStock; © Telnov Oleksii/ShutterStock; 61 © Agb/ShutterStock; 62–69 *bricks* © Tobias Machhaus/ShutterStock; *ink blot* © Kirsty Pargeter/ShutterStock; 72 © Agb/ShutterStock; © Jupiterimages Corporation; © Kirsty Pargeter/ShutterStock; © Telnov Oleksii/ShutterStock; 76 © Scott Hales/Shutterstock; 77 © Andrey Armyagov/ShutterStock.

UNIT 4
80 © Getty Images; 82 © Jan Erasmus/ShutterStock; © Jupiterimages Corporation; 83 NASA; 103 © Getty Images; 104 Courtesy of HowStuffWorks.com; 105 NASA.

UNIT 5A
110 © Jupiterimages Corporation; 113 © Christopher John Coudriet/ShutterStock; 118 © Jupiterimages Corporation; 120 © 2006 Craig Elevitch.

UNIT 5B
126, 135 © Lottie Davies/Getty Images; 136 © Galina Barskaya/ShutterStock.

UNIT 6
142 © Stephanie Connell/ShutterStock; 145 © Agb/ShutterStock; 146–148 *top* Public Domain; 149 © Vallentin Vassileff/ShutterStock; 156 © Stephanie Connell/ShutterStock; 157 Library of Congress, Prints and Photographs Division; 160–161 Map by GeoNova LLC; 161 © Travis Manley/ShutterStock.

UNIT 7
164, 175 *top row* © Getty Images; © Getty Images; © Getty Images; © Jupiterimages Corporation; *2nd row* © Banana Stock; © Banana Stock; © Banana Stock; © Jupiterimages Corporation; *3rd row* © Getty Images; © iofoto/ShutterStock; © Banana Stock; © Glenda M. Powers/ShutterStock; *4th row* © Jupiterimages Corporation; © Jupiterimages Corporation; © Jupiterimages Corporation; © Jupiterimages Corporation; 176 *top* Courtesy of HowStuffWorks.com; © David Burden/ShutterStock.

UNIT 8A

184 © Jurgen Ziewe/ShutterStock; **186** NOAA George E. Marsh Album/AP/Wide World Photos; Map by GeoNova LLC; **188–190** © javarman/ShutterStock; **188** *left* © Jupiterimages Corporation; *right* © Keir Davis/ShutterStock; **189** *left* © David Shen/SeaPics.com; *right* © Jupiterimages Corporation; **190** *left* © Jupiterimages Corporation; *right* © Douglas Pulsipher/Alamy; *left* © Kelvin Aitken/marinethemes.com; *right* © Kelvin Aitken/marinethemes.com; **192–193** Illustration by Stuart Jackson-Carter/The Art Agency; **196** NOAA George E. Marsh Album/AP/Wide World Photos; Map by GeoNova LLC; **197** © James Steidl/ShutterStock; **198** *top, bottom* © Jupiterimages Corporation; **199** *mouse* © Getty Images; *pig* © Ariusz Nawrocki/ShutterStock; **200** © Getty Images; **201** © Getty Images.

UNIT 8B

204 NASA; **207** The Granger Collection, New York; **214** NASA; **215** *top* © Blaz Kure/Shutterstock; *bottom* © Samuel Kessler/ShutterStock; **216** © Pelham James Mitchinson/ShutterStock; **218** © DigitalVues/Alamy.

Back Cover © Photodisc/Getty Images.